HEART
OF A
CHAMPION
ROGER LIPE

Jenai,

Thanks for your
faithful partnership.

God bless,

[signature]

Proverbs 31:29

Heart of a Champion
Roger Lipe

ISBN 1-929478-70-4

Cross Training Publishing
317 West Second Street
Grand Island, NE 68801
(308) 384-5762

Library of Congress Cataloging in Publication Data in Progress.

Dedication

This book is dedicated to the people of sport in the United States and around the world. Over the last ten years, my life and ministry have been focused on coaches, competitors, trainers, and support personnel in the world of sport. I am continually challenged and encouraged by their commitment, drive and enthusiasm.

I pray that this volume of devotional thoughts will serve as a catalyst to the process of your coming to know Christ Jesus and growing in your relationship with Him. The resulting changes in your heart will further enable you to be the most complete person of sport that you can be.

Acknowledgements

The author would like to acknowledge the profound influence upon his devotional life by two particular men.

Fred Bishop of No Greater Love Ministries in DuQuoin, Illinois has been a tremendous example of a consistent life of devotion for the author and countless others. His faithful encouragement of daily Bible reading and devotional prayer has been transformational.

For over twenty years Oswald Chambers, author of My Utmost for His Highest, has greatly challenged and encouraged the author in his pursuit of God's call.

The author is eternally indebted to these two men of God.

Additionally, the author would like to acknowledge the love and commitment shown to him by his wife of 30 years, Sharon and his son Jason.

Introduction

Daily devotional reading of the Bible is a cornerstone of any person's development as a follower of Christ. This book is written to enhance that process, specifically for the people of sport.

The people of sport embrace the training regimens that their sports require to fully develop as competitors. A similar embrace of the daily reading of these devotional thoughts and the suggested Daily Bible Reading will aid in the development of the competitor's heart toward complete devotion to Christ and a whole-hearted life in sport.

Instructions for Daily Bible Reading Plan

This plan is designed to enable you to read through the entire Bible in a year. Reading can begin at any point in the year and continue until completed. Another way to do the Bible reading is to select one section for reading daily (Gospels, Old Testament, Wisdom Books or New Testament) and thereby to spread the reading over four years.

As you read, ask God to speak to you through the Scripture and to transform your life by the Truth.

"The unfolding of your Word brings light,
It gives understanding to the simple."
Psalms 119:130

Discussion Guide and Questions

Beginning on page 374, you will find a discussion guide followed by a group study questions for each day.

COMPE

I Corinth.

What is the value of the train.
tice? How efficiently could you perfe
n't train well? What are the rewards
scripture addresses these issues for all o.

In the first letter to the Corinthian ch.
writes at chapter 9 and verses 24 and 25, "D.
in a race all the runners run, but only one gets
such a way as to get the prize. Everyone who .
games goes into strict training. They do it to get
will not last; but we do it to get a crown that will la.

Obviously you couldn't perform well at all on ga.
you didn't discipline your mind, you body and your en
You've had to exercise self control over these things throug.
your athletic career with respect to diet, running, weight train
ing, studying video tape and more. Expect it to pay off in today's
competition! Win the crown!

What's more, exercise discipline in the most important areas
of life and you'll find yourself winning championships that don't
fade in importance, collect dust on the shelf or diminish in value.

Bible Reading Plan:
Matthew 1:1-17
Acts 1:1-11
Psalms 1
Genesis 1-2

January 1

SOAR

Isaiah 40:30-31

...rt of your sport comes so easily to you that you ...ortlessly soar in it? When does competition seem to ...rally and relaxed? The prophet Isaiah knew of such ...and writes about them in today's scripture.

...Isaiah chapter 40 and in verses 30 and 31 it says, "Even ...s grow tired and weary, and young men stumble and fall; ...those who hope in the Lord will renew their strength. They ...l soar on wings like eagles; they will run and not grow weary, ...ey will walk and not be faint."

What an exciting promise! As we trust God, as we place our hope in His love for us, we will be renewed and able to soar like eagles. Can you really believe that simply trusting Christ will make a real difference in your performance on the field of competition? What do you have to lose?

As you prepare to compete today, take the chance to ask God for His transforming power in your weary, aching body. Ask Him to strengthen your tired legs and to breathe courage into your fainting spirit. Trust strongly and compete courageously.

Bible Reading Plan:
Acts 1:12-26
Psalm 2
Genesis 3 and 4

January 2

INVESTMENTS

Mark 12:41-44

If athletic talent could be measured in dollars and cents, who would be the richest player that you know? How generous is that player in relation to her teammates? Who would be the poorest player that you know? How generous is that person toward others?

Jesus speaks of a similar contrast between rich and poor in Mark chapter 12 and verses 41 through 44. "Jesus sat down opposite the place where the offerings were put and watched the crowd putting their money into the temple treasury. Many rich people threw in large amounts. But a poor widow came and put in two very small copper coins worth only a fraction of a penny. Calling his disciples to him, Jesus said, 'I tell you the truth, this poor widow has put more into the treasury than all the others. They all gave out of their wealth; but she, out of her poverty, put in everything - all she had to live on."

Why does it seem that often the poorest of us make the deepest investments in the team? It happens all the time. Often the least talented among us are the best teammates and give to others most generously. It's no surprise; Jesus saw it in His day as well.

Let me challenge you today. Whether athletically rich or poor, invest deeply in your team collectively and in your teammates individually. Give it all away in pursuit of a great team victory.

Bible Reading Plan:
Matthew 2:1-12
Psalm 3
Genesis 5-8

January 3

LOYALTY

II Corinthians 7:3

How do you relate to your teammates when they're at their best? You probably congratulate them, look them in the eye, hang around and even embrace them. How about on their worst days? Do you ignore them, avoid them or even run and hide? What does your heart tell you to do?

In Paul's second letter to his friends in Corinth at chapter 7 and verse 3, he wrote, "I do not say this to condemn you; I have said before that you have such a place in our hearts that we would live or die with you." Even in tense, ugly circumstances like those experienced by the Corinthians, we must be loyal to our teammates, friends and family.

A loyal teammate will not run from another who has failed or otherwise fallen from favor. Rather, that loyal one will run straight toward and embrace his/her fallen comrade. Our teammates must occupy such places of honor and respect in our hearts that we believe the best about them and seek their highest good, even at our personal cost.

On his best day honor, respect and embrace your teammate, he's worthy of that. On his worst day, honor, respect and embrace your teammate, he's worthy of that.

As you pray in preparation for today's contest, ask God to fill your heart with commitment and loyalty for your teammates. Win or lose, live or die, be a loyal teammate and friend.

Bible Reading Plan:
Matthew 2:13-23
Acts 2:22-47
Genesis 9-11

January 4

DISCIPLINE

Proverbs 3:11-12

How many of us would say that we have an ideal father? Who among us has a dad 100% without fault or inconsistency? The Lord God is that kind of Father.

In Proverbs chapter 3 and verses 11 and 12 we read, "My son (daughter), do not despise the Lord's discipline and do not resent His rebuke, because the Lord disciplines those He loves, as a father the son in whom he delights."

Most of us know what it is to be disciplined by our coaches. It's something that if not understood, we could soon despise. Our parents may have rebuked us for foolish things we did as children and many of us may have resented their chastening. I don't know how many times I wondered if my coach was crazy while we ran laps after practice for bonehead plays. We often resented the discipline at the moment, but as we grew in our sport, we realized the wisdom in his correction.

That same principle applies to life on a wider scale. God will lovingly correct those whom He loves. He will not sit passively by and let you destroy yourself. He will correct, discipline and sometimes rebuke us. Be careful to not despise His correction, it comes for your benefit and is driven by His profound love for you.

In today's competition, do not resent your coaching staff's correction and discipline. As we work together, we will be more successful that any of us dreamed. Have a great day; compete like a champion!

Bible Reading Plan:
Matthew 3:1-12
Acts 3
Psalms 5

January 5

OPPORTUNITY

Mark 14:3-7

Can you recall a time in your sport career when things were so good that you didn't want them to end? You wanted that winning feeling to last for days, but it was soon gone. Jesus had similar days and we can read about some of them.

In Mark chapter 14 and verses 3 through 7 we read, "...A woman came with an alabaster jar of very expensive perfume, made of pure nard. She broke the jar and poured the perfume on (Jesus') head. Some of those present were saying indignantly to one another, 'Why this waste of perfume? It could have been sold for more than a year's wages and the money given to the poor.' And they rebuked her harshly. 'Leave her alone,' said Jesus. 'Why are you bothering her? She has done a beautiful thing to me. The poor you will always have with you, and you can help them any time you want. But you will not always have me.'"

Focus on the words, "The poor you will always have with you, but you will not always have me," and remember the greatest moments of your athletic career. Think of how precious those feelings and memories are to you. Now when you recognize a similar moment, adopt Jesus' philosophy and drain every drop of good from it.

When another great victory arrives, stay there as long as you can. Savor the moment and grasp its significance. Pay whatever it costs to enjoy every drop of its value and aroma. The necessary, mundane things of life are always there, but moments like these are fleeting and few. Recognize them and enjoy them to the fullest. Compete well today and you may just create such a moment.

Bible Reading Plan:
Matthew 3:13-17
Acts 4:1-22

January 6

KNOWLEDGE

Proverbs 1:7

Everyone who competes needs knowledge. We each need the knowledge of our games, of our positions and of the game plan. We need to know another set of things that are even more important to life off the field.

In the book of Proverbs at chapter 1 and verse 7 we find the theme verse for the whole book, "The fear of the Lord is the beginning of knowledge; Fools despise wisdom and instruction."

Most people, when they hear the phrase, the fear of the Lord, think of a fear of death, that somehow the Lord may get mad at you and kill you. Rather than that, this proverb refers to a reverential awe that profoundly respects God and listens to His wisdom.

What's more, this profound respect is the said to be the beginning of knowledge. This is where real knowledge starts! It's easy to see how God sees people who refuse the starting place for knowledge, He refers to them as fools. Only a fool would despise the real source for wisdom and instruction.

As you pray and prepare for competition today, ask the Lord to fill you with real knowledge. Ask Him to give you wisdom and instruction. All this begins with a healthy, profound respect for the awesome Lord of Creation...Jesus Christ.

Bible Reading Plan:
Acts 4:23-27
Psalms 7
Genesis 18-20

January 7

COURAGE

I Chronicles 28:20

At times it seems like our hard work and commitment will go for nothing. Sometimes we get tired and discouraged. The Bible speaks to these questions and fears very directly.

In the Old Testament historical book called First Chronicles at chapter 28 and verse 20 it says, "David the king also said to Solomon his son, 'Be strong and courageous, and do the work. Do not be afraid or discouraged, for the LORD God, my God, is with you.'" This was a pivotal time in the nation of Israel's history and you are at an equally important time in this team's history.

It's true that the preseason has held a lot of adversity for you and could even lead to your being discouraged. Take heart from King David's words to his son Solomon. Don't be afraid or discouraged, rather be strong and courageous and do the work. Focus on the task at hand and all the distractions will fade away.

The thing that makes all this possible for us is the same as what worked in David and Solomon. It's the strong assurance that the LORD God, my God is with you. That is strong stuff and the source of great strength. Let the assurance of God's love and care for you result in strength and courage, both individually and as a unit.

Bible Reading Plan:
Matthew 4:12-17
Psalms 8
Genesis 21-23

January 8

RESOLVE

Isaiah 50:7

Have you ever known a competitor who seems to have an unbending will to win? One he set his mind on his goal, he would not waiver from it for anything. Perhaps you're like that. Many of the greatest competitors are.

In Isaiah's book of prophecy at chapter 50 and verse 5 we read about such an attitude of resolve, "Because the Sovereign Lord helps me, I will not be disgraced. Therefore have I set my face like a flint, and I know I will not be put to shame."

Some of us are so committed to our goals that, on game day, our faces look like they're carved out of stone. Our resolve is so strong that we're unfazed by outside noises or distractions.

Though he was exposed to possible disgrace and shame, Isaiah pressed on in the pursuit of his goals. He did so because he had a profound trust in God and sensed His help day to day.

As you compete today and as you press toward the completion of this season, set your face like a flint. Focus strongly on your team's goals and let nothing deter you from their fulfillment. Trust in your teammates, your coaching staff and ultimately in your God to help you in this marvelous pursuit.

Bible Reading Plan:
Matthew 4:18-25
Acts 5:17-42
Genesis 24

January 9

STRENGTH

II Thessalonians 2:16

Who are the people in your lives who encourage your heart and strengthen you to do well? Take a moment to recall their faces, their encouraging words and their strengthening presence. What if God was on your list of such people?

In Paul's second letter to his friends in Thessalonica at chapter 2 and verses 16 and 17 we read, "May our Lord Jesus Christ himself and God our Father, who loved us and by his grace gave us eternal encouragement and good hope, encourage your hearts and strengthen you in every good deed and word." Paul's prayer for his friends is that they would be encouraged and strengthened.

To be encouraged is like getting a transfusion of courage for your heart. You're suddenly possessed of more confidence and hope for the situation at hand. To be strengthened is like the hand of a spotter assisting you with that final rep in the weight room. Completing your task is made much easier.

That's my prayer for you as well. May you be encouraged in every good deed and word. May your actions and your speech be full of courage, confidence and hope. May you be strengthened in every good deed and word. May your behavior and your speech reflect the inward strength of your heart.

Prepare for today's competition with courage and strength.

Bible Reading Plan:
Matthew 5:1-12
Acts 6
Psalms 10

January 10

TRUST

As we compete, there is a great deal of trust required from all of us. At times we have to trust our coaches, our teammates, even our own abilities. The most secure person to place one's trust in is certainly the Lord Jesus.

In Proverbs chapter 3 and verses 5 and 6 it says, "Trust in the Lord with all your heart and lean not on your own understanding; in all your ways acknowledge Him and He will make your paths straight."

In competition there are always things that are beyond our control and things that are beyond our understanding. Rather than leaning on our understanding, this scripture leads us to lean on the understanding of the Lord. He's the Creator of the universe, He certainly has sufficient understanding for today's competition.

The call is to trust Him with all our hearts. Let's commit everything to Him and lean wholly upon His understanding and His love for us. Make your prayer today a whole hearted commitment of everything you are to the Lord Jesus.

Bible Reading Plan:
Acts 7:1-38
Psalms 11
Genesis 27-28

January 11

BETRAYAL

Mark 14:17-19

Have you ever felt betrayed by a coach or a teammate? Maybe something told in confidence was spoken to others or a promise went unfulfilled. Such feelings of betrayal hurt deeply. Imagine if betrayal were to lead to one's death. Such was the case in the life of Jesus.

We read about how Jesus handles a betrayal that hasn't even occurred yet in Mark chapter 14 and verses 17 through 19, "When evening came, Jesus arrived with the Twelve. While they were reclining at the table eating, he said, 'I tell you the truth, one of you will betray me - one who is eating with me.' They were saddened and one by one they said to him, 'Surely not I?'"

Jesus' twelve teammates were all together at something very similar to a pre-game meal when He dropped a bomb on the group. He said that He was aware that one of them would betray Him. It's curious that they would each ask him, "Surely not I?" But it makes sense when we consider that each of them was fully aware that he was certainly capable, given the right circumstances.

These men knew that betrayal is easy, but loyalty is tough. It's easy to betray a confidence, to forward gossip or to turn our backs on our teammates. It's much tougher to be loyal in hard times and to hang in with teammates who perform poorly.

As you prepare for today's competition, be loyal like John. Don't betray your teammates like Judas. Even more, be ready to love extravagantly, like Jesus.

Bible Reading Plan:
Matthew 5:21-32
Psalms 12
Genesis 29-30

January 12

PAIN

Mark 14:35-36

What is there about your life in sport that is so difficult or painful that you wish it would just go away? Maybe it's a nagging injury, the pain of mounting losses or strained relationships with coaches or teammates. Any of these can rip the joy from life.

Jesus faced a similar situation, but the consequences were far greater. We read about it in Mark chapter 14 and verses 35 and 36, "Going a little farther, he fell to the ground and prayed that if possible the hour might pass from him. 'Abba, Father,' he said, 'everything is possible for you. Take this cup from me. Yet not what I will, but what you will."

In His last night on the earth, Jesus stared death in the face and knew that He'd be dead in less than 24 hours. As any of us would, He asked that He be spared such pain and suffering. Thankfully, He also had the self-discipline to submit His will to God's.

As you face your every day pains, look for God's will in the matters of life. Don't deny your feelings or hide your displeasure, God knows that it hurts. Talk with Him about it and commit yourself to His purposes in the situation.

In today's competition, take the same attitude toward pain and suffering that Jesus did and press through them to achieve your goals.

Bible Reading Plan:
Matthew 5:33-48
Acts 8:1-25
Genesis 31

January 13

RISK AND DANGER

John 13:34

What is the most reckless, dangerous and risky thing you've ever done? Please don't answer out loud! If you said it was to love your family, friends and teammates, you're thinking like Jesus.

In John's Gospel at chapter 13 and verse 34 we read these challenging words, "A new commandment I give to you, that you love one another; as I have loved you, that you also love one another."

These words are remarkable for a couple of reasons. Jesus says them while Judas, who would the same evening betray Him, is still in the room. He also says these words to His disciples, His teammates, who within hours will go into hiding and one will even deny knowing Him. His love was rather risky, but very deep.

We have the same challenge and opportunity as the disciples had. We can also choose to love our teammates, coaches and families without reservation, all the way. We can love them as we reflect Jesus' love toward them. Love with this kind of abandon is not safe. Love with this kind of sacrifice is not cheap. This is love with commitment it doesn't look for an escape. That's what we need for team unity and loyalty.

Let's exhibit this kind of teamwork in today's competition as we love one another as Jesus has loved us.

Bible Reading Plan:
Matthew 6:1-15
Acts 8:26-40
Psalms 14

January 14

WISDOM

I Corinthians 1:25

As athletes we are often looking for an edge over our opponents, something that will provide an advantage and lead to a win. Sometimes we think that comes by being smarter and other times we think that being stronger will lead to victory. The Bible points to a person who overcomes both great human wisdom and the power of physical strength.

In Paul's first letter to his friends at Corinth at chapter 1 and verse 25 he says, "For the foolishness of God is wiser than man's wisdom, and the weakness of God is stronger than man's strength." There is more to strength than what can be measured in the weight room, more to quickness than can be measured with a stop watch. There's more to wisdom than what can be attributed to a degree or a g.p.a.

There is strength and wisdom available to us that comes from a whole other dimension, because it's the strength and wisdom that comes from God. Live in that dimension today.

Ask the Lord to fill you with His wisdom, the ability to know the right thing to do. Ask Him to fill you with His strength, the power to carry out what is best.

Play with great passion and enthusiasm. Use the Lord's wisdom and strength to achieve excellence on the field of competition.

Bible Reading Plan:
Matthew 6:16-24
Acts 9:1-19
Psalms 15
Genesis 34-35

January 15

JOY AND PEACE

Isaiah 55:12

Which of these is a better descriptor of your frame of mind in competition; joy and peace or anxiety and rage? I've known competitors from both camps and I know which ones were more successful and were better teammates.

Isaiah wrote these words in chapter 55 and verse 12, "You will go out in joy and be led forth in peace; the mountains and hills will burst into song before you, and all the trees of the field will clap their hands."

Though many competitors pursue their sport in anger, full of anxiety and rage; this scripture presents another alternative. If we go out in joy and are led in peace, we find the whole course of life more pleasant and we receive great favor with those around us.

Joy is simply emotional stability. That's most important during competition as we experience the inevitable swings of momentum from one team to the other. If we go out in joy, we have the emotional stability to react appropriately to each situation that arises.

Peace is the capacity to be calm in the midst of chaos and confusion. Competition is full of moments of confusion and we're too often overcome by it. Peace gives you the ability to keep your mind focused on your assignment even when everything seems to be coming unglued.

As you compete today, let peace and joy rule your hearts. Pray for the capacity to remain calm and under control, even in chaotic situations. Seek God's character of joy to keep your emotionally afloat in the midst of a turbulent sea of momentum shifts. Compete with a joyful, peaceful heart today.

Bible Reading Plan:
Matthew 6:25-34
Acts 9:20-43
Genesis 36

January 16

ABANDONED

Mark 15:33-34

Have you ever felt abandoned by your team during competition? You look around and wonder, "Where did everybody go? I feel like I'm out here all alone!" Imagine how Jesus felt on a very dark day in His life.

This darkest of days is recorded in Mark chapter 15 and verses 33 through 34, "At the sixth hour darkness came over the whole land until the ninth hour. And at the ninth hour Jesus cried out in a loud voice... 'My God, my God, why have you forsaken me?'"

This was the biggest, most important day of Jesus' life. This was the culmination of His life's purpose. In such a moment, He'd been abandoned by His followers, was even betrayed by one. Worst of all, He felt abandoned by God. In spite of how He felt, He fully completed His mission and honored God to His last breath.

Competition at the highest levels is not always pleasant. It is surely not always fun. You'll occasionally feel like you're all alone in the fight. Don't give in to discouragement and the temptation to quit. You could be on the threshold of a breakthrough for yourself and for your team.

Compete strongly today. Press through your feelings and honor God with your life as a competitor.

Bible Reading Plan:
Matthew 7:1-14
Acts 10:1-23
Psalm 17
Genesis 37-38

January 17

GUARD YOUR HEART

Proverbs 4:23

To whom have you given your heart? Your boyfriend or girl-friend? An intimate friend and confidant? Family? The Lord Jesus? Be careful...

In the book of Proverbs at chapter 4 and verse 23 it says, "Guard your heart with all diligence, for from it flow the springs of life."

Why would a person's heart be of such value that the Bible would say to guard it with all diligence? The verse says that from it flow the springs of life. The things that keep our life fresh and clean, like spring water, flow from our hearts. If our hearts are pure and unspoiled, we can honor God with all of our lives. However if we're polluted in our hearts, everything about us is unclean and lacks life giving freshness.

So what shall we do? Guard your heart. Be careful who you choose for friends. Consider prayerfully the people you date and be very sober and sure about choosing a spouse. Guard your heart. If you compromise the purity of your heart to make a friend or to impress a lover, you're in peril of polluting the spring.

In today's prayer time, commit your heart to the Lord. Ask Him to help you guard it with all diligence and to maintain its purity.

Bible Reading Plan:
Matthew 7:15-29
Acts 10:24-48
Psalms 18:1-24
Genesis 39-40

January 18

UNITY

Acts 4:32

Take a moment to recall a team from your past which had great team unity. What were the key attitudes from which that unity sprang? What made that team so special? Today's scripture shows us some attitudes that lead to a unified team.

In the book of Acts at chapter 4 and verse 32 it says, "All the believers were one in heart and mind. No one claimed that any of his possessions was his own, but they shared everything they had." What a team! These people were winners.

Note some important things about this group. They were one in heart – that is they shared the same values driven by the Spirit of Christ. They were one in mind – their goals and the strategy for achieving them were unified. They shared everything – they were totally selfless, each one looking out for the other's best interest.

Your team can achieve the same unity. You will be one in heart when you share the same set of values for your team. You will be one in mind when you each align your personal goals with those of the team. You will be fully unified when you compete selflessly and seek the team's best over your personal achievement.

As you prepare today, ask God to unify your team. Commit yourselves to being of one heart and mind.

Bible Reading Plan:
Matthew 8:1-13
Acts 11:1-18
Psalms 18:25-50
Genesis 41

January 19

OVERCOMING STRIFE

Proverbs 10:12

Does your team seem divided at times? Is strife at work to tear your teammates apart and to cause disharmony? How do we bring about the healing of relationships and restoration of teamwork?

In Proverbs chapter 10 and verse 12 it says, "Hatred stirs up strife, but love covers all transgressions." Hatred seems like such a harsh word for the things we see dividing our teams. Most people wouldn't even admit to hating anyone. Look at what causes the strife on your team and you'd probably say it's self-ishness, which is simply a soft word for hate.

The good news is that there's a solution. According to the scripture, Love covers all transgressions. Not just a few trans-gressions, all of them. What a powerful thing love is. What's more, it's proven in the life of Christ. His love for us has covered our transgression for all time and has ushered us into an eternal relationship with God.

Love is the key to good relationships on your team. Let love, selfless giving to each other, counter the strife born of selfish-ness. Let love rule your conduct in practice, on the field of com-petition and in the classroom. Cover your teammates' short-comings by loving them and seeking their best, even when it comes at your cost.

Pray for the Lord to heal your team's divisions and to fill you with His love. Ask the Lord to cover others' transgressions by His love expressed through you.

Bible Reading Plan:
Matthew 8:14-22
Acts 11:19-30
Psalms 19
Genesis 42-43

January 20

GOD'S WILL

Mark 3:35

What is it that we as Christian athletes can do to bring about a more intimate relationship with the Lord? Is there some program to work through, some book to read, a tape to listen to? What makes for a closer walk with Christ?

In Mark's gospel at chapter 3 and verse 35 Jesus says, "For whoever does the will of God is My brother and sister and mother." Jesus says this just as His family is outside the house, ready to take him home. They think He's lost His mind and is in need of real help.

Jesus flips the whole idea of who is most closely related to Him by using these powerful words. He says that the ones to whom He is most closely related are those who do God's will. People with whom He has no blood relation can enjoy a deep, personal, intimate relationship with the Lord in a way that mere relatives can never even understand.

Let's join these to whom Jesus spoke and be the Lord's most intimate family members. Let's do what Jesus says makes that happen. Let's do the will of God.

As you pray today, ask the Lord to reveal His will to you. Ask Him to make your relationship with Him rich and personal.

Bible Reading Plan:
Matthew 8:23-34
Acts 12
Psalms 20
Genesis 44-45

January 21

DIRECTION

II Thessalonians 3:5

When does your heart need direction? Do you ever feel like you've gone adrift or that you're wandering through life with no clear path? Today's scripture will help our hearts to have a road map for living.

In the second letter Paul wrote to the Thessalonians at chapter 3 and verse 5 we read, "May the Lord direct your hearts into God's love and Christ's perseverance." Paul is very simple with his directions; he says we should steer toward God's love and Christ's perseverance.

God's love is the source for every good thing in life. All that our hearts long for can be found in Him. Let Him direct your heart toward such love, security, peace and joy.

Christ's perseverance is beyond our wildest imaginations. He can help us push through the pain of injury, the disappointment of failure, the sting of loss, the ache of loneliness. The perseverance of Christ enables us to do the right thing even when everything in our minds and our bodies scream that we should just give up.

As you prepare to compete today, follow you heart as God directs it toward His love and the perseverance of Christ. The best things in sport and all of life are awaiting your arrival.

Bible Reading Plan:
Matthew 9:1-13
Acts 13:1-25
Psalms 21
Genesis 46-47

January 22

PRAYER

Isaiah 59:1

What do you pray about your life in sport? Do you regularly talk with God about each situation or just when things seem out of control? Which kind of prayer do you think God hears well? My answer may surprise you.

Isaiah the prophet wrote about prayer at chapter 59 and verse 1, there we read, "Surely the arm of the Lord is not too short to save, nor His ear too dull to hear."

It's exciting to me to know that God doesn't discriminate between my weakest prayers of panic and my most serene prayers of thanksgiving. He clearly hears both kinds. What's more, He is responsive to both with His strong arm of protection and deliverance.

In today's competition, invite the Lord into each moment of the game. Pray during pre-game, asking for His help and protection. Pray as the competition reaches its height, seeking His power and wisdom for excellence. Pray after it's all over, give thanks for the privilege of competing and for the win or the loss.

God's more than willing to hear from you on your best day or at your worst moment.

Bible Reading Plan:
Matthew 9:14-26
Acts 13:26-52
Psalms 22:1-11
Genesis 48

January 23

FLEE AND PURSUE

II Timothy 2:22

Can you recall an instance when a great player was disqualified from competition due to poor off-field decisions? I can think of dozens. What do you suppose was driving their hearts to make such foolish decisions? Many times it's simply the strong, destructive, desires of youth. Today's scripture warns us about such desires.

In Paul's second letter to his friend Timothy at chapter 2 and verse 22 we read, "Flee the evil desires of youth, and pursue righteousness, faith, love and peace, along with those who call on the Lord out of a pure heart."

There's no need to list the evil desires of youth, you probably have a few of them in your mind presently. The point is to flee from them. Don't just stand idly by them, that's the easiest way to be run over by such things.

Further, we're called to pursue four principles of wise living from a pure heart. Let your pure heart lead you to pursue righteousness – doing what you know to be right. Pursue faith – actively trust God, your coaches, your teammates, and your friends. Pursue love – seek the best for others, even at your personal cost. Pursue peace – work to keep your relationships open and honest.

As you prepare to compete today, run away from the foolish desires that would compromise your ability to compete well and to contribute to the life of your team. Pursue the best things of life from a pure heart.

Bible Reading Plan:
Matthew 9:27-38
Acts 14
Psalms 22:12-31
Genesis 49

January 24

DISCIPLINE

Proverbs 10:17

No one likes to be corrected by his coach or teammate. Everyone wants to think that he competes at the highest level of his ability every time out. The problem is, most of us never approach that level of competence and thus need correction.

In Proverbs chapter 10 at verse 17 it says, "He who heeds discipline shows the way to life, but whoever ignores correction leads others astray."

We've all probably had teammates who ignore the correction that the coaches give them. They give verbal agreement when the coach is speaking, but go on doing everything the way they were. This scripture says that in doing that they do a great disservice to not only themselves, but the whole team. Here it says they lead others astray by their actions.

The promise of this scripture is that if we listen closely to discipline, or correction, that we will show others the way to life. When we make adjustments when corrected by our coaches, parents, pastors, friends or teammates, we provide a rich example of humility and grace to all those around us.

As you pray today, ask the Lord to give you the grace to heed discipline and to enable you to show all those around you the way to rich, full, abundant life in relationship with Christ Jesus.

Bible Reading Plan:
Matthew 10:1-20
Acts 15:1-21
Psalms 23
Genesis 50

January 25

ISOLATION

Mark 1:12-13

Do you ever feel isolated, cut off, all alone? Though you're surrounded by people, you may still be lonely. Jesus knew that feeling and we can draw some courage and comfort from his experience.

We read about it in Mark's gospel at chapter 1 and verses 12 and 13. "At once the Spirit sent him out into the desert, and he was in the desert forty days, being tempted by Satan. He was with the wild animals and angels attended him."

Now I'm sure none of us has ever been sent out into a desert to be the personal whipping boy for Satan, but I'm sure we've all known some loneliness. Notice who cared for Jesus in his loneliness, the text says that wild animals were with him and angels attended him.

Who is with you on your loneliest days? Probably it's your teammates. Who attends to you when you're at your lowest points? That's probably friends and family. The loneliness comes to everyone; the issue is how we deal with it.

As you prepare for today's competition, lean on your teammates and coaching staff for support in the same way Jesus would have depended on those attending angels. Even in the loneliest moments of this season, look for consolation and companionship from friends and family as an oasis might appear in the desert. Compete strongly today.

Bible Reading Plan:
Matthew 1:18-25
Acts 2:1-21

January 26

TALKING TRASH

Proverbs 10:19

Trash talking on the field of competition has become more and more pervasive in the last few years. How should we as Christians approach this issue? The Scriptures are full of wisdom related to speech. One such verse follows.

In Proverbs chapter 10 and verse 19 it says, "When words are many, sin is not absent, but he who holds his tongue is wise."

As we speak more and more, our chances of speaking foolishly certainly increase. You probably know someone who talks too much and in doing so speaks in ways that cause harm to himself or to others. That's what is meant by, "sin is not absent." Talk long enough and the best of us will sin with our tongues.

The other side of this is that when we remain silent in certain discussions, we display an uncommon wisdom. Some people speak when there is nothing to say. We would do well to speak only when it is appropriate and when the situation is enhanced by our comments. "He who holds his tongue is wise."

As you pray today, ask the Lord to guard your mouth. Ask Him to help you control what you say, when you speak and to choose appropriate settings for your speech.

Bible Reading Plan:
Psalms 4
Genesis 12-14

January 27

COMPETITION

I Corinthians 9:24

Competition is a great thing as it moves people to greatness and beyond mediocrity. The Bible is full of instances where the life of faith is likened to an athletic contest. One of those follows.

In First Corinthians chapter 9 and verse 24 it says, "Do you not know that in a race all the runners run, but only one gets the prize? Run in such a way as to win the prize." I like that! It's said very simply, "Run in such a way as to win the prize."

Your coaching staff has outlined for you the way to win the prize today. Your part is to run that way. Your part is to follow their direction and to compete to the greatest extent of your ability. Invest all that you have and all that you are in the pursuit of the team's goals.

As you compete today, do so in such a way as to win!!! Strive to honor Him in all that you do.

Bible Reading Plan:
Matthew 4:1-11
Acts 5:1-16

January 28

COURAGE

Joshua 1:6-7

When does your sport demand courage of you? Is it when you face superior competition? Does playing through injuries require courage? Is courage a factor in overcoming fatigue? What role does courage play in overcoming adversity? Today's scripture links strength and courage in a powerful combination.

In the historical book of Joshua in the first chapter and verses 6 through 7 we read, "Be strong and courageous, because you will lead these people to inherit the land I swore to their forefathers to give them. Be strong and very courageous. Be careful to obey all the law my servant Moses gave you; do not turn from it to the right or the left, that you may be successful wherever you go."

Joshua had just taken leadership of his people after Moses had died and this was what God told him as he assumed this most intimidating role. Twice God said to be strong and courageous. The second time He said to be very courageous. Courage would obviously be a most important quality for Joshua's leadership.

What are the situations in today's competition that may require you to be strong and very courageous? You probably thought of some as we opened the issue earlier. Some of those could be as scary to you as replacing Moses would have been to Joshua.

The Lord's word to you today is the same as it was to Joshua, several millennia ago. He would say, "Be strong and very courageous." Walk boldly into today's competition with strength and confidence. Take on your opponent with great courage and determination to win.

Bible Reading Plan:
Psalms 9
Genesis 25-26

January 29

EVIDENCE

Acts 11:23

Payday for your coaches comes when they see evidence that their team "gets it." When she sees that the team understands and does what she wants, that's as good as it gets. She's enthused, happy, thrilled and renewed in her commitment to the team. Today's scripture shows us an example of this dynamic.

In the book of Acts at chapter 11 and verse 23 we read, "When he arrived and saw the evidence of the grace of God, he was glad and encouraged them all to remain true to the Lord with all their hearts." Paul was thrilled to see these people doing so well and encouraged them to love God with all their hearts.

Paul the Apostle and your coaches know that doing things with all our hearts is the key to achievement. He saw evidence that his goals for them were being achieved and it thrilled him. Your coaches see such evidence in you and they encourage you to give all your hearts in pursuit of your goals. These are the great rewards of coaching.

I'd like to join Paul and your coaching staff as we encourage you to give your absolute best today. Compete in total abandon. Pursue a victory with all your heart. Sell out 100% to your teammates, your coaches and to pursue God's best.

Bible Reading Plan:
Matthew 5:13-20
Acts 7:39-60

January 30

PEACE

John 14:27

From where does peace come for your life? Is it found in quiet weekends with your family? Maybe you get it from music or good books to read. Could it be there is a source of tranquility that is internal rather than based on circumstances?

Jesus talks about such a source of peace in John chapter 14 and verse 27. It reads, "Peace I leave with you, My peace I give to you; not as the world gives do I give to you. Let not our heart be troubled, neither let it be afraid."

Jesus was about to leave His disciples and was walking straight toward His death. Everyone around Him was scared to death! They needed someone to give them some peace. Jesus stepped up and gave an extraordinary kind of reassurance.

The world gives peace in rather weak ways. The world gives peace externally...it's easily brushed off. The world gives peace temporarily...constantly in need of refreshment. The world gives peace with strings attached...there's a hook on the end of that line.

God's peace calms our fears and erases our anxieties. He gives peace like Jesus demonstrates here on the last day of His earthly life. He was unhurried and unafraid. His peace is internal and won't wear out with time.

Play today's game with this sense of peace ruling your life. Play like Jesus; unhurried and unafraid. May the Lord's peace be yours in today's contest.

Bible Reading Plan:
Psalms 13
Genesis 32-33

January 31

SELF-CONTROL

I Corinthians 9:25

What would it be like to compete for something that will not tarnish on your bookshelf? All my trophies are collecting dust and fading in their importance. What would be a prize worth striving for that never fades, but requires great effort and concentration of will to achieve? The Bible speaks of such a prize.

In Paul's first letter to his friends in Corinth at chapter 9 and verse 25 it says, "And everyone who competes in the games exercises self-control in all things. They do it to receive a perishable wreath, but we an imperishable one." We all need some self-control.

Some of us need self-control over our tongues, for others it's with our tempers, with others it's our appetites or our time or study habits or something else.

Why is self-control so important? It keeps us from living our lives in an out of control way and from losing focus on the most important matters of life. Without some self-control our lives would resemble a skidding car headed for the ditch and a horrible crash.

The writer spoke of competing for a prize. In today's competition you'll be pursuing a prize and it will require self-control for you to maximize your gifts and abilities toward the goal of winning the contest.

Pray for the fruit of self-control to be evident in your life today and approach the field of competition with great confidence in its presence. Let's compete in such a way that leads to winning prizes, both perishable and eternal.

Bible Reading Plan:
Matthew 10:21-42
Acts 15:22-41
Psalms 24

February 1

VICTORY

To whom do you look for guidance? Your coaches, your teammates, your parents? Who helps you make good decisions? What would be the consequences of your not seeking the wisdom of others? Let's look to the Scriptures for an answer.

In the book of Proverbs at chapter 14 and verse 11 Solomon writes, "Where there is no guidance, the people fall, but in abundance of counselors there is victory." Obviously none of us want to fall, so where does this guidance and counsel come from?

We get guidance from our coaches, from our teammates, from Bible reading, from church attendance, from family and friends. We need guidance to guard against falls, both individual and corporate.

It says that in abundance of counselors there is victory. Let's see our coaches and teammates as our counselors during competition today. Let's trust that in such an abundance as we have, there will be victory.

You have the counselors to achieve victory and to avoid the falls that come from a lack of guidance.

Bible Reading Plan:
Acts 16:1-15
Psalms 25
Exodus 4-6

February 2

FEAR

Have you had times of competition that assaulted your belief in your teammates, your game plan or even in your own abilities? What do we have to believe in when our strengths are called into question? The Scripture for today brings us strong encouragement.

In Mark's gospel at chapter 5 and verse 36, Jesus is talking to a man whose daughter has been critically ill and has just been told that she had died. He says to the father, "Do not be afraid any longer, only believe." Sometimes we can be overcome by a sense of fear when we see the vision of things we hope for dimmed by present circumstances. Jesus' word to us is the same as to the father of the little girl, "Do not be afraid any longer, only believe."

This man's faith was assaulted by the news that his daughter had already died. Our faith is sometimes assaulted by newspaper articles, t.v. reports, or second guessing and negative talk by classmates. Jesus calls us to maintain a trust regarding our goals and the things we hope for in our lives.

He says "only believe." Believe what? Believe in a concept or a set of ideas? No, Christ calls us to believe a person, Himself. In the same way as you believe your friends to tell you the truth, we believe God to tell the truth about the real affairs of life. I believe Him.

When you compete today, do not be afraid of anything, rather only believe! Believe in what God's doing in you. Believe in your coaches and teammates. Trust God to do great things in you.

Bible Reading Plan:
Matthew 11:20-30
Psalms 26
Exodus 7-9

February 3

ADVERSITY

Micah 7:8

How do you react when you're losing by a wide margin and your opponent rubs salt in your wounds with some trash-talk? How does it feel to lose and to hear the snickers of the winners on their way to the locker room? What should your attitude be in the face of such disrespect?

The prophet Micah had encountered such attitudes and writes about it in chapter 7 and verse 8, "Do not gloat over me, my enemy! Though I have fallen, I will rise. Though I sit in darkness, the Lord will be my light."

Micah advises his triumphant enemy that it would not be wise to gloat over him. He will come back. He also says that though he knew the experience of sitting painfully in the darkness of despair, he would trust the Lord to give him direction for the future.

I love it when a competitor comes back to defeat an earlier trash-talking opponent through perseverance and self-control. I'm impressed by the team that suffers quietly a disappointing loss, only to strengthen their resolve and to compete courageously the next time.

As you prepare for today's competition, guard your heart from the foolish pride that comes with an early lead. Don't gloat over your enemy. Even if you're on the short side of the scoreboard, maintain your attitude and press through to the end, trusting the Lord to be your light to victory.

Bible Reading Plan:
Matthew 12:1-21
Acts 17:1-15
Exodus 10-12

February 4

INTIMIDATION

Joshua 5:1

What advantages are yours when you know your opponents are intimidated by you and your teammates? Do you ever sense their fear? Can you see them hesitate or compete tentatively? Have you watched as the intimidated team was overcome by a momentum shift? Such intimidation is not limited to the arena of sport. In today's scripture, we see it in the Bible.

In the Old Testament book of Joshua at chapter 5 and verse 1 it says, "Now when all the Amorite kings west of the Jordan and all the Canaanite kings along the coast heard how the Lord had dried up the Jordan before the Israelites until we had crossed over, their hearts melted and they no longer had the courage to face the Israelites."

Did you hear how Joshua described the intimidation felt by his opponents? He said their hearts melted and they no longer had the courage to face them. This happened because of the stories being told by others.

This happens all the time in sport. Teams read the newspaper or watch the polls on the web and hear stories of how powerful their upcoming opponents will be. Often, just hearing the news is enough to melt their hearts and to drain every drop of courage from their souls.

As you approach today's competition, expect the news about your team to have made it to your opponent's locker room. Watch for the ferocity of your competitive drive to melt their hearts. Look for the opportunity to drive the courage from the souls of your opponents and to achieve a great victory.

Bible Reading Plan:
Matthew 12:22-37
Acts 17:16-34
Psalms 28

February 5

PREPARATION

I Peter 1:13

How do you prepare for competition? How do you bring your mind into focus? What do you think about and how do you keep your goals in sight as the season moves along? The Bible has some great instruction for such questions.

In Peter's first letter to his friends, in chapter 1 and verse 13 he says, "Therefore, prepare your minds for action; be self-controlled; set your hope fully on the grace to be given you when Jesus Christ is revealed."

Here's what you must do in approaching today's competition:

1) Prepare your minds for action. Bring some focus to your play. Don't be distracted by the officials' calls, the trash talking of other players, the fools in the stands or anything else. Prepare your minds for action.

2) Be self-controlled. Control your emotions and so avoid foolish penalties. Control your mouth and so improve your teamwork. Control your attitude and focus on accomplishing your task, not on placing blame for missed plays.

3) Set your hope fully on Jesus Christ. Ultimately the only person who can fully enable you to do all these things is Christ Jesus. He has the power to bring a focussed mind, self-control and real hope. Trust Him in prayer, give yourself fully to Him and He will never fail you.

As you pray today, prepare your mind for action, be self-controlled and set your hope fully on Jesus Christ. He is the ultimate winner in all things!

Bible Reading Plan:
Matthew 12:38-50
Acts 18:1-17
Psalms 29
Exodus 16-18

February 6

WISE ADVICE

Proverbs 12:15

Some people compete in the ways that they always have and never improve or learn new ways. Others continually innovate and look for new and better ways from their coaches and teammates. The Bible speaks about these two avenues for competition.

In Proverbs chapter 12 and verse 15 it says, "The way of a fool seems right to him, but a wise man listens to advice."

Those who shun their coaches' advice and the counsel of their peers are called fools. The fool is betrayed by his attitude and his actions. He follows the way that seems right to him and disregards the wisdom of his leaders and the helpful concern of his teammates and friends.

People who are wise listen to the advice of those who care for them. We are wise when we listen closely to our coaches, teammates, parents and friends. Their counsel and wisdom can keep us from being fools who have a poor perspective on life and walk down the path of foolishness.

In your prayer prior to competition today, ask the Lord to make you a person of wisdom who listens to advice. Ask Him to not let you live like a fool who stumbles along in the way that seems right to his own blinded eyes.

Bible Reading Plan:
Matthew 13:1-23
Acts 18:18-28
Psalms 30
Exodus 19-20

February 7

RECRUITING

Mark 1:16-18

During the recruiting process, what would be the most important factors in your decision to attend a university? Would it be something like the beauty of the campus, the prospects for the team or another factor like a perfectly matched field of study? Jesus was an outstanding recruiter and we read today about one of his recruiting calls.

Mark records this exchange between Jesus and some of his soon-to-be disciples at chapter 1 and verses 16 through 18. "As Jesus walked beside the Sea of Galilee, he saw Simon and his brother Andrew casting a net into the lake, for they were fishermen. 'Come follow me,' Jesus said, 'and I will make you fishers of men.' At once they left their nets and followed him."

The remarkable thing about how Jesus recruited was that he appealed to these men squarely within their life calling... they were fishermen and so he spoke to them in fishermen language. He talked to them about fishing. He simply shifted their focus from fish to men.

It's the same for you. Your coaches are shifting your focus from one level of sport and the limited area of competition to a higher level and to greater levels of skill and intensity. It's a big shift and requires a strong focus from each of you.

The question for today is, how will you respond to the call? Will you respond as these men did and follow, 'At once...'? Or will you hedge and hesitate to commit to your team? Let me encourage you to commit fully to your coaching staff, to your team leaders and to each member of your team.

Bible Reading Plan:
Matthew 13:24-43
Acts 19:1-22
Psalms 31
Exodus 21-23

February 8

DISTINCTIONS

Acts 15:9

What distinctions are easily made between your teammates? Surely you're different in terms of size, strength, speed, agility, skill, intelligence, background and more. What can be done to override these distinctions and to unify your team? Today's scripture gives us an idea of what God uses to unify people.

In the 15th chapter of Acts at verse 9 we read, "He made no distinction between us and them, for he purified their hearts by faith." Here's Peter, a formerly terribly bigoted man, appealing for others to accept people that he would have hated just days before. His heart was changed and he helped unify a very diverse set of people.

They key to such unity is a heart made pure by faith. Faith is active trust. A pure heart can see past the distinctions to the hearts of his teammates. A heart, made pure by faith, can see through the external differences to the essence of another.

As you prepare for today's competition, purify your heart by faith. Actively trust God to change your heart. Trust your teammates as you pursue a victory. Trust your coaching staff to enable you to compete at your best.

Bible Reading Plan:
Matthew 13:44-58
Acts 19:23-41
Psalms 32
Exodus 24-26

February 9

DILIGENCE

Proverbs 12:24

Would you characterize yourself as a hard worker in practice or as a lazy player? What would your coach say? How about your teammates? Today's scripture provides a warning for the lazy and a promise for the diligent.

Solomon wrote in Proverbs chapter 12 and verse 24, "Diligent hands will rule, but laziness ends in slave labor." Obviously none of us wants to labor like a slave, that is with no reward for our investment of time and energy.

The Proverb says that slave labor is the inevitable outcome of laziness. Let's be diligent in our work and we will reap the reward that comes with diligence... ruling. Ruling means to have success and authority in our spheres of influence.

As you compete today, be diligent in your preparation and in the execution of your responsibilities. Your diligence, concentration and hard work will result in your ruling.

Bible Reading Plan:
Acts 20:1-12
Psalms 33
Exodus 27-29

February 10

GIFTS

I Peter 4:10

As an athlete you're a gifted person. From where do these gifts come? How is it that you're given certain abilities and others do not possess them? How much of your talent is a gift and how much is cultivated skill? How should we use our gifts and abilities in relation to our teammates and coaches? The Scripture has some insight into all these questions.

In Peter's first letter to his friends in Asia, in chapter 4 and verse 10 he writes, "As each one has received a special gift, employ it in serving one another, as good managers of the grace of God in its various forms." What special gift have you received? How are you specially gifted? How well do you manage the gifts with which you've been entrusted?

The key message for me in this sentence is that I'm to use my giftedness in the service of others. The fact of my being gifted has very little to do with me, but everything to do with Him who gives the gifts. These are gifts, not merit badges. I'm called to exercise my gifts in the service of others. Think for a minute about how to use your giftedness in the service of your teammates.

Where sports are concerned, some of you are gifted at ball handling, others at rebounding, others at running, others in encouraging, others at defense, others at passing, still others at developing a game plan. The key for us all is to not exercise these gifts selfishly, but in the service of all the others. The Giver of the gifts is best honored by this kind of selfless, humble, effective, management.

Pray and ask Him to give you the strength to serve your teammates through the exercise of your gifts.

Bible Reading Plan:
Matthew 14:22-36
Psalms 34

February 11

POWERFUL TEAMMATE

Joshua 5:13-14

Have you ever had a teammate of whom you'd say, "I'm glad he's on our team? I really don't want to be his/her opponent." There is a story in the Bible of just such a person.

In Joshua's book of history at chapter 5 and verses 13 and 14 it reads, "Now when Joshua was near Jericho, he looked up and saw a man standing in front of him with a drawn sword in his hand. Joshua went up to him and asked, 'Are you for us or for our enemies?' 'Neither,' he said, 'but as commander of the army of the Lord I have come.' Then Joshua fell facedown to the ground in reverence, and asked him, 'What message does my Lord have for his servant?'"

Joshua didn't really understand to whom he was talking as he encountered this man. It didn't take long, however, for him to get a clear picture of who was the greater person.

It may be the same with you and your teammates. After just a few practice sessions you probably knew who the superior athletes were. Your probably saw right away who the leaders were. With such people, it's not a matter of them being for or against us; it's more a matter of being sure we're on their side.

In today's competition, be sure to closely align yourself with your teammates and coaching staff. They're for you. Be thankful them and the privilege you have of being on their team. I'm praying that we're all with the commander of the Lord's army. He's the ultimate victor.

Bible Reading Plan:
Matthew 15:1-20
Acts 21:1-26
Psalms 35
Exodus 32-33

February 12

ANXIETY

Proverbs 12:25

As we approach a competition, many times we're burdened by anxiety and worry. Often we wonder how well we'll perform, how good our opponent is, how well we know our assignments and other concerns. While these are legitimate concerns, they can serve to hinder our athletic performance.

In Proverbs chapter 12 and verse 25 it speaks of this dynamic, "An anxious heart weighs a man down, but a kind word cheers him up."

It's like our heart becomes lined with lead or our legs are made of rubber, when we are overcome with anxiety we are weighed down. Suddenly we're weighed down by doubt, confusion and frustration. All these lead to a less than our best performance during competition.

There is also a great promise in this scripture. It says that a kind word cheers one up. Encouragement is a powerful tool for the athlete. A simple word, a kind expression of thanks, a well timed compliment can put a charge in a teammate or a coach and thus will lift the weight that he's been carrying.

In your time of prayer today, ask the Lord to lead you to someone whom you can encourage. Ask Him for a chance to speak the kind word that cheers up your teammate, coach or friend.

Bible Reading Plan:
Matthew 15:21-39
Acts 21:27-40
Psalms 36
Exodus 34

February 13

BELIEF

Mark 9:23

What are the limiting factors for you in relation to achievement? What is the greatest thing you think you're capable of accomplishing? Do you believe you're able to achieve everything God has called you to do?

In Mark's gospel at chapter 9 and verse 23, Jesus speaks to a man with a great problem, "If you can believe, all things are possible to him who believes."

This man was faced with his son's terrible affliction and struggled to believe the Lord would free him from it. Jesus tells him that all things are possible to him who believes. Believes in what? In this case in the goodness, compassion and mercy of God.

What is it you're having trouble believing? What is there about life that keeps you from fully trusting the Lord? Look fully upon the Lord Jesus and trust Him. He says to you the same words He said to that man.

In your prayers today, ask the Lord to help your unbelief. Ask Him for more grace to trust Him. Tell Him that you believe in Him and in all that He can do in you. Commit yourself fully to Him for all of life.

Bible Reading Plan:
Matthew 16:1-12
Acts 22
Psalms 37:1-22
Exodus 35-37

February 14

EMERGING LEADERS

Judges 11:4-7

How do leaders emerge from among your teammates? Is there a personality type or a position on the team that automatically makes one a leader? Be careful, sometimes the best leaders appear from the most unlikely places. One such leader is seen in today's scripture.

In the book of Judges at chapter 11 and verses 4 through 7 we read, "Some time later, when the Ammonites made war on Israel, the elders of Gilead went to get Jephthah from the land of Tob. 'Come,' they said, 'be our commander, so we can fight the Ammonites.' Jephthah said to them, 'Didn't you hate me and drive me from my father's house? Why do you come to me now, when you're in trouble?'"

Jephthah was an illegitimately born child who nobody cared for, but he grew up to be a mighty warrior. Suddenly, when the people were in trouble, they came to him to be their leader. There must have been something special about Jephthah for the people to reach beyond their prejudice to seek his leadership.

It could be the same among you. Watch and listen to your teammates. Look for and encourage the leaders who emerge, even if they don't fit into your previous leadership profile. These leaders are often God's gift to a team.

As you compete today, respect and loyally follow your team leadership. Your coaching staff and the leaders among your teammates may lead you out of real trouble and into tremendous victory.

Bible Reading Plan:
Matthew 16:13-28
Acts 23:1-11
Psalms 37:23-40
Exodus 38-40

February 15

POSITION

I Peter 5:6

What is the key to attaining a position of power and influence? How do leaders and other people of prestige and authority attain their places? It is shown throughout the Bible that God sets people in places of prominence and power after they have taken the lower position to serve others and the Lord.

In Peter's first letter to his friends, in chapter 5 and verse 6 he writes, "Humble yourselves, therefore, under the mighty hand of God, that He may lift you up at the proper time." Peter calls us to maintain an attitude of humility, both before God and among our teammates. There seems to be no room for self promotion or arrogant attitudes in God's kingdom.

The promise that Peter offers in this verse is that as we maintain a spirit of humility, God himself will lift us to prominence at just the right time. I'm sure God is smarter than me and it's probably true that He's smarter than any of us. Let's trust Him and His timing for our coming into positions of prominence.

Hold your ambitions in check, He's guarding your best interests, at all times. Conduct yourself with humility toward each other and certainly in relation to God's plan for you. Trust Him to deliver you right on time.

Bible Reading Plan:
Acts 23:12-35
Psalms 38
Leviticus 1-4

February 16

LAZY OR DILIGENT?

Proverbs 13:4

Would you characterize yourself as a diligent, hard worker in practice or do you lean toward doing just enough to get by? What might be the eventual outcomes of each of those attitudes toward training?

In the Proverbs chapter 13 and verse 4 it says, "The soul of the lazy craves and gets nothing, but the soul of the diligent is full satisfied." It's true in all of life that some people will be lazy and will find their needs going unmet, while others who are consistently working hard will be rewarded with success.

This seems to be true of more spiritual matters as well as it says the soul of these people is the subject. If we will be faithful in prayer, consistent in Bible reading, committed to our friends and teammates, we'll find that the real stuff of life is supplied in great abundance. Our souls will prosper and be in good health as we diligently do the things that please God.

As you pray and prepare for competition, ask the Lord for diligence in all the affairs of your life. To be diligent in the classroom, in practice, in the weight room, in your relationships, with your teammates and certainly in relation to spiritual disciplines, will result in a fully satisfied soul. You'll find real happiness and great success.

Compete today with the focus and intensity befitting your abilities and your satisfied soul.

Bible Reading Plan:
Matthew 17:14-27
Acts 24
Psalms 39
Leviticus 5-7

February 17

COMMITMENT

Mark 1:19-20

What have you left behind to pursue your athletic career? Many of you left your families hours away. Many more left your best friends and possibly even a relationship with a potential spouse. What do you suppose that Jesus' disciples left when he asked them to follow him? We get to see the price of such decisions in the writings of Mark.

At chapter 1 and verses 19 and 20, Mark writes, "When he had gone a little farther, he saw James son of Zebedee and his brother John in a boat, preparing their nets. Without delay he called them, and they left their father Zebedee in the boat with the hired men and followed him."

These men walked away from their family business and their whole careers as fishermen to follow this man Jesus. That's what total commitment looks like.

You've shown similar commitment and you are to be commended for it. You walked away from your family, friends, everything that was familiar and comfortable to you to come to a strange place and strange people.

We must now show the same kind of commitment to our team and to the coaching staff that we've always shown to our family and friends. Demonstrate family-like commitment and loyalty to your teammates as you compete strongly together today.

Bible Reading Plan:
Matthew 18:1-14
Acts 25:1-12
Psalms 40
Leviticus 8-10

February 18

PRIVILEGE

Psalm 16:5-6

How much are you a student of your sport? Do you know its history and traditions? Who are the key figures in your own program's history? The Bible is full of stories and even poetry that recount the history of God's people.

In the Hebrew book of Poetry called Psalms at chapter 16 and verses 5 and 6 we read, "Lord, you have assigned me my portion and my cup; you have made my lot secure. The boundary lines have fallen for me in pleasant places; surely I have a delightful inheritance."

The writer was well aware of his blessed heritage. He credited God with putting him in position to be even further blessed. He described his place in life as secure, pleasant and delightful.

As you are in preparation for today's competition, let your mind page back through the players and coaches from this program's past. Remember their names and the heritage in which you now live. Recall the achievements of those who have gone before you. You'll probably join the psalm writer in seeing your position as secure, pleasant and even delightful.

Bible Reading Plan:
Matthew 18:15-35
Acts 25:13-27
Leviticus 11-13

February 19

UNITY

Colossians 3:15

What are the attitudes that rule your hearts? Are you ruled by fear, doubt, rejection, or pride? Or maybe it's peace that rules your hearts.

In Paul's letter to his friends in Colossae at chapter 3 and verse 15 we read these words, "Let the peace of Christ rule in your hearts, since as members of one body you were called to peace. And be thankful."

It's no coincidence that the word "hearts" is plural. Paul was writing to a group and he is making an appeal for them to be unified in heart. He is calling them to let the peace of Christ rule their hearts, collectively.

On the field of competition, that looks like a team which is focused on their collective goals over personal achievement. It's a team whose leaders work for harmony and reconciliation among teammates. It's a coaching staff that openly communicates with each member of the team. The peace of Christ rules their hearts, leading to their operating as one body.

As you prepare for competition, take some time to pray that the peace of Christ will rule your hearts, both individually and collectively. Work together in harmony and achieve greatly as one heart, one mind, and one body.

Bible Reading Plan:
Matthew 19:1-15
Acts 26:1-18
Psalms 42
Leviticus 14-15

February 20

PUBLIC ATTENTION

Mark 1:27-28

How many newspaper clippings have your parents collected about your athletic career? I imagine each of you have scrapbooks filled with photos and articles written about how you excelled in your sport. Did you ever wonder at the attention you received for playing your game? Jesus had a similar experience in his life, a few centuries before newspapers.

Mark writes about this incident at chapter 1 and verses 27 and 28, "The people were all so amazed that they asked each other, 'What is this? A new teaching - and with authority! He even gives orders to evil spirits and they obey him.' News about him spread quickly over the whole region of Galilee."

Jesus had recently done some amazing things and the news about him was spreading like wildfire. There was a buzz all over the region about this guy and the awesome works he was performing.

It's fun to be in the newspaper, to see your face on television and to be the topic of conversation at the local restaurants on the morning after a great night of competition. Jesus knew that exhilaration just like you.

As you compete today, focus your mind and prepare your body in order to give people something to talk about. Give your absolute best effort on the field of competition and who knows, you might be the talk of the town.

Bible Reading Plan:
Matthew 19:16-30
Acts 26:19-32
Psalms 43
Leviticus 16-17

February 21

ANXIETY

I Peter 5:7

Have you ever approached a competition filled with worry and apprehension because you didn't know if you would be successful? Have you ever faced an opponent who seemed unbeatable and wondered who could possibly be concerned for your feelings? The Bible speaks of one who knows your worries very well and is doing something about them.

In Peter's first letter to his friends, at chapter 5 and verse 7, he says, "Cast all your anxiety upon Him because He cares for you." During the first half of a season we all have anxiety about things like who will play, how many minutes will I get, will I be able to score well, and can I keep up with the player I'm asked to guard?

The exciting part of this verse is the promise that we can take all that anxiety and roll in onto the Lord. We can take all of life's worries to Him and rest in the assurance of His real and active care for us.

Today as you prepare to play, take a moment to pray and to cast all your cares, anxieties, worries and doubts upon the Lord. He genuinely cares for you and is more than able to work in your behalf. Let the assurance of His care and provision for you lead to your playing with great confidence and power.

Bible Reading Plan:
Matthew 20:1-16
Acts 27:1-26
Psalms 44
Leviticus 18-20

February 22

GAME PLAN

How clearly does your coaching staff outline your game plan? How well do you study and implement each one? Clarity of communication on each end will enable us to compete at the highest level.

The prophet Habakkuk speaks of clear communication in chapter 2 and verse 2, "Write down the revelation and make it plain on tablets so that a herald may run with it."

The Lord told the prophet that his communication should be so plain that it could be written on big signs carried by a man on the run and those who saw him could easily understand the message.

Your season of sport moves like a herald on the run. There is a ton of information coming your way every day. Thus each competition's game plan must be expressed very plainly so everyone may understand it fully and your focus must be clear in order to strongly fulfill it.

As you compete today, concentrate tightly on the game plan. Explain it and execute it to perfection for greatest success.

Bible Reading Plan:
Matthew 20:17-34
Acts 27:27-44
Psalms 45
Leviticus 21-23

February 23

PRIDE

Do you have any teammates who you'd call arrogant, boastful or proud? Might others describe you in that way? How should we view ourselves with respect to others on our team? The Holy Scripture has some advice.

In the book of Proverbs at chapter 13 and verse 10 it is written, "Through pride comes nothing but strife, but with those who receive counsel is wisdom."

Pride in our abilities, our intelligence, our looks, or whatever else leads us to boasting seems to have the same result... strife. This kind of boastful pride only serves to divide our team and to hurt our relationships with teammates and coaches. This is different than confidence, pride calls attention to itself and puts others down as inferior.

Wisdom calls us to not set ourselves up as greater than others, but to receive the wise advice of our friends, family, coaches and teammates. To have a unified team and to enjoy success as a team, we will each have to put down our individual pride and work together with our teammates.

In your prayer time, ask the Lord to expose your areas of pride. Ask Him to change those and to make you a person of humility and wisdom.

Bible Reading Plan:
Matthew 21:1-11
Acts 28:1-16
Psalms 46
Leviticus 24-25

February 24

SOLITUDE

Mark 1:35-37

What do you do to quiet your mind and to keep some perspective about your life? Where do you go to relax, reflect and to meditate? How do you stay true to who you are when everybody is praising you? We'll read today about how Jesus did all of these.

Mark writes about Jesus' life of solitude and focus at chapter 1 and verses 35 through 37, "Very early in the morning, while it was still dark, Jesus got up, left the house and went off to a solitary place, where he prayed. Simon and his companions went to look for him, and when they found him, they exclaimed, 'Everyone is looking for you.'"

Jesus had a unique quality in his life that most of us miss. He valued solitude over popularity. He maintained clarity of thought about who He was, about His values and about His life goals while in quiet reflection, free from the flattering crowds. He knew that it's very easy to pander to a crowd of people who tell you that you're great. He was more concerned with pleasing His Father in Heaven.

We can each carry a similar commitment related to our team. Let's be more committed and responsive to our teammates and coaching staff than we are to the fickle opinions of fans and sportswriters. Let's remember to value those who know us privately and their commitments to us. Let's value them more than those who only know us from what they see on game day and in public. Compete powerfully today and honor those who are most committed to you.

Bible Reading Plan:
Matthew 21:12-22
Acts 28:17-31
Psalms 47
Leviticus 26-27

February 25

TRUST

Psalm 20:7

On what basis do your opponents or teammates boast? Do they brag about their size and strength? Maybe they talk loudly about their skills, technique or knowledge. Does anyone you know boast in the power of his God?

That's exactly what we hear from David in Psalm 20 and verse 7, "Some trust in chariots and some in horses, but we trust in the name of the Lord our God."

God's power is greater than a whole division of chariots. His strength is mightier than a thousand horses. To David the warrior, God's name is better than all the finest military equipment on the planet.

When your opponent boasts of his speed, God is faster. When your teammate is bragging about his power in the weight room, remember that God is most powerful. When the media boasts of your most recent victories, think about the eternal nature of God's wisdom.

In today's competition, if you must brag at all, make your boast in the one unchanging, immovable person – God almighty.

Bible Reading Plan:
Matthew 11:1-19
Acts 16:16-40

February 26

ENLIGHTENMENT

Ephesians 1:18

Are there ever opportunities to score or to make a great play that escape your notice? It was there, but somehow you just couldn't see it. Are there other times when it seems like someone is shining a giant flashlight on the situation and the whole game slows down for you? Today's scripture will enlighten our hearts to great treasure.

In the book of Ephesians at chapter 1 and verse 18 it says, "I pray also that the eyes of your heart may be enlightened in order that you may know the hope to which he has called you, the riches of his glorious inheritance in the saints and his incomparably great power for us who believe." How well do the eyes of your heart see?

Paul prays that these people's hearts would be enlightened toward three things – hope, an inheritance and power. Hope is confidence in the future. An inheritance is provision from someone who loves us. Power is the ability to do what's right.

This same prayer is applicable for us in the world of sport. I pray that the eyes of your hearts are enlightened to know the hope you can have, in this life and in the next. I pray that your hearts are enlightened to know the inheritance that is yours presently in the marvelous opportunity to compete and to have such teammates and coaches. I also pray that your hearts are enlightened to the power that is yours to make choices that honor your family, your team and even your God.

As you prepare to compete, echo this prayer for enlightenment and then watch for its fulfillment in this very day.

Bible Reading Plan:
Psalms 27
Exodus 13-15

February 27

CELEBRITY

Mark 1:45

Has your success in athletics and the resulting popularity ever led to a loss of privacy for you? Many people of sport who achieve highly become celebrities and thus lose the ability to move about freely in society. You might be thinking, "I'd like to have that problem." We can watch that happen to Jesus as we read from Mark's gospel.

At chapter 1 and verse 45 we read, "Instead he went out and began to talk freely, spreading the news. As a result, Jesus could no longer enter a town openly but stayed outside in lonely places. Yet the people still came to him from everywhere."

Jesus had just done some seemingly impossible things in town and the man that was most affected couldn't help but talk about it. Jesus asked him to keep it quiet, but the man's excitement couldn't be contained. All this resulted in a level of celebrity for Jesus that began to rule his life, he couldn't go anywhere without a crowd gathering.

Even if this season results in you and your teammates becoming big celebrities, stay connected to your coaches and friends. Your teammates are the ideal support system. Practice and competition can be your escape from the crush of the public. The people you want in your life can still find you and you can enjoy the more private places for retreat, like Jesus did.

Let's compete today in a tremendous way and give everyone a reason to treat us like celebrities.

Bible Reading Plan:
Matthew 14:1-21
Acts 20:13-38
Matthew 17:1-13
Psalms 41

February 28

ATTITUDE

I Thessalonians 5:16-18

As athletes we're subject to having good days and bad days. Sometimes you win and sometimes you lose. I always like winning better than losing. Enough losses in a row and any of us can get a little blue. So how do we maintain a joyful life? The Bible gives us some good answers.

In Paul's first letter to his friends in Thessalonica at chapter 5 and verses 16 - 18 he writes, "Rejoice always, pray without ceasing, in everything give thanks; for this is the will of God in Christ Jesus for you."

In these verses there are three directives and one reason that combine to show us the way to a joyful life.

1) Rejoice always: More than a command, this is a reassuring encouragement that we can find something to be joyful about in every circumstance. Lead with your will and let your emotions follow along.
2) Pray without ceasing: If you took this seriously you'd never sleep, eat or study. That's probably not what he meant. Surely he meant that there is never a situation for us in which prayer is not proper and powerful.
3) In everything give thanks: Not for everything, but in everything. In all situations give thanks to the Lord and you'll cultivate a joyful, thankful attitude that rises above any circumstances.

Why? This is the will of God in Christ for you. The Lord joins you in your rejoicing, He communes with you when you pray and He blesses you when you thank Him. He is most desirous of an intimate, personal relationship with you and He knows that these things serve to deepen that relationship.

Bible Reading Plan:
Matthew 21:23-32
Romans 1:1-17
Psalms 48
Numbers 1-2

March 1

DESTINY

Habakkuk 2:3

Have you ever been a part of a team that seemed destined to win? How confident were you as you approached each competition? The prophet Habakkuk wrote about destiny in today's scripture.

At chapter 2 and verse 3 of Habakkuk we read, "For the revelation awaits an appointed time; it speaks of the end and will not prove false; Though it linger, wait for it; it will certainly come and will not delay."

It often seems that our dreams and goals from preseason will go unfulfilled and disappointment will surround our team. Habakkuk would encourage us to not give up so easily.

His attitude is incurably positive and forward looking. He says that success is awaiting our arrival. We should remain confident and hopeful for it will certainly come and will not delay.

That's my encouragement to you today. Live with a sense of destiny. Expect the best to happen rather than the worst. Expect your teammates to make great plays instead of waiting for them to collapse. Even in the worst of times, trust God to bring your marvelous destiny to full fruition.

Bible Reading Plan:
Romans 1:18-32
Psalms 49
Numbers 3-4

March 2

ENEMIES AND ALLIES

Mark 3:6

Do you ever think about the irony that accompanies some of the videotape exchange between your opponents? Some of the bitterest rivals in your conference exchange the best film they have of your team because they both want to beat you. In the world of sport, mortal enemies become momentary allies in order to defeat a common opponent. There was at least one similar instance in the life of Jesus.

In Mark's gospel at chapter 3 and verse 6 we read, "Then the Pharisees went out and began to plot with the Herodians how they might kill Jesus." The Pharisees and Herodians were bitter political enemies, but they found themselves with a common opponent – Jesus of Nazareth.

In your sport, there are times when natural enemies share information in order to beat another team with whom they both must compete. Usually, that team's above them both in the standings. Sometimes their conspiracy of information may even lead them to compromise ethical standards.

What are you to do? Be who you are. Maintain your integrity and compete fairly, even when your opponents cheat and conspire. That's what Jesus did and it's what He would do today.

As you compete today, do so within the rules and to the absolute best of your ability. We'll all be proud if you do and they'll all be sorry.

Bible Reading Plan:
Matthew 22:1-14
Psalms 50
Numbers 5-6

March 3

JOY

Psalm 21:1-2

What is there in sport that can match the joy of winning? Probably nothing. The feelings of excitement, joy, fulfillment and satisfaction in sport that come with a win are conspicuously absent in a loss. This truth was also known by the great people of the Bible.

We read a description of such victories in Psalm 21 and verses 1 and 2 where it says, "O Lord, the king rejoices in your strength. How great is his joy in the victories you give! You have granted him the desire of his heart and have not withheld the request of his lips."

Did you hear who the writer credits as being the source of these victories? It surely wasn't himself.

For the king and for us, the great joy in victories comes as a gift from God. Both David and our team rejoice in the strength we feel in sport. God has granted us all the deep desires of our hearts, we're greatly blessed just to be here.

As you pray in preparation for today's competition, trust that the Lord will not withhold the request of your lips, and then compete in great freedom and joy.

Bible Reading Plan:
Matthew 22:15-33
Romans 3
Numbers 7-8

March 4

STRENGTH AND POWER

Ephesians 3:16

Who is the strongest, most powerful player you've ever competed with or against? What seemed to be the source of that strength and power? If you could access an even greater, limitless source of strength and power for your life, would you want some? Today's scripture tells of such a source.

In his letter to the church at Ephesus at chapter 3 and verse 16, Paul wrote, "I pray that out of his glorious riches he may strengthen you with power through his Spirit in your inner being, so that Christ may dwell in your hearts through faith." Paul's prayer for those in Ephesus and for us today is for God to give us the strength and power for Christ to fill our hearts through faith.

The strength and power of the greatest competitors comes from within. Their real strength is not found in their muscles or even in their mental capacity. Strength and power are found in their hearts, then they find expression outwardly.

God is gloriously rich in both strength and power so we should expect that we will be given them in abundance. As Christ dwells in our hearts through faith, this is a very natural occurrence.

As you compete today, do so with your whole heart. Trust that God will provide the strength and power to enable you to give your absolute best.

Bible Reading Plan:
Matthew 22:34-46
Romans 4
Psalms 52

March 5

HOPE

Proverbs 13:12

What goals have you set that are still unachieved? For what have you hoped and been disappointed? How did these times affect you? The Bible speaks of such times.

In the book of Proverbs at chapter 13 and verse 12 it says, "Hope deferred makes the heart sick, but desire fulfilled is a tree of life."

When a dream doesn't come true, when a goal is not achieved, when a hope is deferred it makes our hearts sick. We hurt inside when we have had the desired goal within our grasp, only to see it slip away. This scripture serves as a reminder along the way to your goals. Here's a road sign that encourages you to work hard and give your best, because failure is a bitter pill to swallow.

The marvelous promise here is that the fulfillment of our desires is like a tree of life. Can you imagine a tree which has as its fruit, life itself? Better than apples or oranges, the very stuff of life hangs from its branches. This verse says that's what we find when we have our desires fulfilled.

Pray in commitment today. Give the Lord all that you have today to see your goals achieved, your dreams come true, your hope fulfilled.

Bible Reading Plan:
Romans 5:1-11
Psalms 53
Numbers 12-14

March 6

PLEASING TO GOD

Matthew 3:16-17

Some athletes play to please their parents, others to please their boyfriend or girlfriend. Some play to please the Lord. But what really pleases the Lord? Further, what makes us pleasing to Him?

In Matthew's gospel at chapter 3 and verses 16 and 17 it says, "Then Jesus, when he had been baptized, came up immediately from the water; and behold the heavens were opened to Him and He saw the Spirit of God descending like a dove and alighting upon Him. And suddenly a voice came from Heaven, saying, 'This is my beloved Son, in whom I am well pleased.' "

What a day this must have been! I've never seen anything like this on my days of competition. What must have Jesus achieved on this day that merited such a powerful display of affection by the Lord? Nothing!! He didn't do anything but be baptized by John.

To this point Jesus had no followers, had done no miracles, had healed no one, had no great achievements. So why would the Lord say He is well pleased with Him? It's simple, He says that He is His beloved Son and He's well pleased with Him.

It's the same with us. Because of our relationship with Christ, we too are pleasing to the Lord. It's not because of our achievements, or in spite of our failures. If you have a relationship with the Lord God, you too are His beloved child and He is well pleased with you.

In your pre-game prayer today, thank the Lord for the marvelous privilege you have as His child. Thank Him for the great security you have in your relationship with Him. Compete today knowing that He is well pleased with you.

Bible Reading Plan:
Matthew 23:13-24
Numbers 15-17

March 7

CALLING

I Thessalonians 5:24

Have you ever had a sense that God was calling you to do something? Did the task seem too great or your resources seem too small? Did the call of God overwhelm you and cause you to doubt whether you had really heard Him at all? The Scripture speaks directly to our fears and doubts related to God's call.

In Paul's first letter to his friends in Thessalonica at chapter 5 and verse 24 it says, "Faithful is He who calls you, and He will also bring it to pass."

This is a marvelous promise for those who hear God's call. It says nothing about the abilities of the hearer, but says volumes about the One who does the calling. He is called faithful, that is fully reliable to do that which He promised. That's encouraging! Further it says that He will bring it to pass. That's a whole lot better than saying that He'd watch as I bring it to pass.

This powerful verse causes me to trust in the Lord all the way through this marvelous process called pursuing the Lord's will. He does the calling and the carrying out of His will. My part is to answer His call and to make myself available for His service.

In today's time of prayer, ask the Lord to make His call clear in your life. Commit your life to Him, trusting in His power for both the hearing and the doing of His will.

Bible Reading Plan:
Matthew 23:25-39
Romans 6:1-14
Numbers 18-20

March 8

DESIRE

Psalm 37:3-4

In what parts of your sport do you find real delight? Which situations or settings give you a wide grin? Maybe it's when you first walk onto the field or court to warm up. Maybe it's the opening minutes of competition. Or maybe it's the look on your opponent's face when he knows you're going to win. Such things are often delightful to people of sport.

King David writes about delightful things in Psalm 37 and verses 3 and 4 where it says, "Trust in the Lord and do good; dwell in the land and enjoy safe pasture. Delight yourself in the Lord and he will give you the desires of your heart."

To this former shepherd, David, to dwell in a land and to enjoy safe pasture would be a great delight. Safety and security would give him a broad smile and a contented heart.

We can experience similarly delightful days when we follow David's instruction. The key seems to be that we trust God and follow his ways. As we place our faith in Him and follow His ways, we will find fulfillment and security in our sport and among our teammates. As we delight ourselves in God's love, we'll see the desires of our hearts come to full fruition.

Compete today in the freedom and security that accompanies those who trust and delight in God.

Bible Reading Plan:
Romans 6:15-23
Psalms 56

March 9

OBEDIENCE

Ephesians 6:6

Here's a heart check – do you do what pleases your coaches all the time or only when they are watching? Do you do the right thing just to win their favor or because it's right? Today's scripture continues the heart check.

At chapter 6 and verse 6 of the book of Ephesians we read, "Obey them not only to win their favor when their eye is on you, but like slaves of Christ, doing the will of God from your heart." Paul is rather direct with these people about their work ethic.

I often watch teams closely during practice and as they warm up prior to competitions. I always see players who give a great effort when the coach is watching, but as soon as the coach's head is turned, some of those players immediately start cutting corners and cheating on drills. Their hearts are not fully with their coaches or their teammates. They fail the heart check.

My challenge to you is to give the same effort when no one is watching as you do when the head coach is right beside you. That is called integrity. A whole heart will lead you to do the right thing whether anyone is watching or not.

As you prepare to compete today, give a whole-hearted effort to the pursuit of a great team victory. When you compete with integrity you don't waste any time looking over your shoulder.

Bible Reading Plan:
Matthew 24:15-35
Psalms 57
Numbers 23-25

March 10

CHOSEN

Mark 3:13

How did you come to be a part of this team? Did you just show up and volunteer or were you chosen? Certainly most of you were recruited by the coaching staff and given a personal invitation to join this team. When game day arrives, those who compete are all chosen for specific roles on the team. It was the same for those who walked with Jesus.

In the book of Mark at chapter 3 and verse 13 we read, "Jesus went up on a mountainside and called to him those he wanted and they came to him." Though surrounded by thousands of people and certainly hundreds of willing volunteers, Jesus consciously chose the people to whom He would commit himself.

There are thousands of people who compete in your sport at lower levels, why aren't they all here today? It's simple, they were not chosen. Since you were chosen, you have the privilege of looking at your sport like a life calling. Such a calling comes with certain privileges and responsibilities that those countless others can't even begin to think about.

Some of those privileges can be exercised in today's competition. Compete with great joy as you revel in the privilege that comes with your position. The responsibilities of your calling relate to your teammates, your coaching staff, and your family. Represent them well as you compete honorably today.

Bible Reading Plan:
Matthew 24:36-51
Romans 7:13-25
Numbers 26-27

March 11

RECURITING

Who's the best recruiter you've ever seen? What was it that made him/her special? How good would Jesus be at recruiting?

In Matthew's gospel at chapter 4 and verse 19 he writes, "Come, follow me,' Jesus said, 'and I will make you fishers of men.' At once they left their nets and followed Him." Was Jesus a great recruiter or what? These guys left family businesses right there and followed Jesus into a new life.

These guys took a tremendous risk to pursue something they thought was important. You've each done much the same. You've left your families, hundreds of miles away for many of you, as well as friends in pursuit of a diploma and athletics. You are to be commended for having the guts to take risks with life.

What could have gripped these men deeply enough for them to leave their livelihood and to follow instantly? They surely sensed that Christ was more than just a man, more than another teacher, more than a religious leader. May we all be so gripped that we follow Him passionately, risking all to find real life.

In today's competition, faithfully follow your team's leadership. They've called you, now follow them. Be sure to answer the Lord's call when He asks you to follow Him.

Bible Reading Plan:
Matthew 25:1-13
Romans 8:1-17
Psalms 59

March 12

FRUITFUL LIVES

John 15:4

How successful is a star player without his teammates and coaches? How well could that player compete if he took on the opposing team by himself? The answers are obvious and Jesus paints an even clearer picture of our dependence in today's letter.

In John chapter 15 and verse 4 we read, "Abide in Me, and I in you. As the branch cannot bear fruit of itself, unless it abides in the vine, neither can you, unless you abide in Me."

What do you call a branch that's separated from the vine? Firewood! It's no good for bearing fruit if it's been cut off from its source of life.

It's the same with the players on a team. No matter how productive the player has been, he cannot be fruitful if cut off from the team. The star running back cannot succeed without his offensive linemen. The outstanding volleyball hitter cannot score without an effective pass and set. The greatest basketball player cannot compete if the scheme is one on five.

We can only be fruitful if we remain attached to our source. For us as players, it's the team and coaching staff that provides us the opportunity to be fruitful as players. For each of us in life, it's to stay attached to Jesus. He's the giver of real life. Make this a very fruitful competition by staying firmly rooted in the life of your team.

Bible Reading Plan:
Matthew 25:14-30
Romans 8:18-39
Psalms 60
Numbers 31-32

March 13

PAIN AND INJURY

II Corinthians 4:7

Why do some athletes seem so fragile? Some seem to constantly be in the training room with pulled muscles, sprains, stingers, bruises, scratches or other maladies. Often the greatest players seem to be playing through pain and injuries. We see a similar picture in the Bible.

In Paul's second letter to his friends in Corinth at chapter 4 and verse 7 it says, "But we have this treasure in earthen vessels, that the excellence of the power may be of God and not of us." It seems there are three ideas needing investigation here.

1) This treasure: What is the treasure? In this case it's the Spirit of God. The very life God gives us is a treasure. He puts in us the very life that filled Jesus of Nazareth, a life of power, grace and mercy.

2) Earthen vessels: Like clay pots, we're rather fragile. We're easily broken; physically, emotionally, psychologically, spiritually and other ways. More like paper cups than fine china, we're not the most noble vessels for containing the great treasure.

3) The excellence of the power: With such a weak container for a marvelous treasure, which do you think is seen as greater, the vessel or the treasure? If the vessel was perfect, the treasure might be overshadowed. As it is the vessel is hardly even seen as the treasure eclipses it with its brilliance.

God has chosen earthen vessels like you and me to be carriers of His great treasure. Thank Him in prayer. Let's be sure to highlight the treasure and not the vessel. Ask Him to show the excellence of His power through your life.

Bible Reading Plan:
Matthew 25:31-46
Romans 9:1-18

March 14

SKILL

How would you rate the skills possessed by your teammates and yourself? Are you so skilled that people will be reading about you in 1500 years? Such were the abilities of the mighty men of David.

We read about these mighty men in First Chronicles chapter 12 and verses 1 and 2. There it reads, "These were the men who came to David at Ziklag, while he was banished from the presence of Saul son of Kish (they were among the warriors who helped him in battle; they were armed with bows and were able to shoot arrows or to sling stones right-handed or left-handed; they were kinsmen of Saul from the tribe of Benjamin.)"

These men were ambidextrous with any kind of implement of battle and were very experienced. That's a great team to have if you're on the run from the king.

I'd like to challenge you to work hard in every facet of your sport. Continually make constant improvements in your technique, strength, conditioning, mental preparation and teamwork. Apply yourself fully to every skill and tactic with great diligence.

Compete skillfully in today's contest and maybe we'll be reading about you for a long time.

Bible Reading Plan:
Matthew 26:1-16
Romans 9:19-33
Psalms 62
Deuteronomy 1-3

March 15

MISUNDERSTOOD

Mark 3:20-21

Are you sometimes misunderstood by your family and friends because of your high commitment to sport? Do they occasionally think you've lost your mind? Jesus' family thought the same of Him.

Mark wrote about a strange incident at chapter 3 and verses 20 and 21, "Then Jesus entered a house, and again a crowd gathered, so that he and his disciples were not even able to eat. When his family heard about this, they went to take charge of him, for they said, 'He is out of his mind.'"

Imagine this, here came Mary and Jesus' brothers and sisters to take him away thinking that he had lost touch with the real world. I know my parents thought I was nuts when I'd skip meals, run miles in sweat clothes and stay after practice every day, just to be a better wrestler.

You are no doubt misunderstood by classmates, friends and even your family when you make sacrifices, prefer teammate relationships to others who don't understand your sport, and when you commit deeply to your team's success over your own convenience or comfort.

That's what winners look like. They commit to their teams and coaches in spite of misunderstanding and questioning. Do like Jesus did and pursue excellence and authentic relationships in today's competition.

Bible Reading Plan:
Matthew 26:17-35
Romans 10
Psalms 63
Deuteronomy 4-5

March 16

COMMITMENT

Psalm 37:5-6

To whom and to what are you most committed? What do you expect to come from those committed relationships? Today's scripture tells of a person who is worthy of such commitment and one who rewards commitment greatly.

In Psalm 37 at verses 5 and 6 we read, "Commit your way to the Lord; trust in him and he will do this: He will make your righteousness shine like the dawn, the justice of your cause like the noonday sun."

As we commit ourselves to God and trust him with the details of life, he's very faithful to reward us and to even make us look good. This text says that our righteousness will shine like the dawn. Just like the rising son, the issues of life become plainer and we know exactly what to do. It says that the justice of our cause will shine like noonday. Even those around us will see the shining result of our commitment and trust as we justly pursue God's will.

In today's competition, commit everything about yourself to God's wise care. He's fully trustworthy with every part of life, even sport. Entrust your whole life to him and watch as he strongly supports you in every way.

Bible Reading Plan:
Matthew 26:36-56
Romans 11:1-24
Psalms 64
Deuteronomy 6-8

March 17

ENDURANCE

Hebrews 12:3

Take some time to think of someone you know from sport that inspires you because of how he has endured opposition, but stayed true to his principles. Do you know anyone like that? The Bible is full of such characters and today's scripture points to one in particular.

In the book of Hebrews at chapter 12 and verse 3 we read, "Consider him who endured such opposition from sinful men, so that you will not grow weary and lose heart." The author is referring to Jesus Christ as his example of faithful endurance.

Christ endured terrible opposition from nasty people during his life, but held tightly to the guiding light of his life. We are challenged to consider his example and to gather encouragement for our hearts from him.

We who compete encounter opposition in every contest, that's normal. We sometimes even meet opposition from our own minds and bodies as they break down due to fatigue or injury. Let's not lose heart as we meet these foes, rather let's follow Christ's example, enduring the opposition while our hearts refresh our bodies and sharpen our minds.

In today's competition, meet your opposition head on. Consider the examples of others who have endured, do not grow weary or lose heart.

Bible Reading Plan:
Matthew 26:57-75
Romans 11:25-36
Psalms 65
Deuteronomy 9-12

March 18

WISDOM

Proverbs 14:12

What would it be like to be going down the road, fully confident of being on the right highway, but you're actually heading straight for a washed out bridge that crosses a 1,000 foot cliff? The Bible paints a similar picture in one of the Proverbs.

In Proverbs chapter 14 and verse 12 it says, "There is a way that seems right to a man, but in the end it leads to death."

Just like the road that leads to the washed out bridge and an awful crash, many of our choices can lead us to death or certainly to trouble and heartache. Most of the time these decisions seem to make good sense... to us. Our problem is that we lack enough perspective on the situation. We can't always see that the bridge is out and without a warning, we could plunge right over the cliff.

As you pray before competition today, ask the Lord for the wisdom and grace to accept guidance and instruction from your coaches. Ask Him for the ability to work well with your teammates. They can add to your perspective and you can help them to avoid the washed out bridges and the tragedies that lie ahead.

Bible Reading Plan:
Matthew 27:1-10
Romans 12:1-8
Psalms 66
Deuteronomy 13-17

March 19

MEEKNESS

Matthew 5:5

When you think of power under control, what images do you see? Which people? What words come to mind?

In his gospel at chapter 5 and verse 5, Matthew writes, "Blessed are the meek, for they will inherit the earth." Most athletes hear the word meek, immediately think weak and don't want any part of this. This is a misconception.

Meekness is best described as power under control. Imagine a powerful, horse being ridden by a skillful equestrian. This is a great image for one who is meek. The meek person is possessed of great power, but he's also very disciplined.

Today's game will require both great power and tremendous self control. As you exercise both you will realize the promise in this verse. Jesus says that the meek will inherit the earth. There is no limit to our inheritance when we keep our power in check and employ discipline in our quest to achieve.

Drain every ounce of power from your bodies as you play today, focus your minds fully on the game, keep your emotions in check and watch for your inheritance to appear. Have a great game.

Bible Reading Plan:
Matthew 27:11-26
Romans 12:9-21
Psalms 67
Deuteronomy 18-21

March 20

REPRESENTATION

II Corinthians 3:2

You're in a unique position to represent your school, your club or your community in the world of athletics. Even more than that, you reflect your family, coaching staff and others of influence in your lives. Today's scripture speaks to that dynamic.

In Paul's second letter to the church at Corinth in chapter 3 and verse 2 he says, "You yourselves are our letter, written on our hearts, known and read by everybody." This is a heart-felt affirmation from a leader to his friends.

It's like when you go places, people can see the signatures of the people from whom you've learned and with whom you've worked and played. They see your mother's smile, your coaches' expressions, and sometimes they see Christ's character.

In today's game, compete in such a way that everyone who's been an influence on you is plainly evident as you represent them with grace, power, excellence and tenacity. You really are our letter, written on our hearts, known and read by everybody.

Bible Reading Plan:
Matthew 27:27-44
Romans 13
Psalms 68
Deuteronomy 22-26

March 21

SECURITY

Psalm 37:23-24

How secure do you feel in your game? Is your position on the team rock-solid and secure or a little tenuous? From where does your security for life in sport and life in general come?

King David shares with us the source of his security in the words of Psalm 37 and verses 23 and 24. There we read, "If the Lord delights in a man's way, he makes his steps firm; though he stumble, he will not fall, for the Lord upholds him with his hand."

This man was far from perfect; in fact he had some terrible character flaws. However, he maintained his relationship with God as first priority. Because of that he was very secure.

Some of us find our security in our strength, speed, skills or technical abilities. The problem is that none of those will endure for ever. They will all dissipate over time.

The key to real security over time is relationship. As we maintain our relationships with teammates, we find greater security on our team. As we commit strongly to friends and family, we're ever more secure off the field of competition. As we build a deep, loving relationship with Christ Jesus, all of life is upheld by the secure, strong hands of God.

Bible Reading Plan:
Matthew 27:45-56
Romans 14
Psalms 69:1-18
Deuteronomy 27-28

March 22

PERFORMANCE

Mark 4:24-25

How do you measure an athlete's performance? What is your standard of measure for a player's effort? How do you gauge a competitor's commitment, loyalty or teamwork? Jesus had some sobering comments related to measuring such concepts.

Mark recorded these words of Jesus at chapter 4 and verses 24 and 25, "Consider carefully what you hear." He continued. 'With the measure you use, it will be measured to you – and even more. Whoever has will be given more; whoever does not have, even what he has will be taken from him."

Jesus seemed to be more concerned with faithfulness than fairness. Fairness would have everyone receive and have the same amount of everything. Jesus rewards those who are faithful with whatever they have. They receive even more, while those who are unfaithful squander even what they have.

We've all seen this in athletes with whom we've competed. The faithful competitor demands the same level of commitment that he gives. He gives the same measure of loyalty that he asks of his teammates. He shows the same kind of teamwork that he expects of his teammates. For the unfaithful, sadly, the principle is still true. They neither give nor receive sufficiently.

As you compete today, you can expect great commitment and teamwork from your teammates, if you have shown the same every day in practice. You can expect great loyalty and effort, if you have given them greatly all through the season. Give your absolute best effort today and watch your teammates reciprocate.

Bible Reading Plan:
Matthew 27:57-66
Deuteronomy 29-31

March 23

WARRIORS

I Chronicles 12:8

How do you describe your teammates and opponents who compete greatly? You might say things like, "He runs like a ...." "She's as strong as an ...." "That guy is a ...." You may have dropped in words like, gazelle, ox or animal in those blanks. The Bible talks about some warriors so fierce that they looked like lions.

We read about these men in the book of First Chronicles at chapter 12 and verse 8, "Some Gadites defected to David at his stronghold in the desert. They were brave warriors, ready for battle and able to handle the shield and spear. Their faces were the faces of lions, and they were as swift as gazelles in the mountains."

I want those guys on my team! Imagine having teammates whose courage makes them look like lions. How great would it be to have the athletic grace and speed of gazelles to carry into competition? That's how these men are described.

As you prepare to compete today, show the strength of a Clydesdale. Run like a deer. Focus as sharply as an eagle and soar over your opponents. Give your absolute best effort today and leave the description of your performance to the media.

Bible Reading Plan:
Matthew 28:1-10
Romans 15:14-33
Psalms 70
Deuteronomy 32

March 24

FLAVOR

Matthew 5:13

Have you ever chewed some gum until the very last drop of flavor was gone? What did you do with it then? I'm sure I know.

In Matthew's gospel at chapter 5 and verse 13 he writes, "You are the salt of the earth. But if the salt loses its saltiness, how can it be made salty again? It is no longer good for anything, except to be thrown out and trampled by men."

What makes salt valuable as a seasoning? Its distinctive taste seems to be what Jesus is driving at here. He even says that if it loses its saltiness, its distinctiveness, it's no good for anything. You are the salt of the earth. If you lose your distinctiveness your value to the team is diminished.

We'd be a pretty bland team if each player was just a clone of all the others. Each player brings a unique flavor to the team and contributes to its success.

As you pray prior to today's competition, thank God for your unique role on this team. Thank Him for your teammates and the gifts they bring to your team's life. Employ each of those gifts in pursuit of a great victory.

Bible Reading Plan:
Matthew 28:11-20
Romans 16
Psalms 71
Deuteronomy 33-34

March 25

QUICK TEMPERS

Proverbs 14:29

Do you have any short tempered teammates? Do you know anyone who gets angry at the drop of a hat? How even tempered are you? Are you easily angered? What does God think about these things?

In the Proverbs at chapter 14 and verse 29 we read, "He who is slow to anger has great understanding, but he who is quick-tempered exalts folly."

To exalt folly is to act as though foolishness is good. Some people act like being easily angered is a good thing. They think that they're better competitors when they play in a rage. They take offense at everything said to them and often draw penalties and technical fouls due to their out of control play. They exalt folly by their quick-tempered natures.

When you compete with a cool temperament, not easily angered, under control, you display great understanding. You can think more clearly, make better decisions, have fewer distractions and honor God with your wisdom. Let's exercise self control as we compete and resist the temptation to lose our temper.

Ask the Lord to keep your temper under control as you compete. Ask Him for a cool spirit, a mind of understanding and a heart of love for God.

Bible Reading Plan:
Matthew 21:33-46
Romans 2

March 26

GRACE

Hebrews 13:9

For decades the news has been full of stories about athletes who have resorted to counterfeit sources of strength to enhance their athletic performance. These counterfeit sources had short-term effectiveness, but in the end led to their disqualification and shame. Today's scripture draws a strong distinction between wise and foolish sources of strength.

In the book of Hebrews at chapter 13 and verse 9 we read, "Do not be carried away by all kinds of strange teachings. It is good for our hearts to be strengthened by grace, not by ceremonial foods, which are of no value to those who eat them."

Whether they are performance enhancing drugs or even superstitions about pregame meals, these things are of no value to our hearts or to our bodies. They are counterfeits.

Rather than trusting in those things, it's good for our hearts to be strengthened by grace. Grace is the receiving of something you don't deserve and could never merit. We have received abundant grace from God just to be here competing. We receive grace daily to live and to pursue our goals.

As you compete today, rest in the grace that has been given to you. Trust in the strength that comes from that grace and compete with all your heart.

Bible Reading Plan:
Psalms 51
Numbers 9-11

March 27

LEADERSHIP

Mark 4:39-40

Have you ever had a coach or a teammate who could instantly bring peace and order to a chaotic situation? Jesus was that guy for His disciples.

Mark records a remarkable story at chapter 4 and verses 39 through 41, "He got up, rebuked the wind and said to the waves, 'Quiet! Be still!' Then the wind died down and it was completely calm. He said to his disciples, 'Why are you so afraid? Do you still have no faith?'"

In the middle of a furious storm, Jesus was sleeping below the deck of the boat. The panic-stricken disciples woke Him up and thought He didn't care that they were about to die. Jesus calmly dealt with the situation and brought calm from the chaos.

As you compete today, there may be times when chaos and turmoil try to take over your team. There will certainly be some stormy situations that could wreck your team's ship. Who will be the one to restore peace and to speak to the situation?

You can be the person on your team to speak to the chaotic situation in order to restore order. Be the one who says, "Quiet! Be still!" to the situation that's bringing fear to your teammates. Speak confidently and lead your team to a great victory.

Bible Reading Plan:
Matthew 23:1-12
Romans 5:12-21

March 28

LEADERSHIP

I Chronicles 12:22

Who among your teammates leads in such a way that others will naturally follow along? What difference does that make in your team's performance? In today's scripture we see great leadership in the person of David.

David's leadership is described in First Chronicles chapter 12 and verse 22 this way, "Day after day men came to help David, until he had a great army, like the army of God."

Here's David, a great leader assembling an outstanding team. Day after day people joined him in his pursuits. His team could only be compared with the army of God. That's remarkable leadership.

As you prepare to compete today, be the kind of team that defies comparison. Don't be satisfied with the most natural comparisons to last year's team or the team presently leading the conference. Lead and follow in a way that can only be compared with the army of God.

Bible Reading Plan:
Psalms 55
Numbers 21-22

March 29

SUFFERING

II Corinthians 4:17

Have you ever wondered in your mind, "What's the use, we're not doing very well, why put up with the suffering of losing?" Maybe you're struggling through an injury that nags your every step and you're wondering when this begins to pay dividends. The Scripture has some comforting and encouraging words for those days.

In Paul's second letter to the Corinthians in chapter 4 and verse 17 it says, "For momentary, light affliction is producing for us an eternal weight of glory far beyond all comparison." Sometimes in competition we encounter what seems like far more than "momentary, light affliction." When illness or injury comes your way, you can choose how we react to it.

It's true that injuries can make us lose heart, become depressed and lose sight of our goals, but it doesn't have to be that way. The writer of this verse was severely injured many times, but he knew how to make these things work in his favor.

Let the momentary, light affliction of your life turn your attention to your goals and to trusting in God's ability to complete them in you. Be assured that these hard times prepare us for days of greatness in the future.

The Lord is working in us to make "an eternal weight of glory beyond all comparison." He uses these hard times to prepare us for receiving the glorious times with grace and humility.

Pray to see the Lord's purposes accomplished in your life and in the lives of your teammates. Trust Him to use affliction and adversity to make glorious times and quality character for us all.

Bible Reading Plan:
Matthew 24:1-14
Romans 7:1-12

March 30

SACRIFICES

Psalm 51:16-17

What attitudes are most respected and appreciated by your coaches and team leaders? We'd probably list qualities like a strong work ethic, loyalty, teamwork, a willingness to sacrifice and more. What do you suppose would be the attitude most respected by God?

The writer of Psalm 51 answers that question very directly in verses 16 and 17, "You do not delight in sacrifice, or I would bring it; you do not take pleasure in burnt offerings. The sacrifices of God are a broken spirit; a broken and contrite heart, O God, you will not despise."

The writer has found that God's not really impressed with the normal religious sacrifices. Rather, God is very impressed with two primary attitudes. A broken spirit and a contrite heart are of great value to Him.

Those attitudes would serve us well in our pursuit of excellence in sport. A broken spirit is the very opposite of the arrogance so often seen in highly achieving people of sport. A contrite heart is essential to maintaining good teamwork. When one admits his failures or claims the fault for an error to his teammates, he's exhibiting a contrite heart.

As you compete today, maintain a broken spirit and your attitude will win the hearts of your teammates. Compete with a contrite heart and you'll build loyalty and commitment in everyone.

Bible Reading Plan:
Psalms 58
Numbers 28-30

March 31

WORDS

Proverbs 15:1

Words are a powerful tool and the attitudes we convey by our tone of voice can be equally strong. The Bible speaks about these ideas in many places and one of the most insightful follows.

In the Proverbs at chapter 15 and verse 1 it says, "A gentle answer turns away wrath, but a harsh word stirs up anger."

I'm sure we've all seen how a harsh word can stir up a person's anger. It's like striking a match and throwing it into a pool of gasoline. The situation is immediately inflamed. This happens all the time during competition. As the heat of intensity increases our fuses shorten and we often say things we wouldn't normally say. We often speak in tones we normally wouldn't use with our friends and teammates. It's easy for a harsh word to stir up anger and thus harm our relationships.

The marvelous promise contained here is that we can choose to answer gently and thus deflect the anger or wrath that is coming our way. It's like having a big fire extinguisher in our hands, we can put out the fire of harsh words by answering gently or kindly. A smile, a chuckle, a compliment and subdued, calm tones are like throwing cold water on hot, angry words. The wise use of gentle words can preserve relationships with coaches and teammates that are often in jeopardy of damage through intense situations.

Pray today for the Lord to use you as a speaker of gentle answers and for Him to keep you from speaking harsh words that stir up anger.

Bible Reading Plan:
Mark 1:1-8
I Corinthians 1:1-17
Psalms 72
Joshua 1-2

April 1

INVESTMENT

Matthew 6:21

In whom have you made a great investment? A family member? A friend? Your teammates or coaches? What happens between you and those in whom you make such investments? The Bible is full of insight into such human relations matters. One such instance follows.

In Matthew chapter 6 and verse 21, Jesus tells his followers, "for where your treasure is, there will your heart be also." We might say the same thing in our culture as, "your heart will have affection for the things in which you invest yourself."

What sort of things do you give your heart to? To what kinds of people? If you look closely I believe you'll find that you have the greatest affection for the things and people in whom you've made the deepest investments of your time, money and emotion.

So what should we do today? Commit yourself to investing deeply in your teammates, in the team as a whole. Buy into the team's goals, follow the coaching staff's leadership. Make a solid investment in anything and you'll find that you grow in your affection for it.

Jesus is very smart. He knows that where our treasure is, there our hearts will be also. Make your investment on the floor today. Empty your soul's pockets of everything you brought to the competition. Sell out in your effort, invest everything you have, in any way can for your team/family. Your collective goals will be realized as you each make your individual investments.

Bible Reading Plan:
Mark 1:9-20
I Corinthians 1:18-31
Psalms 73
Joshua 3-5

April 2

OBSTACLES

John 11:41

Do you have any teammates or friends who seemed trapped by something? They may have something blocking their way to great performance in competition. There may be something that blocks them from knowing freedom in living. What could you possibly do to remove the obstacle from their paths?

Jesus knew about this and we can read about it in John chapter 11 and verse 41. It says, "Then they took away the stone from the place where the dad man was lying. And Jesus lifted up His eyes and said, 'Father, I thank You that You have heard Me.'"

Jesus' friend Lazarus had been dead and buried for four days when Jesus returned to town. Here He says an incredible thing, "Take away the stone." Martha complains that the body will smell horribly after four days in a Palestinian grave. Jesus however had other plans for Lazarus.

As they rolled the stone away, they were removing the obstacle that prevented the crowd from seeing the marvelous thing that God was about to do. That's what Jesus could see that no one else could.

What can you do to remove an obstacle for a friend or teammate? Is there something that God wants to do for your friend that no one can see but you? How can we pave the way to our friend's breakthrough?

Let's do the same in today's competition. Let's make great plays in setting our teammates up to score. Let's make the sacrifice that enables our teammates to excel. Be a great team player today!

Bible Reading Plan:
I Corinthians 2
Psalms 74
Joshua 6-7

April 3

WEAKNESS

II Corinthians 5:16

Might one of your teammates have a glaring weakness? Maybe it's a part of his game that's incomplete or maybe it's a character flaw. Do you make that weakness the defining characteristic of the person?

Paul wrote to his friends in Corinth in his second letter at chapter 5 and verse 16, "So from now on we regard no one from a worldly point of view." I would paraphrase like this, "So from now on I will not let someone's personal weakness be that person's defining characteristic."

Just as we wouldn't focus totally on a person's limitations physically, I am committed to the same attitude in matters of faithfulness to commitments. I'm committed to pray for you and to encourage you when you act wisely and when you act foolishly. I'm committed to you when you do right and when you do wrong. On your good days and on your bad days. Your bad day behavior will not deter me from loving you and seeking God's best for you.

Take this attitude to heart and employ it in relation to each other on your team. This is what love looks like, whole-hearted commitment. Take that into today's competition for a day marked by great performances and even greater character.

Bible Reading Plan:
Mark 1:35-45
Psalms 75
Joshua 8-9

April 4

TRUST

Psalm 56:3-4

What situations in your sport tend to produce fear in you or your teammates? How do you deal with fear when it appears? Who can we trust when we're assaulted by fear and anxiety?

David, the psalmist, wrote the following words in Psalm 56 and verses 3 and 4, "When I am afraid, I will trust in you. In God, whose word I praise, in God I trust; I will not be afraid. What can mortal man do to me?"

You'll notice that he didn't say that he was never afraid. Rather, he said that when he was afraid, he would trust in God. He trusted in one who is far greater than any mortal man.

There are plenty of moments in sport that produce fear. We may find ourselves afraid of injury. Many of us compete, nagged by a constant fear of failure. Others may even fear their opponents.

In any case, when we are afraid, let's put our trust in God. He's with us every moment and is able to dispel every fear and doubt from our minds.

As you pray in preparation for this day's competition, commit yourself to God's care. Trust Him with every detail of your sport. In His care you're safe, what can mortal man do to you?

Bible Reading Plan:
Mark 2:1-12
I Corinthians 4
Joshua 10-12

April 5

RESPECT

Mark 6:4

How much respect do you get when you go back to your hometown to visit family and friends? Do they understand who you've become? Jesus knew that we don't automatically get the respect that we're due in our hometowns. It was the same for Him in His day.

We read about it in Mark chapter 6 and verse 4 where it says, "Only in his hometown, among his relatives and in his own house is a prophet without honor." Even for Jesus, the Son of God, this truth of human relations was true.

You can be the player of the year, a hall of fame performer, the MVP on your team and people back home will still remember you as the person you were in grade school. Family will still refer to you as your parents' child. It seems a little disrespectful and it's frustrating to endure.

What should we do when this occurs? Be who you are and don't worry about it. It's just natural for them to think this way. Many times, the folks back home just don't get it. Rather than taking offense, treat it like your little secret. Love them and relate to them in a way they can handle. Sooner or later, they'll wake up to who you are and you'll be afforded the respect you deserve.

As you compete today, do so in a way that deserves such respect and give the home folks something to be proud of. Even more than that, compete in a way that deserves God's respect.

Bible Reading Plan:
I Corinthians 5
Psalms 77

April 6

PURPOSE

Acts 13:36

Do you ever wonder about what God's purpose for you might be? Have you ever contemplated why God would have you born in this generation and not a hundred years earlier, or later? How will our great-grandchildren see our lives long after we've died?

In the Acts of the Apostles at chapter 13 and verse 36, the Apostle Paul says, "For David, after he had served the purpose of God in his own generation, fell asleep, and was laid among his fathers, and underwent decay."

Paul, many generations after King David had died, says of him that he served the purpose of God in his own generation. What a marvelous legacy! How great would that be for you and me, to know that we had served God's purpose in our own generation. How do we approach such matters? What shall we do to insure our success in this pursuit?

Let's do as David did and give ourselves fully to seeking God's face and to serving Him only. Let's give the very best of all that we are and all we have to loving God. Then as we sleep with our fathers, we shall have confidence that our descendents will look upon us as having served the purpose of God in our own generation.

As you pray today, ask the Lord to show you His purpose for you in this generation. Ask Him further for the power and wisdom to carry it out.

Bible Reading Plan:
Mark 2:18-28
Psalms 78:1-39
Joshua 15-17

April 7

VIGILANCE

Proverbs 15:3

Do you ever feel like the Lord must be on vacation? Does it seem that your plight has gone unnoticed? Does it seem to you that everybody but you gets the breaks? The Bible speaks clearly about how vigilant our Lord Jesus is.

One such passage is in Proverbs chapter 15 and verse 3, "The eyes of the Lord are everywhere, keeping watch on the wicked and the good."

The Lord is not limited by space and time as we are. He can see and hear everything in all places at once. This scripture says that His eyes are everywhere. It is comforting to me to know that nothing that concerns me has escaped His notice.

The Lord keeps watch on both the wicked and the good. It seems He keeps watch on the wicked to reward them according to their deeds and he watches the good to protect them and to provide for them.

As you pray today, thank the Lord for His carefully watching over your life. Compete today with the assurance that the Lord's eyes are everywhere and they're watching over you.

Bible Reading Plan:
Mark 3:1-19
I Corinthians 6:12-20
Joshua 18-19

April 8

FOUNDATIONS

Matthew 7:24-25

Which would provide a better foundation for your home, solid rock or a sandy beach? What kind of foundation does your team have?

In chapter 7 and verses 24-25 of Matthew's gospel we read, "Everyone who hears these words of mine and puts them into practice is like a wise man who built his house on the rock. The rain came down, the streams rose, and the winds blew and beat against that house; yet it did not fall, because it had its foundation on the rock."

Here's a house on a good foundation, let's talk about a team on a good foundation. This is a team built upon principles of truth put into practice. That team will not crumble when it encounters adversity.

Adversity will come, but it cannot harm the team or the individuals within it. Just as the winds and rain couldn't harm the house or its inhabitants, the team that is built upon principles of truth put into practice, will not fall. That team has a rock hard foundation.

In your time of prayer today, ask the Lord to solidify your team's foundation. Ask Him to build your team upon a foundation that will not give way to even the most powerful adversity.

Bible Reading Plan:
I Corinthians 7:1-16
Psalms 79

April 9

CONFIDENCE

II Corinthians 7:16

Whom have you known long enough to have acquired an unshakable confidence in them? What do you suppose is in John Stockton's mind when he passes the ball toward Karl Malone in the middle of a pick and roll? Complete confidence! Do you have that kind of confidence in your teammates? Why is that so?

In Paul's second letter to the church at Corinth at chapter 7 and verse 16 he writes, "I am glad I can have complete confidence in you." How rich would it be to have your friend and mentor to say that of you?

There is a confidence that comes from knowing people in their good times and in their bad times. We gain confidence in our teammates when we see them perform well under pressure. We grow in trusting our coaches when they make good decisions at trying times. We also gain confidence in our God when He comes through for us in times of great sorrow and confusion.

Your coaches have grown in their confidence in you, individually and as a group. That makes them glad, seeing you like daughters and sons who are maturing and growing into outstanding young people. They are glad they can have complete confidence in you, on and off the field of competition. Have your best game of the season today. I have complete confidence that you will.

Bible Reading Plan:
Mark 4:1-20
I Corinthians 7:17-40
Psalms 80
Joshua 22-23

April 10

OPPORTUNITY

John 12:7-8

You're certainly aware that this competition or any game could be your last opportunity to put on the uniform and to compete. Any number of things could bring one's career to an end. Not the least of those is graduation and the end of one's eligibility. Jesus gives us some wisdom for how to handle opportunities toward the end of a season.

The situation is recorded in John's Gospel at chapter 12 and verses 7 and 8, where we read, "Then Jesus said, 'Let her alone; she has kept this for the day of my burial. For the poor you have with you always, but Me you do not have always.'"

Mary had done something very expensive and very extravagant as an expression of her devotion to Christ. One person in the room didn't react very well, thinking she was foolish and wasteful. His name was Judas. He didn't realize the significance of the moment like Jesus did.

It could be the same with you and your team today. Be aware of the significance of the moment, the import of the day and take full advantage of the opportunities you have to express appreciation to those who are helpful to you and your team.

Be a little extravagant in expressing your thanks to your coaches, to your teammates and to those most highly committed to your team. In so doing, you'll be like Mary, knowing this moment will not always be available. Have a great day of competition.

Bible Reading Plan:
Mark 4:21-41
Psalms 81
Joshua 24

April 11

PRESSURE

When do you feel the pressures of your life of competition most greatly? Is it on game day, in practice or when surrounded by reporters and fans? Jesus and His followers felt similar pressures and He knew how to handle them.

Let's watch how He deals with the pressing crowd in Mark chapter 6 and verses 30 and 31. "The apostles gathered around Jesus and reported to Him all they had done and taught. Then, because so many people were coming and going that they did not even have a chance to eat, He said to them, 'Come with me by yourselves to a quiet place and get some rest.'"

Jesus' apostles were coming back from a victorious road trip and they were reporting to Jesus about their successes. They were tired, but excited and had gathered quite a crowd of others who were awed by their accomplishments. Jesus knew just what to do for His most devoted followers.

Rather than hang around with the crowd and its pressures, He calls them away to a more private, quiet place so they could rest. Some of us might be tempted to hang around indefinitely after an important home win, but it might be more prudent to get away with some teammates and close friends for some quiet time of relaxation.

Compete today with great energy and intensity. Pursue excellence in every moment of this contest. But after it's all over, make time to relax, to rest and to unwind with teammates and friends who appreciate you and help take the pressure out of your life. Choose your friends wisely and find peaceful places to relax, far from the foolish, nagging questions and frivolous demands.

Bible Reading Plan:
Mark 5:1-20
I Corinthians 9:1-12

April 12

REFUGE

Psalm 57:1

Where and with whom do you seek refuge when the pressures of competition are getting to you? Do you seek out family, friends, solitude? All those can be good sources of refuge. Where do you suppose is the best?

Psalm 57 and verse 1 reveals a most secure place of refuge. There we read, "Have mercy on me, O God, have mercy on me, for in you my soul takes refuge. I will take refuge in the shadow of your wings until the disaster has passed."

The psalmist sought protection and comfort from God in the middle of a great disaster. He begged for God to be merciful and to hide him.

We might encounter disaster in any number of forms during a season of sport. It could come through injury or illness. It might be a losing streak or a coaching staff transition. The question remains, where will we find refuge when disaster strikes or pressures mount?

May I challenge you to trust God's immeasurable power and protection as a secure place of refuge? He will cover you with his love and compassion until the disaster has passed.

Let God's mercy and love cover you as you compete today. Trust Him to be a rock of refuge from the daily storms of life.

Bible Reading Plan:
Mark 5:21-43
I Corinthians 9:13-27
Psalms 83
Judges 4-5

April 13

GOD'S HELP

Acts 26:22

Have you ever had a sense that God was helping you as you competed? Do you remember having healed from an injury more quickly than normal? Have you obtained help from God? Have you told anyone about it?

In the Acts of the Apostles at chapter 26 and verse 22, the Apostle Paul says to Festus the governor, "And so, having obtained help from God, I stand to this day testifying both to small and great, stating nothing but what the Prophets and Moses said was going to take place."

Here is Paul in chains before the people who could free him or could send him on to Rome and ultimate death. What does He talk about? He speaks of how God has helped him and how Jesus is the fulfillment of everything spoken by the prophets and Moses. Has your relationship with Christ so changed your life that it consumes your conversation with both great and small?

Let's join Paul in speaking of the times in which we've sensed the Lord's help. Times of recovery from injury, grief from a friend's death, hope in the midst of despair, displays of power when you feel weak.

As you pray and prepare today, ask the Lord for His help. He is ever present. Ask Him also for the opportunity to speak of Him to both the great and the small. He will be honored by your witness, as He was by Paul's.

Bible Reading Plan:
Mark 6:1-13
I Corinthians 10:1-13
Psalms 84
Judges 6-7

April 14

NO GREATER LOVE

John 15:13

What is the standard for measuring commitment, loyalty and teamwork? How about for a family? How about for friendship? Let's see what Jesus says in today's letter.

In John chapter 15 at verse 13 we read, "Greater love has no one than this, than to lay down one's life for his friends."

There it is again, the recurring theme of self-sacrifice and service. Jesus again challenges us to give ourselves up in preference of our teammates' best and highest good.

How does one lay down his life? Let's think it through:

To sacrifice your personal goals for your team's goals.

To sacrifice your selfish dreams of glory for the good of your team.

To play fewer minutes to help develop other players.

To sacrifice your body to make a play for the team.

To sacrifice your ego to praise your teammates and coaches.

To love and serve your team over seeking your own pride and glory.

Let's play today with these attitudes and give everyone an example of the love Jesus says is without equal.

Bible Reading Plan:
Mark 6:14-29
I Corinthians 10:14-33
Psalms 85
Judges 8

April 15

COACHES AND ATHLETES

Matthew 10:24-25

Who are your heroes in this game? Who has mentored you in your career? Wouldn't it be great to be like that player? Wouldn't you like to emulate your mentor?

In Matthew chapter 10 at verses 24 and 25 it says, "A student is not above his teacher, nor a servant above his master. It is enough for the student to be like his teacher, and the servant like his master." Jesus seems to want these relationships kept in a proper order.

We'd be fools to presume to have knowledge, skills and wisdom beyond that of our heroes. We'd be way out of line in boasting about our abilities in the presence of our mentors.

In the same way we should guard our attitudes with our coaches, our team leaders and others associated with the team. We should watch closely how we speak and relate to each one. It would be great for us just to be mentioned in the same breath as some of those around us.

We should certainly seek to emulate our teacher and master Jesus Christ. To be like Him would be the accomplishment of a lifetime. Give your absolute best effort today to honor your leaders, mentors and coaches. The Lord Jesus will be honored as well.

Bible Reading Plan:
Mark 6:30-44
I Corinthians 11:1-16
Psalms 86
Judges 9

April 16

UNDERDOGS

I Samuel 17:48-50

What's the greatest mismatch in competition that you've ever experienced? On which side of the mismatch were you? Were you the underdog or the heavy favorite? What was the outcome?

We read about such a conflict in First Samuel chapter 17 and verses 48 through 50, "As the Philistine (Goliath) moved closer to attack him, David ran quickly toward the battle line to meet him. Reaching into his bag and taking out a stone, he slung it and struck the Philistine on the forehead. The stone sank into his forehead, and he fell facedown on the ground. So David triumphed over the Philistine with a sling and a stone; without a sword in his hand he struck down the Philistine and killed him."

Here in one of history's greatest mismatches – the underdog, the little guy, David – kills the overwhelming favorite – the giant, Goliath with a sling and a rock. Notice David's attitude in competition, he ran quickly toward the battle line to meet the giant. No fear, no hesitation, no intimidation. He was ready and willing to give his all.

As you compete today, cast off any fear or intimidation that you may feel of today's opponent. Compete with confidence, sling your stone, slay the giant then cut off his big, ugly head.

Bible Reading Plan:
Mark 6:45-56
I Corinthians 11:17-34
Psalms 87
Judges 10-12

April 17

SOWING AND REAPING

II Corinthians 9:6

How about a simple exercise in reason today? If one farmer sows 100 pounds of seed and another sows 10,000 pounds, which one will have the greater harvest? Simple, huh? How about another one?

In the second letter to the Corinthians at chapter 9 and verse 6, Paul the Apostle writes, "Remember this: Whoever sows sparingly will also reap sparingly, and whoever sows generously will also reap generously." That seems simple enough, invest lots and you'll get lots in return. Sounds kind of like what investors hope for in the stock market.

This law applies to all of life; work, money, study, relationships, practice, everything. In sowing and reaping; we always reap after we sow, we always reap more than we sow and we always reap exactly what we sow. As you have sown generously in practice, you should expect to reap greatly on game day. If you have sown sparingly on the practice floor, you should expect to reap sparingly during the game.

I trust that you've invested generously into the life of this team. Therefore I expect you to reap a generous reward in this game. Expect the hours of work, study, sweat and effort to produce a great victory today.

Bible Reading Plan:
Mark 7:1-23
I Corinthians 12:1-13
Psalms 88
Judges 13-15

April 18

LEADERSHIP

Mark 6:46-51

In your life as a competitor, have you ever experienced great courage and an unnaturally calm spirit in the midst of tremendous struggle and fear? Many of us have and so did Jesus.

We read about such an instance in Mark's gospel at chapter 6 and verses 46 through 51. There it says, "After leaving them, He went up on a mountainside to pray. When evening came, the boat was in the middle of the lake and He was alone on land. He saw the disciples straining at the oars, because the wind was against them. About the fourth watch of the night He went out to them, walking on the lake. He was about to pass by them, but when they saw Him walking on the lake, they thought it was a ghost. They cried out because they all saw Him and were terrified. Immediately He spoke to them and said, 'Take courage! It is I. Don't be afraid.' Then He climbed into the boat with them, and the wind died down."

Great team leaders are aware of the team's condition. Jesus saw that His team was straining at the oars and walked out to check on them. Great team leaders speak strong words of encouragement to their teammates. Jesus said three simple sentences to His terrified disciples and thus quelled their fears. He said, "Take courage! It is I. Don't be afraid." That was enough.

Great team leaders calm their teammates simply by being present. As soon as Jesus climbed into the boat, the wind died down. Some of you calm things down for your teammates by simply entering the contest. Your very presence in the lineup makes your team more confident.

Be such a team leader in today's competition and the whole team will be successful.

Bible Reading Plan:
Mark 7:24-37
Psalms 89:1-18

April 19

HARD WORK

Colossians 3:23

How do you approach the sport in which you compete? Is it just a game to you or is there more to it than that? How do you practice? Do you apply all you have and all that you are to improving your game or do you just try to get through practice and do what it takes to keep the coach off your back? The Bible gives us some encouraging words about work and practice.

My favorite verse related to work is from Paul's letter to his friends at Colossae at chapter 3 and verse 23. Here he says, "Whatever you do, do your work heartily, as for the Lord rather than for people." In your case this may be related to your chosen field of competition. How should we approach these things? Heartily, that is with all our hearts.

We might say that we should pour out our guts in pursuit of achieving excellence. Give all that you are to doing the work that's before you. Why? Because ultimately we're serving God in this rather than just the coaching staff or our schools.

God is honored by our whole hearted pursuit of excellence in our work. Let's honor Him today in the way we go about our work of competing and let's trust Him with the results. Give all that you've got to your competition today.

Bible Reading Plan:
Mark 8:1-13
I Corinthians 13
Psalms 89:19-52
Judges 17-18

April 20

RENEWED STRENGTH

Psalm 61:1-3

When, in the course of a season, do you begin to lose a little steam? When are you starting to run low on energy? What can you do to regain your strength and vitality?

In Psalm 61 and verse 1 through 3, we hear a poetic prayer for renewed strength. There we read, "Hear my cry, O God; listen to my prayer. From the ends of the earth I call to you, I call as my heart grows faint; lead me to the rock that is higher than I. For you have been my refuge, a strong tower against the foe."

The writer felt totally alienated and exposed. He felt like he was at the edge of the earth and called out to God as his heart grew more and more faint. He saw God as a rock, as a refuge and a strong tower to protect him from his enemies.

You may feel similarly when your strength is waning and all your muscles ache. You may be physically, mentally and emotionally worn out by practice and competition. What are you to do when your hearts grow faint?

As you prepare to compete today, follow the writer's example and cry out to God as a refuge and a strong tower against your foe. Today, that foe may be fatigue or pain. Pray right where you are and He'll be there to support and to protect you.

Bible Reading Plan:
Mark 8:14-21
I Corinthians 14:1-25
Psalm 90
Judges 19

April 21

REST

Matthew 11:28

Do you ever get tired, a little leg weary? Of course you do. Does it ever seem like you're dragging an anchor back and forth through practice? It doesn't have to be that way.

Jesus' words are recorded in Matthew chapter 11 and verse 28 this way, "Come to me, all you who are weary and burdened, and I will give you rest. Take my yoke upon you and learn from me, for I am gentle and humble in heart, and you will find rest for your souls. For my yoke is easy and my burden is light."

When we take on the Lord's yoke, we lay down the one we've been carrying. This is like taking the anchor off your neck and replacing it with a lovely necklace. Rather than being a burden to you, it's an adornment. It graces your life with beauty and freedom.

As you encounter fatigue and even exhaustion, rest in the assurance that the Lord Jesus' yoke is easy and his burden is light. Find rest for your soul in His gentle, humble heart. Learn from Him and your energy and passion for sport will be renewed as well.

Bible Reading Plan:
Mark 8:22-30
I Corinthians 14:26-40
Psalms 91
Judges 20-21

April 22

PLANS

Proverbs 16:3

What are your plans for this season? Do you have goals for your team or for yourself? What are the keys to seeing your goals achieved?

In Proverbs chapter 16 and verse 3 we find an important principle, "Commit to the Lord whatever you do, and your plans will succeed."

How does one commit to the Lord everything that he does? Simply said, that would be to approach all of life's activities and pursuits with prayer and attention to doing things God's way. Commit all of your life to pursuing God's will and His ways in school, in practice, in competition, in family life, in friendships and dating relationships. Commit it all to Him.

The promise is that when we do this, He works in us to see that our plans succeed. That assumes that you have some plans. Make a plan that will honor God, then commit everything about yourself to Him. The Lord is faithful and His promise is that He'll work to see our plans succeed.

As you pray, make those first commitments to the Lord. Commit this day's competition to Him and watch for Him to make your plans successful.

Bible Reading Plan:
Mark 8:31-38
I Corinthians 15:1-28
Psalms 92
Ruth 1

April 23

STRENGTH AND WEAKNESS

II Corinthians 12:9

Have you heard about Kareem Abdul Jabbar's college basketball career? I'm old enough to have watched it. In those days college hoop had a "no dunking rule." Though he was over seven feet tall, his highest percentage shot was taken away. However, the rule that could have weakened his game caused him to develop his jump shot, the sky hook, better post moves, and more; making him the dominant player of his era. His perceived weakness became the strength of his career.

In Paul's second letter to his friends in Corinth, he encourages them with similar thoughts at chapter 12 and verse 9, "But He said to me, 'My grace is sufficient for you, for My power is made perfect in weakness." Paul quotes the Lord's word to him regarding his personal weakness.

Sometimes the Lord uses our perceived weaknesses as the platform for displaying His great power. God makes His greatest evidences of power through some of the weakest looking people. It is God's way to show His strength in the middle of our weaknesses.

In today's game, when it seems like all your strength is gone, look up!! You're now in position for God to show His power in your life. He is ready to reveal His strength when we've exhausted all our natural resources. When we come to the end of ourselves, there He is. Give your best today, then watch for the Lord to empower you to even achieve even more greatly.

Bible Reading Plan:
Mark 9:1-13
I Corinthians 15:29-58
Psalms 93
Ruth 2-3

April 24

RESPECT

Have you ever heard a disrespectful comment or seen a gesture by a competitor inflame the competitive edge in his opponent and lead to his/her team's defeat? It happens more often than you can imagine and today's scripture tells about a similar instance.

In the Old Testament book of Second Kings at chapter 1 and verses 13 and 14 it says, "So the king sent a third captain with his fifty men. This third captain went up and fell on his knees before Elijah. 'Man of God,' he begged, 'please have respect for my life and the lives of these fifty men, your servants! See, fire has fallen from heaven and consumed the first two captains and all their men. But now have respect for my life!'"

This man was much wiser than the two who preceded him. They showed terrible disrespect for the Man of God and were consumed with fire. He knew that Elijah was not someone to be messed with and he took an appropriate posture.

As we compete, we might be better off letting sleeping dogs lie. If your opponent is struggling and seems to be a little off his game, don't trash talk him into a better performance. Rather than showing him up with your mouth, give him proper respect and maybe he won't destroy you in the second half.

Bible Reading Plan:
Mark 9:14-32
I Corinthians 16
Psalms 94
Ruth 4

April 25

STRENGTH

Psalm 73:26

Take a moment to recall a time when you've competed to the point of total exhaustion. Your body, mind and soul were fully spent in pursuit of a victory. How does one continue to compete, even when at the point of physical breakdown and total collapse? The writer of today's psalm knew what it was for his flesh and his heart to fail.

In Psalm 73 and verse 26 we read, "My flesh and my heart may fail, but God is the strength of my heart and my portion forever."

The writer had lived through times when he had totally exhausted the capacity of his body to fight, but had lived on. He had been to the very end of his heart's ability to love, but found renewed strength of soul.

At the end of your body's natural ability to compete, God is a limitless source of strength. When your heart is poured out like so much water, God is a river of life to your soul.

As you compete today, don't simply rely on the power of your flesh to carry you. Look to God as a continual source of power and strength. Look for His wisdom and joy to carry you through the momentum shifts of the sport. Compete with great strength and passion.

Bible Reading Plan:
Mark 1:21-34
I Corinthians 3

April 26

TRADITIONS

Every sport has a set of traditions or practices that are a part of its culture and history. Do any of those things ever violate your conscience or cause you to wonder if you should be involved in them? Jesus had some tough things to say to people in His day about similar things.

Let's listen as He confronts some people about foolish traditions in Mark chapter 7 and verse 9, "You have a fine way of setting aside the commands of God in order to observe your own traditions!" Jesus took these people on as they rationalized their way around the simple commands of God in order to make themselves look good for other people.

If we think everyone else cheats in recruiting, does that make it alright for us to do so? If your sport has a tradition of violently hazing young players, does that make it a good idea? From whom shall we take our cues for ethics within the world of sport? These are all tough questions that we need to consider.

Jesus points straight to the most enduring source of truth in regards to ethical standards. It's the Word of God. The Bible speaks straight to us in relation to all of life, even competition and the ethics we need to compete with fairness and justice.

In today's competition, compete strongly and fairly. Compete with great passion and within the rules of the sport. Compete in a way that honors your teammates, your coaches, your family and even honors God.

Bible Reading Plan:
Psalms 76
Joshua 13-14

April 27

REWARDS

Colossians 3:24-25

The rewards for performing well in sport are numerous. You probably thought of things like trophies, rings, medals and ribbons. You may have also had thoughts of more intangible rewards like satisfaction, fame, and exhilaration. The other side of performance based rewards is that when you perform poorly, there are less attractive rewards attached. Who among us hasn't felt the sting of disappointment, pain and disgust after a bad competition? We all have memories of being rewarded for a poor performance with second-guessing, ridicule or embarrassment. Both kinds of rewards for athletic performance are given without regard to our position or prestige as competitors.

The Apostle Paul wrote about rewards in his letter to the Colossians at chapter 3 and verses 24 through 25, "...since you know that you will receive an inheritance from the Lord as a reward. It is the Lord Christ you are serving. Anyone who does wrong will be repaid for his wrong, and there is no favoritism."

The exciting thing about this scripture is that it tells of another basis for reward that's more secure than your latest performance on the field of competition. The reward that comes from inheritance is not based on your performance, but on your relationship with God through Christ Jesus. Christ rewards those related to Him with gifts like love, peace, security, patience and self-control. Competitors who love God find these rewards to be more enduring and of infinitely greater value than those which come from performance.

As you prepare for this competition, give all that you have to perform at your very best. You owe that to your team, to yourself and ultimately to the Lord Christ you are serving.

Bible Reading Plan:
Mark 2:13-17
I Corinthians 6:1-11

April 28

PROVIDENCE

Proverbs 16:9

Have you ever wondered why your path seems to zig zag sometimes? Why am I here? How did I end up in this place when I was going over there? Lots of athletes ask those kind of questions as they consider their paths in pursuit of athletic goals.

In Proverbs 16 and at verse 9 we find a possible answer, "The mind of a man plans his ways, but the Lord directs His steps."

Every athlete I know sometimes lays on his bed and dreams about what he'd like to achieve, the awards he'd like to win, the career he'd like to pursue. In his mind he plans his way.

But, somewhere along the way to those dreams being accomplished, he gets sidetracked and before long he's not sure how he got here. Here's the comforting word in this scripture. It's the Lord's way to direct our steps along the path to the fulfilling of His purposes in our lives. The Lord sees very clearly the best path for us. He sees very clearly what we need in preparation for our ultimate place of serving Him. Sure we can make plans, and that is good, but it's the Lord's place to direct our steps along the way.

Pray in thanksgiving for the Lord's direction of your life. Ask Him to help you plan your way and for the grace to trust Him all along the way.

Bible Reading Plan:
Psalms 78:40-72
Joshua 20-21

April 29

BLESSINGS

Matthew 13:16

Yours is a unique privilege. How many people around the world would love to compete in your sport? How many would love to see what you see and hear what you hear?

In Matthew chapter 13 and verse 16, Jesus says, "Blessed are your eyes because they see, and your ears because they hear." Sure you can all see things and hear sounds, on the physical level, but there's more to this.

Be thankful on another level all together. There are untold thousands of people who would love to see what you see and to hear what you hear on a daily basis. To see sports from the bench, rather than from the seats. To hear what can't be heard from the top row of the stadium is what some people dream about.

On still another level, you have a unique privilege to be on a team and to experience the depth of relationship that is much rarer in the non-sport world.

As you prepare to compete today give thanks for what your eyes see and your ears hear. Look for the inspirational performances by your teammates. Listen for the encouraging words from coaches. Listen also for the Lord's blessing.

Bible Reading Plan:
Mark 3:20-35
I Corinthians 8

April 30

IN THE FLOW

Deuteronomy 28:2

Have you ever stood in a stream and felt the power of the current pulling everything downstream? Have you ever tried to outrun the wind on a March afternoon? These are similar ideas to how Moses describes the flow of God's blessings for those who obey Him.

In Moses' book called Deuteronomy at chapter 28 and verse 2 it says, "All these blessings will overtake you and will accompany you if you obey the Lord your God." It is as if Moses is saying the blessings of God will come upon us just by our standing still if we are obedient to God's will.

Picture this for how this works. It's like you're standing in a river bed on hot, dry ground and you hear a sound coming up behind you. It's a cool, refreshing stream coming down the river bed and enveloping you in its wake. Moses is saying that God's blessings will overtake you like a river when you pursue His will and obey His commands.

In today's competition make it your goal to have your best performance of the year, this would be fitting with God's desire for you. As you run, look over your shoulder once in a while and don't be surprised if God's blessings are coming up behind you and even overtaking you. He loves you dearly.

Bible Reading Plan:
Mark 9:33-50
II Corinthians 1:1-11
Psalms 95
I Samuel 1-2

May 1

PERSECUTION

Have you ever taken some heat for your convictions? Have you been criticized for doing the right thing? Jesus spoke about such things often.

In another verse of the Beatitudes in Matthew chapter five and at verse 10 it says, "Blessed are those who are persecuted because of righteousness, for theirs is the kingdom of heaven." How could anyone feel blessed when he's being persecuted? Seems silly doesn't it? It's not if you understand what it is to be blessed.

There is a sense of being content that is ours when we are taking heat for doing the right thing. When we come under fire for doing the unpopular and the proper, we find an unusual sense of peace. That's what Jesus calls being blessed. You can probably remember a time when you chose to do the right thing, even when it was unpopular.

Why does that feeling come to us? Jesus says that it's because when we do, ours is the kingdom of heaven. We're acting like citizens of heaven when we choose godly behavior, even in the face of criticism and accusations.

As you prepare for today's competition, set your mind and heart to doing the right thing in every situation. Choose the best, even when you know you'll be criticized, accused or even persecuted. In doing so you'll be blessed and you'll be living in possession of the kingdom of heaven.

Bible Reading Plan:
II Corinthians 1:12-24
Psalms 96
I Samuel 3-5

May 2

PRIVILEGE

Psalm 84:10

Have you ever considered how very fortunate you are to participate in sport? There are countless millions of people who would give all they have to be in your positions of privilege.

The writer of Psalm 84 felt such privilege as he wrote the following in verse 10, "Better is one day in your courts than a thousand elsewhere; I would rather be a doorkeeper in the house of my God than dwell in the tents of the wicked."

This person fully realized his great privilege and position. He made very strong comparisons to express it.

If I were to paraphrase his expressions into the language of sport, I might say, "Better is one day on the field of competition than a thousand games watching from the bleachers. I would rather be serving water on the sideline than to watch from the best luxury box in the stadium."

As you prepare to compete today, thank God for the high privilege of being where you are. Rejoice in your position and compete powerfully yet humbly. Be mindful that nearly everyone watching you would give his eye teeth to be where you are. You are truly blessed.

Bible Reading Plan:
Mark 10:17-34
Psalms 97
I Samuel 6-8

May 3

CORRUPTION

Mark 7:14-16

Have you ever felt that you were personally tainted by the cheap shot taken by a teammate or by the unethical tactics or gamesmanship of your coach? Jesus understood that feeling and clarified the truth about it in Mark chapter 7 and verses 14 through 16.

There it reads, "Listen to me, everyone, and understand this. Nothing outside a man can make him 'unclean' by going into him. Rather, it is what comes out of a man that makes him 'unclean.'" Jesus was speaking with the most legalistic people of His time who spent all their time worrying about who was and who was not 'clean' enough for proper relationship with God.

Jesus cut through all the surface level nonsense and went straight to the heart of the matter. He knew that rather than being polluted by our surroundings, our greater problem is the corruption in our own hearts. From the hatred in our hearts come mean-spirited words. From our internal envy comes the motivation to steal or to cheat.

Jesus' words give us all pause when we would point the finger and shift blame for our feelings of guilt or shame. Rather than point to the errors of others, we should look closely at our own hearts and confess to our own faults.

In today's competition, compete in a way that leaves no room for anyone to point a finger or to place blame. Make this competition one of great excellence and purity.

Bible Reading Plan:
Mark 10:35-52
II Corinthians 3
I Samuel 9-10

May 4

POWER, LOVE AND DISCIPLINE

II Timothy 1:7

Every once in a while we encounter an opponent in competition who by all accounts is unbeatable and it prompts fear in our team. Some opponents seem to grow larger and larger as we approach game day. The media reports and word of mouth reports have us thinking these people are giants. How shall we approach such an opponent?

In Paul's second letter to his timid friend Timothy, at chapter 1 and verse 7 it says, "For God has not given us a spirit of fear, but one of power, love and a sound mind." Your opponents on the athletic fields are good and worthy of your respect. They are not, however worthy of fear!! The work of God's Spirit within us does not bring fear, but courage.

Instead of fear, here is what God has given us:

1) Power... not just physical power, but power that comes from within.

2) Love... not an emotional attraction to a guy or girl, but a powerful force that seeks the highest good for those around us. Concern and sacrifice for teammates, coaches, family... that's real love.

3) A sound mind... not just doing well in school, but mental soundness related to doing the right things and to correct assessment of the truth.

As you approach your competition, be assured that your opponents are not worthy of fear. Beyond that, exercise power, love and soundness of mind in a day of greatness in competition.

Bible Reading Plan:
Mark 11:1-11
II Corinthians 3
Psalms 99

May 5

PATIENCE

Proverbs 16:32

How well do you control your emotions during competition? Do you blow up on occasion or do you stay under control? Might the Bible have anything to say about these matters?

Proverbs chapter 16 verse 32 states, "Better a patient man that a warrior, a man who controls his temper than one who takes a city." Sometimes the greatest battles that we fight take place between our ears.

It's often the struggle over who controls our minds and emotions that is the foremost factor in our success or failure. In this scripture, patience and self-control are valued even more highly than physical strength or military power.

As you compete today, ask the Lord to enable you to master your mind and emotions. Ask Him to take control of them for His purposes. Compete with patience and in full control of your temper and tongue. As the proverb says, these qualities make us better than the mighty warrior and even stronger than the one who can overthrow a city.

Bible Reading Plan:
Mark 11:12-26
II Corinthians 5
Psalms 100
I Samuel 14

May 6

KINGDOM OF HEAVEN

Matthew 13:45

What is your most prized possession? What did it cost you? How valuable is it to you?

In Matthew 13 and verse 45, Jesus spins a great tale about values, "The kingdom of heaven is like a merchant looking for fine pearls. When he found one of great value, he went away and sold everything he had and bought it."

What is there in your life that's worthy of your whole hearted devotion? What is so valuable to you that you'd sell everything you have to obtain it? This is how valuable Jesus says the kingdom of heaven is.

Knowing God in a deep, personal way is worth giving 100% of yourself in pursuit of that relationship. Conversely, God is pursuing you by having already given all He has to win you.

You are, collectively and individually, God's pearl of great value. He loves you greatly and has paid an infinite price to know you personally.

Play this game with the confidence that comes from being supremely loved. That is a place of great security and freedom.

Bible Reading Plan:
II Corinthians 6
Psalms 101
I Samuel 15-16

May 7

GOOD FIGHTS

II Timothy 4:7

I imagine that everyone thinks about how they will finish this season. Will we have that dream season, undefeated and champions? Will we be winless and disheartened? Will we be somewhere in the middle and somewhat mediocre? We all start the same, but how will we finish?

In the Apostle Paul's second letter to his friend Timothy he wrote in chapter 4 and verse 7, "I have fought the good fight, I have finished the course, I have kept the faith;"

Paul talked about fighting a good fight. It seems that to fight the good fight is to contend for things that really matter. Paul challenges us all to fight the good fight.

Paul said that he had finished the course. I'm sure he meant that he had completed all that God had called him to do. How many of us will say at the end of our lives that we've fulfilled God's purpose for our lives. Paul challenges us to finish the course.

Paul said that he had kept the faith. Faith is something that some people keep forever, while others seem to have it escape their grasp. Faith - active trust in God - can only be kept through maintaining a relationship with Christ through prayer, study, fellowship and sharing that same faith. Paul challenges us to keep the faith.

In preparing for your competition, keep Paul's challenges in mind. Fight the good fight - do the right things for the right reasons. Finish the course - finish the season well and strongly. Keep the faith - maintain a strong trust in your coaches, teammates and your collective goals.

Bible Reading Plan:
Mark 12:1-12
Psalms 102
I Samuel 17-18

May 8

TEAMWORK

Ecclesiastes 4:9-10

How critical is good teamwork to your individual success? How much of your success can you directly tie to your teammates and their support? Few of us ever achieve greatly on our own and today's scripture outlines two reasons why.

In the fourth chapter of the book of Ecclesiastes at verses 9 and 10 we read, "Two are better than one, because they have a good return for their work; If one falls down, his friend can help him up. But pity the man who falls and has no one to help him up!"

Number one: Two are better than one because they don't just add to each other, nor do they simply multiply their work, instead two have an exponentially better return for their work. Amazing things can be accomplished by people who align themselves to achieve a goal.

Number two: Even in failure, they're able to recover and to press on toward their goals. If one falls down, the other can help him up, encourage him and the two continue on their way. If we fail while isolated, we're in real danger of being left behind and unable to complete the race.

In preparation for this day's competition, be thankful for your teammates. Be confident in the exponential increase that comes through your unified teamwork. Watch for your stumbling teammate and be ready to help him through the rough spots in the season. Together, we'll achieve more highly than any of us could individually.

Bible Reading Plan:
Mark 12:13-27
II Corinthians 8
I Samuel 19-20

May 9

ACHIEVEMENT

Mark 7:36-37

Who is the greatest player you've ever known? Did he do everything well or was there one small flaw in his game? How do you think people perceived Jesus when He was on the earth?

Let's read about how Jesus asked people to act after they had witnessed some of his most amazing deeds of compassion. It's recorded in Mark's book at chapter 7 and verses 36 and 37, "Jesus commanded them not to tell anyone. But the more He did so, the more they kept talking about it. People were overwhelmed with amazement. 'He has done everything well,' they said. 'He even makes the deaf hear and the mute speak.'"

Even when Jesus tried to keep people quiet, they couldn't help but talk about Him. It could be the same with you. When you achieve highly, they'll talk about you too. Even when you play down your accomplishments, they'll still talk.

When that happens, watch your attitude. When they won't quit applauding your achievements, maintain some humility. When your photo is in the paper every day and you're the feature story on the television, remember how fickle the crowd is.

Keep these things in mind as you compete today. If you'll take on Jesus' attitude of humility, you'll not be overly impressed by yourself and you'll be in a perfect position to continue with high levels of achievement and superior performance.

Bible Reading Plan:
Mark 12:28-34
II Corinthians 9
Psalms 104

May 10

WISDOM

At this point in your sport career, in how many games have you competed? Could you count them? Looking into the future, how many more do you think you have left? That's a sobering question.

Moses, one of the greatest leaders in history, raised a similarly sobering thought in Psalm 90 and verse 12. There it says, "Teach us to number our days aright, that we may gain a heart of wisdom."

Moses could certainly count the days that he had lived in the past, but he also had a grasp of how few he might have left to live. That became the basis for wise living.

Wisdom would have us grasp the significance of each contest. Wisdom would lead us to value every moment we get to spend with our teammates and coaching staff. If our hearts are full of wisdom, we will be aware of the brevity of our careers in sport and will drain every drop of good from them.

As you prepare for competition, take some time to pray and to thank God for all the days of your past. Ask Him to fill your heart with wisdom as you seek to grasp the significance of each moment, every practice and today's contest.

Bible Reading Plan:
Mark 12:35-44
II Corinthians 10
Psalms 105
I Samuel 24-25

May 11

MOMENTUM

Deuteronomy 28:7

Have you ever been in a competition and observed how momentum swings from one team to the other? It's like the wind is changing direction and with it the power to win. At times it seems like the power goes out for one team and the other team's power is multiplied by seven. The Bible speaks of that dynamic.

In Moses' book called Deuteronomy at chapter 28 and verse 7 it says, "The Lord will grant that the enemies who rise up against you will be defeated before you. They will come at you from one direction but flee from you in seven." Your enemies are a little different than those who opposed Moses, but the principle is the same. If we are obedient to the Lord, we'll see success and our enemies will flee from us.

Notice also that even though the enemy comes from one direction, they flee from us in seven. God's at work in us to multiply by seven times our successes over against our challenges.

Tonight, play with great confidence and power. Trust that even though your opponents come against you, they'll be defeated seven times over. Take the game to these people and play your game at all times.

Bible Reading Plan:
Mark 13:1-13
II Corinthians 11:1-15
Psalms 106:1-23
I Samuel 26-28

May 12

COURAGE

Matthew 14:27

Have you ever been afraid for your life? Fear can paralyze us to inaction and resignation. Courage can vanish in an instant.

Matthew chapter 14 and chapter 27 records Jesus' words to His disciples during a violent storm, "Take courage! It is I. Don't be afraid." These men were struggling to keep their boat afloat as they were being tossed around by the wind and waves. They thought they would all drown.

In the middle of their fear and intimidation, Jesus speaks three phrases of great encouragement:

1) Take courage! Not just an injunction to stop being fearful, but a call to courage.

2) It is I. The courage comes from His presence. Just knowing Jesus was with them breathed courage and confidence into the formerly fearful disciples.

3) Don't be afraid. Having the Lord with them filled them with courage and dispelled their fear. They need not be afraid now; the Lord's presence replaced their doubts and anxiety with courage and confidence.

These are also Jesus' words to you today, "Take courage!" As you prepare to compete today listen for the Lord's voice bringing courage, his presence inspiring confidence, and his love dispelling all fear.

Bible Reading Plan:
II Corinthians 11:16-33
Psalms 106:24-48
I Samuel 29-31

May 13

TEAM UNITY

Have you had to battle gossip on your team? One player spreading a rumor about another player or poisoning the opinion of his teammates toward the coaches? How do we deal with this and what results from this kind of behavior?

In the Proverbs at chapter 17 and verse 9 it is written, "He who covers a transgression seeks love, but he who repeats a matter separates intimate friends."

When a player repeats a story with damaging information among his friends and teammates, the results can be catastrophic. Even if the story is true, the telling of it can even shatter the relationship of the most intimate friends. The intent of this kind of speech is invariably selfish and born of jealousy.

The good news in this verse is that when we cover the transgression, when we keep the matter to ourselves and don't spread it around, we're acting with love toward our teammates. If your desire is to have good relationships with teammates, coaches and family, you will do well to not tell everything that you know. If you know some damaging information on someone, keep it to yourself. You'll promote loving relationships on all sides by your silence.

In your prayers today, ask the Lord to help you cover the transgressions of others. Ask Him to guard your tongue and to keep you from divisive speech.

Bible Reading Plan:
Mark 13:32-37
Psalms 107
II Samuel 1-2

May 14

INTEGRITY

Mark 8:36-37

What would it take for you to compromise your integrity? How much money would it take for your to shave points for gambling interests? What would be the consequences of such actions?

Jesus knew and spoke about such matters in Mark's gospel at chapter 8 and verses 36 through 37, "What good is it for a man to gain the whole world, yet forfeit his soul? Or what can a man give in exchange for his soul?" The obvious answers to these questions are, "No good. Nothing."

No matter the price tag on the item, it cannot equal the value of a clear conscience and a pure soul. Nothing in the world is worth the forfeit of one's integrity.

If you exchange your integrity for any price – you lose!

If you cheat in the classroom to get a grade – you lose!

If you shortcut workouts in practice – you and your team lose!

As you compete today, keep your conscience clean by competing within the rules of your sport. Maintain the purity of your soul through integrity and accountability within your team. Compete thusly and you'll experience great rewards with no pangs of a sullied conscience or a tainted soul.

Bible Reading Plan:
Mark 14:1-11
II Corinthians 12:11-21
II Samuel 3-4

May 15

DREAMS

Ephesians 3:20

Every year I look at the schedule during pre-season and start to calculate wins and losses. "We can beat them. We'll probably lose there. This one is a toss up. We'd better beat them!" I'm sure all of us lie on our beds at night and dream about championships and M.V.P. awards. What's exciting to me is that God can do immeasurably more than even those things.

In Paul's letter to his friends in Ephesus at chapter 3 and verse 20 he writes, "Now to Him who is able to do immeasurably more than all we ask or imagine, according to His power that is at work within us..." How big can you ask or imagine? How large are your dreams? God's reality is even bigger!!

Could it be that God's plans for me are even greater than I could possibly dream of? Can I trust God to make provision for my life in ways I can't even conceive? Absolutely. The text says that He is able to do immeasurably more than I can even ask or imagine. That's how great God's power is in our lives. He is at work in ways we can't even fathom with our simple minds. His reality is even bigger than our dreams.

In today's game, let the confidence that comes from security make you the player you've always dreamed of being. Step into the reality of God's plans and you'll find life that eclipses your wildest dreams.

Bible Reading Plan:
Mark 14:12-31
II Corinthians 13
Psalms 109

May 16

STREAKS

Psalm 90:15

What's the longest losing streak you can remember suffering through? How long does your best winning streak seem in comparison? Why does it seem that losing streaks drag on, but win streaks just whiz by?

Moses knew those dynamics during his lifetime and he wrote about it in Psalm 90 and verse 15. There we read, "Make us glad for as many days as you have afflicted us, for as many years as we have seen trouble."

Moses was just asking for a winning streak to come along to offset the terrible times that they had seen in the recent past. He was not asking to go undefeated, just to get back to the .500 mark.

This encourages me. I am much more comfortable asking God for success as I read this psalm. The Lord knows we grow tired and discouraged when we face a number of losses in a row and He's not offended by prayers like this one He heard from Moses.

As you pray on game day, ask the Lord to reward your work and your persistence. Ask Him to match your losing streaks from the past with similar sized winning streaks in the future. Let's join Moses in his heart-felt prayer to God.

Bible Reading Plan:
Mark 14:32-42
Galatians 1
Psalms 110
II Samuel 8-10

May 17

SERVANT-LEADER

John 13:5

What is the most appropriate posture for a team leader? Is it standing confidently? Maybe it's sitting with poise like one sits on a throne? Perhaps it's something radically different...

In John chapter 13 and verse 5 we read Jesus' take on this, "After that, He poured water into a basin and began to wash the disciples' feet, and to wipe them with the towel with which he was girded."

Here we see the posture Jesus takes as the supreme leader of a team. He stoops to the floor and washes the dirty feet of his followers. He is on His hands and knees with a basin and towel to serve His teammates in the most menial way.

How could we possibly lead in a similar way? Take a moment and think about how you could humble yourself and serve your teammates well.

Rather than asserting your privilege, take the lower position with a younger player.

Voluntarily sit in the worst seat on the bus, rather than running for the best one.

Carry someone else's bags into the hotel, not just your own.

Help the trainers and equipment managers do their jobs well by serving and encouraging them.

If you'll take on the posture of a servant, you'll find yourself taking on the look of the Savior. Be that kind of a player and teammate in today's competition and both the Lord and I will be very proud of you.

Bible Reading Plan:
Mark 14:43-52
Galatians 2
Psalms 111
II Samuel 11-12

May 18

OVERCOMING UNBELIEF

Mark 9:23-24

What do you have trouble believing when you consider your team's prospects for the season? Can you believe you'll be conference champions? Can you believe you'll have a winning season? Do you believe you'll defeat your strongest rival? Do you really believe you'll win today's contest? Jesus saw a strong link between what we believe and what we achieve.

His words on this are recorded at Mark chapter 9 and verses 23 through 24, "If you can?' said Jesus. 'Everything is possible for him who believes.' Immediately the boy's father exclaimed, 'I do believe; help me overcome my unbelief!"

The father of a terribly tormented child came to Jesus for help, asking if Jesus could do anything. Jesus strongly challenged the father that it was not a matter of ability, but a matter of belief. The man responded well to Jesus' challenge and asked for help in overcoming his unbelief.

The same is true for this team and each of you today. You have plenty of ability to compete at the highest level. The question for us is, "Do we believe it?" What can we do to overcome our unbelief?

Unbelief is overcome through committed relationships. As you commit strongly to your teammates and coaches, your trust and belief in their abilities is strengthened. As you commit to struggling teammates, their own belief in their abilities becomes stronger and more powerful. As you grow the trust and accountability on your team, everyone's unbelief is overcome and you can do anything.

In today's competition, believe and achieve!

Bible Reading Plan:
Mark 14:53-65
Galatians 3:1-14
Psalms 112

May 19

CORRECTION

Proverbs 17:10

How do you respond to your coach's correction? How do you react when a teammate tells you your technique needs improvement? The answers could reveal a lot about your character.

In the book of Proverbs at chapter 17 and verse 10 it says, "A rebuke goes deeper into one who has understanding than a hundred blows into a fool."

How deeply impressed would you be by 100 blows to your back? Pretty deeply I suppose. For athletes this may be 100 laps around the gym floor. I hope it wouldn't take 100 to make an impression. For fools it seems that it takes 100 blows to make a good impression. For people of understanding, it takes something else.

The scripture says that a rebuke makes a greater impression on a person of understanding that running 100 laps would. One correction to a wise person is of greater effect than doing 100 ups-and-downs. One closed door conference with the coach goes deeper into the smart player than 100 trips up and down the bleachers.

In today's prayer time, ask the Lord to make you a person of understanding. Ask Him to give you an attitude of humility and wisdom.

Bible Reading Plan:
Mark 14:66-72
Galatians 3:15-29
Psalms 113
II Samuel 14-15

May 20

A BLANK CHECK

Matthew 18:19

What would you do if you were given a blank check and allowed to write in the amount? Would you write in a big amount or a more modest number?

Matthew records Jesus as saying this at chapter 18 and verse 19, "Again, I tell you that if two of you on earth agree about anything you ask for, it will be done for you by my Father in heaven. For where two or three come together in my name, there am I with them." This verse sure sounds like a blank check onto which we can write our names as payees and can fill in any amount we want. What amount would you write? Champions...MVP...Coach of the Year?

Upon closer inspection we find that when two or three of us get together and pray about something, our Lord joins us with His presence and we find our desires and attitudes changing to match His. We begin to see from His perspective and to desire His will. We pray in line with His desires for us and we see God the Father answering our prayers.

In preparation for today's game, as you pray together, realize that the Lord is present among you. Let the assurance of His presence bring you confidence and courage. Go ahead and ask Him to do something, the blank check may just get cashed.

Bible Reading Plan:
Mark 15:1-15
Galatians 4:1-20
Psalms 114
II Samuel 16-17

May 21

RENEWED STRENGTH

Isaiah 40:28-29

Where do you find strength for competition when you've become weary? Who is your source of power when your legs, arms, back and even your mind is tired? Today's scripture suggests an ideal source.

In Isaiah's book of prophecy at chapter 40 and verses 28 and 29 we read, "Do you not know? Have you not heard? The Lord is the everlasting God, the Creator of the ends of the earth. He will not grow tired or weary, and His understanding no one can fathom. He gives strength to the weary and increases the power of the weak."

Isaiah is confident of the power and strength of God. He knows Him as the Creator of the whole universe, possessed of limitless ability and infinite might. That builds his confidence as he knows God to be gracious and giving of those same attributes.

Everyone who competes becomes weary and feels a loss of power and strength. That is the perfect time to trust God and to commit more than ever to your relationship with Him. He freely gives strength and power. He delights to do so as we simply ask for it and trust Him to supply all that we need.

In your preparation for competition today, ask God for a transfusion of His power in your body. Petition Him for a gift of strength and wisdom for your mind. Pray for and seek more of His love and mercy in your spirit. He'll answer you from His limitless supply, right on time.

Bible Reading Plan:
Mark 15:16-32
Galatians 4:21-31
Psalms 115
II Samuel 18-19

May 22

COMPASSION

Psalm 103:13-14

Have you ever felt like your coaches or teammates expected more from you than you were capable of giving? How do you handle expectations that seem unreasonable? What do you think God expects of us?

In Psalm 103 and verses 13 and 14, we get an idea of how God tempers His expectations of us. There it reads, "As a father has compassion on his children, so the Lord has compassion on those who fear Him; for He knows how we are formed, He remembers that we are dust."

God knows exactly what we're made of and is thus very compassionate toward us. That's good news. He lovingly cares for us like the best possible father would. Trust Him.

In the world of sport, coaches, teammates, parents, media and others may project expectations that you find unreasonable. If they really care for you, they'll also be compassionate and will know what is truly reasonable. They are the ones you can also trust.

As you prepare to compete today, examine your expectations and those of your teammates and coaching staff. Give your absolute best effort to achieve each one of them. Rest assured that those most committed to you will also be compassionate if their expectations go unmet. They know what you're made of and love you completely.

Bible Reading Plan:
Mark 15:33-41
Galatians 5:1-12
Psalms 116
II Samuel 20-21

May 23

FRUIT OF THE SPIRIT

Galatians 5:22

What are the characteristics of your life that show your true nature? Do your actions accurately reflect the condition of your heart? Let's focus our minds on some inward qualities with outward expressions. Let's turn our attention on some transforming character qualities that will lead to victories on and off the field of competition.

In Paul's letter to the Galatians at chapter 5 and verse 22 he writes, "But the fruit of the Spirit is love, joy, peace, patience, kindness, goodness, faithfulness, gentleness and self-control." As apples are the fruit of an apple tree, these qualities are the fruit of a lover of God.

These qualities that are held inside a person's character are expressed in one's speech and conduct:

Love - giving sacrificially to others without expectation of return.

Joy - Emotional stability in turbulent times.

Peace - Clear minded thinking in the middle of chaos.

In today's game, employ love for your teammates in sacrificially giving all you have to achieve a win. Exhibit joy in overcoming the emotional roller coaster that rides through the day. Rest in the peace that comes with trusting God through the chaos of competition. Bear some fruit in today's game, everyone will see the source and they'll honor your God.

Bible Reading Plan:
Mark 15:42-47
Galatians 5:13-26
Psalms 117
II Samuel 22

May 24

FRUIT OF THE SPIRIT

Galatians 5:22

We are again talking about inwardly held character qualities with outward expression. This time they're relational in nature... dealing with how we relate to our teammates, coaches and friends.

In Paul's letter to the Galatians at chapter 5 and verse 22 he writes, "But the fruit of the Spirit is love, joy, peace, patience, kindness, goodness, faithfulness, gentleness and self-control." How would fruit be evident on your life's branches?

Check your relationships to see if these kinds of fruit are hanging there:

Patience - bearing with the unbearable. Do you know anyone like that?

Kindness - Giving the best to the undeserving. To whom do you show kindness?

Goodness - Emulating God's character of moral purity. Is that evident in your relationships?

In today's game, be patient with each other's failings. Show kindness to each other, sacrifice to give your best to the undeserving. Be good. Express yourself with purity of motive and intention. These qualities make for great relationships and for great teams. Be one today!

Bible Reading Plan:
Mark 16
Galatians 6
Psalms 118
II Samuel 23-24

May 25

FRUIT OF THE SPIRIT

Galatians 5:22

Once again we're talking about character. The fruit of God's Spirit in us. Today's list of three qualities relates to lifestyle commitments.

In Paul's letter to the Galatians at chapter 5 and verse 22 he writes, "But the fruit of the Spirit is love, joy, peace, patience, kindness, goodness, faithfulness, gentleness and self-control." When people talk about you, do the words faithful, gentle and self-controlled come up?

These qualities would be great examples of a transformed life. Let's strive to have these things characterize our life styles:

Faithfulness - Loyalty and fidelity to commitments and relationships. Is that you?

Gentleness - Not softness, but profound strength under control. Does your life look like power under control?

Self-control - Not controlled by some outside stimuli like conditions, circumstances, people, but by one's own will. Are you in control of you?

In today's competition, let's show faithfulness as we hold tightly to our commitments and show loyalty to our teammates and coaches. Let's display gentleness in harnessing our personal strengths in serving others. Let's exercise self-control as we overcome the outside pressures that would rob us of victory. Make this a day of greatness.

Bible Reading Plan:
Mark 10:1-16
II Corinthians 2

May 26

SCOUTING REPORT

Mark 9:30-32

Can you recall a time when your coaching staff told you something about an upcoming opponent that triggered some questions? They're how big? Are they really that good? They're how fast? Why are we playing them? Can we compete with them? Did you dare ask the question or did you bite your tongue, afraid to ask it? Jesus' followers had similar thoughts as they heard some tough information from Him.

We read about this in Mark chapter 9 and verses 30 through 32, "They left that place and passed through Galilee. Jesus did not want anyone to know where they were, because he was teaching his disciples. He said to them, 'The Son of Man is going to be betrayed into the hands of men. They will kill him, and after three days he will rise. But they did not understand what he meant and were afraid to ask him about it."

These men heard some very distressing news from Jesus and were immediately full of questions. They didn't understand what was about to happen, but they were sure it was not good. Why would Jesus even tell them about this? It's like your coaches telling you that your next opponent is unbeatable.

The point of such a discussion is to teach and to prepare. Wise coaches give their teams sobering information about upcoming opponents not to bring them fear, but to lead them to strongly prepare for a great competition.

In today's competition, apply every bit of information you've attained from your coaches, from watching videotape, from each day's practice and let it all lead you to a great victory.

Bible Reading Plan:
Psalms 98
I Samuel 11-13

May 27

SELFISH PLAYERS

Proverbs 18:1

Do you have any teammates who seem to compete for themselves and tend to shun their responsibilities to the team? Is there anything wrong with separating my personal competition from the rest of the team? Should I pursue my personal goals if they conflict with the team's goals?

In the book of Proverbs at chapter 18 and verse 1 it says, "He who separates himself seeks his own desire, and quarrels against all sound wisdom."

If you see a teammate who separates himself from the team, always trying to be an individual rather than part of the team, be sure that he's seeking his own desire. The danger is obvious to the writer of the proverb. This person is fighting against everything that makes sense about team activity.

The Proverbs and the whole Bible are written in the context of relationship. God is our Maker and He knows that we operate best when we work together. The Lord's wisdom is revealed best when we compete in loving, respectful relationships. That's what it is to be a team, to have strong relationships with teammates and to seek the best for the team, not for one's self.

As you prepare for competition in prayer today, ask the Lord to keep you properly related to your teammates and coaches. Ask Him for the grace to not seek your own desire and so separate yourself from the team.

Bible Reading Plan:
Mark 11:27-33
II Corinthians 7

May 28

DREAMS FULFILLED

Psalm 126:1-3

Take a moment to recall a time when your sport dreams were realized. Perhaps it was a championship won, a rival beaten or an individual award achieved. The Bible shares a poetic look at dreams fulfilled in today's scripture.

Psalm 126 and verses 1 through 3 reads, "When the Lord brought back the captives to Zion, we were like men who dreamed. Our mouths were filled with laughter, our tongues with songs of joy. Then it was said among the nations, The Lord has done great things for them. The Lord has done great things for us, and we are filled with joy."

The writer remembered returning home after a long absence. It was almost too good to believe, like a dream. He remembered the laughter and the joyful singing of his friends and family. The people from surrounding countries were amazed. Even more, he remembered the source of these blessings.

It's so much fun for us to see our dreams fulfilled and our goals achieved. Our mouths are filled with laughter and we exult in every victory. Those who watch you compete even join in the fun. Occasionally we'll even remember to thank the ultimate source of all that's good... God.

During today's competition, give your best effort to see your dreams fulfilled and your goals achieved. Don't be surprised when people comment like they did in the psalm, "The Lord has done great things for them." You can echo their comment in grateful prayer with a wide grin on your face.

Bible Reading Plan:
Psalms 103
I Samuel 21-23

May 29

POSSIBILITIES

Matthew 19:26

Which of your preseason goals seem to be presently impossible? Which seem totally beyond your grasp?

In Matthew chapter 19 and verse 26, Jesus says, "With man this is impossible, but with God all things are possible."

There are times when our dreams are shattered and our goals seem beyond human attainment. These are the perfect times to turn to God. God specializes in making the impossible a reality.

Jesus assures us that with men much is impossible, but with God all things are possible. Nothing is beyond His reach or outside His ability.

As you prepare to compete today, ask the Lord to fill you with His infinite ability. Trust Him to help you compete at the highest level of achievement possible.

Bible Reading Plan:
Mark 13:14-31
II Corinthians 12:1-10

May 30

WARNING

John 16:1

When has someone said something to you that saved you lots of pain, heartache and suffering? How did you take the warning? Today, we'll hear a warning from Jesus.

Jesus said this to His disciples in John 16 and verse 1, "These things I have spoken to you, that you should not be made to stumble."

Jesus spoke these words to His disciples just before He was betrayed and arrested, prior to His crucifixion. He was informing His disciples of the events to come so they would not stumble in the hours to come.

You hear lots of words that are meant to keep you from stumbling. Among them are administrative rules, sport federation regulations, e-mails from friends, and admonitions from your coaches. These all keep you from going astray, from wandering off course, they warn us of obstacles in our paths that could cause us to stumble.

Listen carefully when you hear words like this, they are life to you. Listen to the coaching staff's words as you prepare to play today. Those words are life to your team. They are spoken to help you avoid stumbling and to guide you into victory.

Bible Reading Plan:
Psalms 108
II Samuel 5-7

May 31

SECURITY

Proverbs 18:10

Have you ever wanted a refuge, a place to hide from problems or adversity? I'm sure everyone has at one time or another. Where does the Christian athlete go when trouble comes? How do we handle great pressure or turmoil?

In the book of Proverbs at chapter 18 and verse 10 it says, "The name of the Lord is a strong tower, the righteous run to it and are safe."

How is the name of the Lord a strong tower? In the Bible the name of a person is equivalent to that person's character or nature. In this case the name of the Lord is strong like a tower that can protect us from enemies who would attack us. His name is full of all the attributes of God. His name is a place of refuge.

Who can find safety there? The scripture says the righteous run to it and are safe. We are righteous because of our relationship with Christ Jesus. He has made us righteous in the Lord's eyes and we have access to the Lord's name, His very nature is put within us. What a marvelous thought!! What a great place of safety! We are safely held in the Lord's arms like we were in a fortified castle.

When you pray and prepare for competition, thank the Lord for His protection of you. Thank you for His making you righteous in Christ Jesus.

Bible Reading Plan:
Luke 1:1-25
Ephesians 1:1-14
Psalms 119:1-8
I Kings 1

June 1

MORE PRACTICE?

Galatians 6:9

Do you ever get tired of practice? Does it seem that all your hours of training and practice seem to go for nothing? You're not the first to think these thoughts. In the Bible there is confident reassurance for you and your teammates.

In the Apostle Paul's letter to his friends in Galatia, he writes, "And let us not lose heart in doing good, for in due time we shall reap if we do not grow weary." Paul makes an assumption that these people had sown or planted something and they were waiting for it to bear fruit. You have obviously done some planting!! All those miles you run in training. All the practices and hours in the weight room can be seen as sowing seed. It's only natural to expect something to grow from that.

Paul's encouragement is that we will reap the harvest, if we do not grow weary and don't lose heart. How do we do this? As a team you can strengthen each other through encouraging words. We can speak courage to our teammates through challenge and affirmation. We can fuel the hearts of our friends by our presence.

Today as you pray and prepare, see the presence and speech of your teammates and friends as fuel for your heart. Run, shoot and rebound with great power and passion. Don't lose heart if you're tired, press on, we shall reap the harvest if we don't grow weary and give up.

Bible Reading Plan:
Luke 1:26-38
Ephesians 1:15-23
Psalms 119:9-16
I Kings 2-3

June 2

PRACTICE

Ecclesiastes 10:10

Why do we have to practice all the time? Why do we continually run these same drills on fundamentals? Haven't we attained enough experience to do away with all this repetition? The Holy Scripture communicates strongly a value for these kinds of activities.

In the Old Testament book of Ecclesiastes, at chapter 10 and verse 10 Solomon wrote, "If the axe is dull and its edge unsharpened, more strength is needed, but skill will bring success." Obviously he is not just talking about cutting down trees. The key phrase is, "skill will bring success."

You have taken years of your life to sharpen your skills. Your investment of time and hard work to improve your techniques, strength, quickness, shooting, etc... will surely bring success.

It's always good to do some evaluation and to check the sharpness of your skills. How sharp am I today? With a dull set of skills, we must apply a whole lot more muscle and extra effort. Trust the words of Solomon, sharpen your skills and meet success.

Pray for a sharp set of tools for today's game. Watch how easily things work when your skills are finely honed and applied to your game. Be sure to thank God for your tools and their sharpness.

Bible Reading Plan:
Luke 1:39-56
Ephesians 2:1-10
Psalms 119:17-24
I Kings 4-5

June 3

PRACTICE

Psalm 126:5-6

What part of practice and conditioning seems to be just plain old hard work? Has such a workout ever pushed you to the point of total exhaustion and even tears? Today's scripture relates exactly to that level of physical and emotional expense.

In Psalm 126 and verses 5 and 6 we read, "Those who sow in tears will reap with songs of joy. He who goes out weeping, carrying seed to sow, will return with songs of joy, carrying sheaves with him."

These people knew the pain and hardship of working on a farm in the early spring. Lots of hours and draining labor. They also knew the joy and exhilaration of a great harvest in the fall.

You know the value of grueling practice sessions and punishing workouts. They produce a fruitful and even fun reward at season's end. Those brutal preseason days of conditioning pay off in the postseason with exciting victories.

Invest yourself in tough, intense practices and you'll reap a harvest of game days filled with joyous wins. Compete today with confidence knowing that you've made the investments that will pay off in today's contest.

Bible Reading Plan:
Luke 1:57-66
Ephesians 2:11-22
Psalms 119:25-32

June 4

TEAM LEADERSHIP

Mark 9:35

What are some of the foundational principles of your sport? From whom did you learn them? How many of those principles apply to life beyond your sport? Today, we'll hear from Jesus one great life principle as He talks with his team.

This is recorded in Mark chapter 9 and verse 35, "Sitting down, Jesus called the Twelve and said, 'If anyone wants to be first, he must be the very last, and the servant of all.'" This is totally backward from the way things tend to work in our day. People today who want to be first, rush to the front and manipulate their way into the most prominent position.

Jesus turns the whole world upside down by outlining these principles of team leadership:

He called the Twelve – the most highly committed to Himself. Jesus communicates with these people strongly and directly. If you desire to be first – take the lowest position with your teammates. Don't push your way to the front or demand privilege.

Leadership demands that we serve each other and elevate the others on our team. It's very simple, I look best in God's eyes when I make others look good in the eyes of everyone else. When I promote and elevate my teammates, we all achieve more highly and we enjoy tremendous team unity. When I elevate myself and promote my own agenda, I diminish my teammates and divide our team.

As you prepare to compete today, search for ways to lead your teammates to victory by serving them and by lifting them up to higher levels of achievement.

Bible Reading Plan:
Ephesians 3:1-13
Psalms 119:33-40
I Kings 8

June 5

GIFTS

Proverbs 18:16

If you're an athlete you're certainly aware of your giftedness. One of my favorite Proverbs speaks about how our gifts work in our lives.

Proverbs 18 and verse 16 says, "A man's gift makes room for him, and ushers him into the presence of the great." It seems that the gifts or abilities we've been given by our Lord, bring us into the presence of great people.

During today's competition, employ your gifts to their maximum potential. The Lord has invested greatly in you and it's evidenced by your giftedness. It's impossible to see today, but in later years you'll realize that at times this season, you were in the presence of great people. The faithful use of your gifts is what brought you there.

Commit yourself today to taking what has been given you and to drain every drop of potential from your abilities. This will honor not only your family, your team, your coaches and friends, but it also honors the Lord who gave you the gifts.

Bible Reading Plan:
Luke 2:1-20
Psalms 119:41-48
I Kings 9-10

June 6

DEFENSE

Which seems to be the tougher assignment for you, working a double-team or a simple man-to-man defense? The answer would appear to be obvious, but we often seem to prefer individualism to teamwork.

The writer of Ecclesiastes at chapter 4 and verse 12 writes, "Though one may be overpowered, two can defend themselves. A cord of three strands is not quickly broken."

Though this makes perfect sense to us in theory, many times we bristle at the dynamics that accompany good teamwork. We worry about our teammate not executing his portion of the double-team or we worry about our own performance in it. Thus, we'd rather take our chances alone and rely on our own abilities.

The problem is that the principle is still true, "Though one may be overpowered, two can defend themselves." We're much more powerful when we're working in concert with other competitors, despite the perceived problems.

The second sentence is equally powerful as it mentions a cord of three strands. Not just two, but three. On good teams, the coaching staff is the third strand in every alliance of teamwork and unified competition. The coaches' instruction and strategy completes the cord of power and strength that pulls the team to victory.

In the lives of followers of Christ, the Lord Himself is the third strand in every relationship giving purpose, wisdom and life. He unifies and strengthens the lives of those who love Him with the people they love. As you compete today, do so in great unity and rely upon each other's abilities.

Bible Reading Plan:
Luke 2:21-40
Ephesians 4:1-16
I Kings 11

June 7

FIRST OR LAST?

Matthew 19:30

Every year, each team in the league starts the season intending to be first, to be champions. Obviously only one can be. However, Jesus puts a twist on our ideas about first and last places.

He says at Matthew chapter 19 and verse 30, "But many who are first will be last, and many who are last will be first."

Have you seen how some teams rush out to an early lead in a conference race, only to fade near the end? They were first, but finished last. Conversely, have you seen teams that began slowly, but progressed all through the season and finished with a flourish? They may have been last, but they finished first.

In many conferences there is a post season tournament and even the last team to qualify can supplant the regular season champ. They can go from last to first in the space of three ball games.

Play this game with an understanding that if you win, you're not guaranteed anything. Also understand that if you lose, you will get another chance. The important thing is to give your 100% best and to finish this season with a flourish of strength, stamina and passionate play.

Bible Reading Plan:
Luke 2:41-52
Ephesians 4:17-24
Psalm 119:57-64

June 8

COMPETITION

I Corinthians 9:24

Today we'll read one of my favorite scripture passages related to competition. Every time I hear it, I want to play racquetball and wear somebody out.

Paul writes to the Corinthian church in his first letter at chapter 9 and verse 24 saying, "Do you not know that in a race all the runners run, but only one gets the prize? Run in such a way as to get the prize." I like that!

Let's do three things he describes here:

1) Compete - determine to overcome your opponents. Don't give an inch to defeated attitudes.

2) Strive - drain every drop of potential from your abilities. Go after your personal and team goals with all your heart.

3) Focus – Clear your mind of all distractions and train your mind on the ultimate goal... a championship.

In today's competition; compete, strive and focus. Run in such a way as to get the prize.

Bible Reading Plan:
Luke 3:1-20
Ephesians 4:25-32
Psalm 119:65-72
I Kings 13-14

June 9

TRAINING

I Corinthians 9:24-25

What is the value of the training you do every day in practice? How efficiently could your perform on game day if you didn't train well? What are the rewards of such training? Today's scripture addresses these issues for all of life.

In the first letter to the Corinthian church, Paul the Apostle writes at chapter 9 and verses 24 and 25, "Do you not know that in a race all the runners run, but only one gets the prize? Run in such a way as to get the prize. Everyone who competes in the games goes into strict training. They do it to get a crown that will not last; but we do it to get a crown that will last forever."

Obviously you couldn't perform well at all on game day if you didn't discipline your mind, you body and your emotions. You've had to exercise self control over these things throughout your athletic career with respect to diet, running, weight training, studying video tape and more. Expect it to pay off in today's competition! Win the crown!

What's more, exercise discipline in the most important areas of life and you'll find yourself winning championships that don't fade in importance, collect dust on the shelf or diminish in value.

Bible Reading Plan:
Luke 3:21-38
Ephesians 5:1-21
Psalm 119:73-80
I Kings 15-16

June 10

DISQUALIFICATION

I Corinthians 9:24-27

Have you ever competed in track? Do you remember running in a race and seeing someone caught running out of his lane? Was that person disqualified? That's what happens when one runs aimlessly.

The Apostle Paul uses that athletic metaphor in writing to his friends in Corinth at chapter 9 and verses 26 and 27 of his first letter. There he says, "Do you not know that in a race all the runners run, but only one gets the prize? Run in such a way as to get the prize. Everyone who competes in the games goes into strict training. They do it to get a crown that will not last; but we do it to get a crown that will last forever. Therefore I do not run like a man running aimlessly; I do not fight like a man beating the air. No, I beat my body and make it my slave so that after I have preached to others, I myself will not be disqualified for the prize."

If one runs a race in an out of control or aimless way, he's disqualified, thrown out of the competition. If we run out of our lanes, foul out or get ejected by an official, we're of no real use to our team. Let's just stay in the game and give ourselves a chance to win.

In a larger way, our choices regarding life off the field of competition can lead to our being disqualified for really important matters like love, family and friends. Make today's competition a model of disciplined effort and well aimed pursuit of excellence.

Bible Reading Plan:
Ephesians 5:22-33
Psalm 119:81-88
I Kings 17-18

June 11

PATIENCE

Ecclesiastes 7:8

Which is the better part of a baseball game, the first pitch or the bottom of the final inning? Do you prefer to see, a football game's opening kickoff or the "Hail Mary" pass in the last seconds? Does the opening tip of a basketball game or the desperation shot at the buzzer hold more excitement for you? The writer of today's scripture holds the same opinion with one added comment.

In the 7th chapter of Ecclesiastes at verse 8 it says, "The end of a matter is better than its beginning, and patience is better than pride."

Just like in sport, the author had found that the end of matters far surpass their beginnings. It's like that in most of life's pursuits. Retirement parties are more fun than the first day on the job. Golden wedding anniversaries are even better than weddings.

In sport, you probably enjoy post-season tournaments more than pre-season conditioning workouts. No doubt. Championship games are lots more fun than the first scrimmages of the season. That leads to the writer's final comment, "...patience is better than pride."

In pre-season, lots of us are full of pride and arrogance. By the end of the season, the ones with patience are obvious to everybody; they're the ones making key plays. The end is better than the beginning and patience is better than arrogant pride.

As you compete today, realize that it's more important who finishes a game than who starts it. Exercise patience and compete wisely, that's much better than being prideful and foolish.

Bible Reading Plan:
Luke 4:13-20
Psalms 119:89-96
I Kings 19-20

June 12

LOVE

John 11:33-36

How deeply do you love your friends, teammates and coaches? How deeply are you touched by their personal moments of grief and pain? Today we'll see an example to follow in the life of Jesus.

In John's Gospel at chapter 11 and verses 33 through 36 we read about when Jesus visited the grave of his friend Lazarus. There it says, "Therefore when Jesus saw her weeping, and the Jews who came with her weeping, He groaned in the spirit and was troubled. And He said, 'Where have you laid him?' They said to Him, 'Lord, come and see.' Jesus wept. Then the Jews said, 'See how He loved him!'"

Jesus obviously had a deep love for his friends and we see it plainly here as He shares in the grief of Lazarus' death. His friends, Mary and Martha, were terribly shaken and Jesus weeps with them. Those who were observing saw Jesus' love evidenced in His tears.

Our love and commitment to our teammates is often most evident when we share in their grief and sorrow as well as in the excitement of accomplishment. We display our loyalty and trust of each other through the joy of victories and in the pain of losses. The greatest team unity sometimes comes through illness or injury.

Let's commit ourselves again to the team, to the coaching staff and to our collective goals. Let's give a great effort today and then let the world watch in amazement as they say, "See how they love each other!"

Bible Reading Plan:
Luke 4:31-37
Ephesians 6:10-24
I Kings 21-22

June 13

172

GREATNESS

Matthew 20:26-28

In our society, who seems to be the greater, the player who scores 25 points and grabs 15 rebounds a game or the one who carries water to her teammates during time outs?

In Matthew chapter 20 at verses 26 - 28, Jesus says, "Whoever wants to become great among you must be your servant, and whoever wants to be first must be your slave - just as the Son of Man did not come to be served, but to serve, and to give His life as a ransom for many."

Jesus turns the whole world upside down with this thought. Those who are truly great are the ones who sere their teammates, making themselves and their team better in the process.

Service is greater than selfishness and sacrifice gives life to one's team. Let's emulate Christ by serving each other and sacrificing for our teammates.

Play this game in an attitude of selflessness, giving to your teammates and coaches the last full measure of devotion. We'll be like Christ when we serve others and sacrifice for our team.

Bible Reading Plan:
Luke 4:38-44
Philippians 1:1-11
Psalms 119:105-112

June 14

VICTORY

How many hours do you spend in preparation for one game? How about your opponents? Does extra practice always make for more wins? What other factors go in to making a team victorious?

In Proverbs chapter 21 and verse 21 it says, "The horse is made ready for the day of battle, but victory rests with the Lord." Every day at practice you and your team works hard to prepare for their days of competition, but ultimately we all must look to the Lord for victory in the things we cannot control.

Is this to say that it's God who determines who wins and who loses in our competition? No, but it is saying that in the battles we face, there is a whole host of things that are beyond our control. As much as we prepare for anything, there are still things we must trust God to supply.

It's our job to prepare to the best of our abilities, but we must also trust the Lord Jesus to bring the victory to our lives. It's very encouraging to me to know that the Creator of the whole universe wants me to trust Him with all the affairs of my life...even competition.

As you prepare to compete today, give your 100% best effort to every detail... preparation is very important. In addition, trust the Lord with your whole heart and look to Him to deal with the things you cannot control. Ultimately, the Bible says that victory rests with the Lord.

Bible Reading Plans:
Luke 5:1-11
Philippians 1:12-20
Psalms 119:113-120
II Kings 4-5

June 15

TEAMMATES

Galatians 6:2

How can we as athletes fully please God with our efforts? How can we best serve God's will in relation to our teammates and coaches? In the Bible we're given a great example of a transforming attitude.

In Paul's letter to the Galatians at chapter 6 and verse 2 it says, "Carry each other's burdens, and in this way you will fulfill the law of Christ." Here we can clearly see the values that God has for us in human relations. The highest act of loving God can be accomplished by loving the people He's put in our lives.

Who do you know among your family or teammates who has a real burden to bear? How can you help that person bear his load? What can you do or say that will lighten his load or will allow him to share it with you? That is the essence of God's kind of love.

Take this same attitude into today's competition. How can you make your teammates better and more effective in their play? How can you carry the load for a teammate who is injured or otherwise at less than 100%. This is how we fulfill the law of Christ.

Bible Reading Plan:
Luke 5:12-16
Philippians 1:21-30
Psalm 119:121-128
II Kings 6-7

June 16

ANGER

Ecclesiastes 7:9

How quickly are you provoked to anger during competition? Would your teammates say that you are slow to anger or that you have a short fuse? Today's scripture explains why it's better to keep a cool head in competition.

In chapter 7 and verse 9 of Ecclesiastes we read, "Do not be quickly provoked in your spirit, for anger resides in the lap of fools."

It's very common in sport for a hot head to suddenly blow up during a competition. They get provoked by some trash talk, by a cheap shot, by a coach's comment or any number of things. They are provoked in their spirits and erupt in a foolish demonstration of anger. Some people even think they compete better when right on the edge of a fit of rage.

There is one very great problem with that. Such anger and rage rest squarely in the lap of fools. One's rage is more often an indicator of foolishness than of greatness in competition. Such anger more often results in technical fouls and penalties than excellence in technique and strategy.

As you compete today, stay under control emotionally. Do not be quickly provoked in your spirit. Rage and anger will only lead to foolish penalties and terrible consequences.

Bible Reading Plan:
Ephesians 2:1-11
Psalms 119:129-136
II Kings 8-9

June 17

TESTS

Mark 10:21-22

What are the most difficult tests for you as an athlete? Do you find the athletic testing hard? How about academic tests? How well do you measure up when your character is tested?

In Mark chapter 10 and verses 21 and 22, we watch as Jesus gives a man a test in character. "Jesus looked at him and loved him. 'One thing you lack,' he said. 'Go, sell everything you have and give it to the poor, and you will have treasure in heaven. Then come, follow me.' At this the man's face fell. He went away sad, because he had great wealth."

This man failed Jesus' simple test in character. I wonder how well we'd do if given a similar test.

If asked to forfeit our position on the team, would we comply? If asked to give up our prospects of success for the future, would we risk it? If asked to even walk away from playing this sport, would we do it? How badly do we want to achieve our goals?

I'd like to challenge you to pay whatever it costs to pursue your goals. Compete without regard to the personal cost as you seek the best for your team. Give all you have in order to help your team be victorious today. As you do, you'll pass the character test with flying colors.

Bible Reading Plan:
Luke 5:27-32
Psalms 119:137-144
II Kings 10-11

June 18

ATTITUDE

Philippians 2:3

My friend, Jim Hart, played quarterback for 19 years in the National Football League. That's a great accomplishment requiring great athletic ability and no small measure of toughness. That's why I was amazed when he told me of his favorite scripture.

In Paul's letter to his friends in Philipi, at chapter 2 and verse 3 he writes, "Do nothing out of selfish ambition or vain conceit, but in humility consider others better than yourselves." Paul gives us two don'ts and one do.

Don't number 1 - No selfish ambition - check your attitude for ideas like, "what do I get out of this?"

Don't number 2 - No vain conceit - check your attitude for empty self-flattery or an inflated sense of your importance.

Do this - Humbly know your role and fill it to capacity. Consider the team and each member of it ahead of your personal goals and desires. This leads to powerful teamwork and fantastic friendships.

In today's game, put away selfish ambition and empty conceited attitudes and take on a humble attitude that seeks the team's successes, even above your own.

Bible Reading Plan:
Luke 5:33-39
Philippians 2:19-30
Psalms 119:145-152
II Kings 12-13

June 19

TEAM UNITY

Psalm 133:1

How would you describe the sense of team unity experienced by this team? What are the benefits that accompany a team with great unity versus a team that is full of strife, contention and selfish attitudes?

Today's scripture describes such unity in Psalm 133 and verse 1. There we read, "How good and pleasant it is when brothers live together in unity!" Simple, huh? The psalmist says that unity produces an atmosphere that is good and pleasant. It's simple to describe, but harder to produce.

Team unity is good, leading to the best possible performance from everyone related to the team. Unity brings out the best in each player, coach, trainer, equipment manager, etc...

Team unity is pleasant, smoothing out every potential conflict and contention. Every team is made up of vastly different people. It's supposed to be that way. Team unity allows us to maintain a focus on our common goals, aspirations and values. That makes the living together pleasant.

In today's competition, let great team unity produce an atmosphere of goodness and pleasance. Strive together to see each teammate compete to his highest capacity. Keep your focus on unifying words and actions that make the whole process pleasant for everyone concerned. Compete in unified way and you'll be unstoppable.

Bible Reading Plan:
Luke 6:1-16
Philippians 3:1-9
Psalms 119:153-160

June 20

PRIDE

Galatians 6:4

Why do you compete in sport? What is your underlying motivation for competition? How do you view those with whom you compete and how well do you pull your weight for your team? The Scriptures give us some instruction for answering these questions.

In Paul's letter to his friends in Galatia at chapter 6 and verse 4, he writes, "Each one should test her own actions. Then she can take pride in herself, without comparing herself to somebody else, for each one should carry her own load." Every once in a while we need to examine our motives and attitudes. The hard part is to do this without comparing ourselves to anyone else.

We each have a part of the team's load to carry. It's not important for you to evaluate whether or not the others are carrying their parts, but it is vitally important that you faithfully carry yours.

The scripture says that when we test ourselves and evaluate our own attitudes we can take pride in our progress and our achievements.

Today as you pray and prepare, check your attitude at the door. Give yourself fully to carrying your share of the load for the team and to pursuing its success. The end of that process is a heart full of satisfaction and joy in achievement.

Bible Reading Plan:
Luke 6:17-26
Philippians 3:10-14
Psalm 119:161-168
II Kings 16-17

June 21

DEVOTION

Matthew 22:21

Do you enjoy paying taxes? Of course not. Do you pay them anyway?

Jesus was asked about paying taxes in Matthew chapter 22 and verse 21. He answered the question like this. "Give to Caesar what is Caesar's, and to God what is God's." Obviously he said to pay the tax because it was owed to the emperor.

He also said to give to God that which is His. What claim does God have on your life? What do you owe Him? How could you pay Him?

I've chosen to give Him 100% of my life. I've pledged my full devotion to Him. You can do that too. This is how we give to God what is God's, by yielding our lives to His will and trusting Him with our hearts.

In today's game, give to God that which is His. Give Him a 100% effort in body, mind and soul. I know He'll be pleased with that and your friends and family will be thrilled to see you play at your very best.

Bible Reading Plan:
Luke 6:27-36
Philippians 3:15-21
Psalms 119:169-176
II Kings 18-19

June 22

DISCIPLINE

Proverbs 23:12

What are the keys to success as an athlete? What brings about the best life for us as Christians? It seems that these ideas overlap a great deal.

In Proverbs chapter 23 and at verse 12 it says, "Apply your heart to discipline and your ears to words of knowledge." As you press through your season of competition it is imperative that you apply your heart to discipline.

The first part means you must involve your mind, your will, even your emotions in a life of disciple or self-control. It's easy to let your imagination or your emotions get out of control and to thus see your hard work go to waste.

It says to apply our ears to words of knowledge. That's what the coaching staff is for. Apply your ears to those who have invested years in learning their craft. Listen to the words of wisdom that come from your coaches, teachers, parents, ministers, teammates and others.

Lives lived with discipline and knowledge are of great worth and lead to profound success. In today's competition, apply your heart to the discipline of your game with all your heart, soul and mind. Pursue the goals you have set as an individual and as a team. Apply your ears to working out the wise game plan as outlined by your coaches.

Bible Reading Plan:
Luke 6:37-42
Philippians 4:1-7
Psalms 120
II Kings 20-21

June 23

UPSETS

Ecclesiastes 9:11

Can you remember a time when you defeated an opponent which was highly favored over you? You might also remember a time when you were picked to win, but somehow the victory slipped away. How does that happen?

The writer of Ecclesiastes saw this in his life and wrote about it in chapter 9 and verse 11. There it reads, "The race is not to the swift or the battle to the strong, nor does food come to the wise or wealth to the brilliant or favor to the learned; but time and chance happen to them all."

We've all been a part of competitions when we knew that the better team did not win. We've all had days when for some reason, we didn't have our "A game" and we lost to an inferior opponent.

What should we make of all this? Simply put, you're never out of a competition, even when terribly overmatched. Conversely, you can never count your opponent out when you seem to be the clearly superior team. Time and chance conspire to keep the lesser team in the contest and to even bring about amazing upsets.

As you prepare for competition, don't dwell on your being the favorite or the underdog. Rather, focus your mind on bringing your absolute best to this game. Do all you can to take time and chance out of the equation.

Bible Reading Plan:
Luke 6:43-49
Philippians 4:8-13
Psalms 121
II Kings 22-23

June 24

WORLDLY LEADERSHIP

Mark 10:42-43

From whom did you learn your leadership style? Do you tend to emulate a coach or team leader from past teams? Who might we find to be examples of poor leadership? Jesus points to some of each in today's scripture.

At Mark chapter 10 and verses 42 through 43, we read, "You know that those who are regarded as rulers of the Gentiles lord it over them, and their high officials exercise authority over them. Not so with you. Instead, whoever wants to become great among you must be your servant..."

There are plenty of models for poor leadership and Jesus pointed directly at one in this passage. He said, "Don't do it like them!" He then laid out simple, direct ways to lead in a way that most honors God and best honors your teammates.

The world's supposed leaders pull rank all the time – don't do that!

Their poor leaders lead purely by position and power – you don't have to!

Not so with you – don't give in to that lowest and most crude level of leadership!

If you want to be great – be a servant to your teammates!

That ethic certainly seems upside down to us, but it is full of wisdom. Jesus knows that the greatest leaders don't need to push their way around with position and power, but they lead by seeking the best for their teammates.

As you compete today, be team leaders like Jesus and seek the best for your team and for individual teammates. As you do, you'll find yourself becoming a great leader and you'll find your team being greatly successful.

Bible Reading Plan:
Luke 7:1-10
Philippians 4:14-23

June 25

FREEDOM

Galatians 5:13

What is the difference between freedom and license? How are liberty and anarchy different? When does one cross the line from living freely to taking advantage of others? Today's scripture has some guidelines for good team relations.

Paul in writing to his friends in Galatia, writes at chapter 5 and verse 13, "You, my brothers, were called to be free. But do not use your freedom to indulge the sinful nature; rather, serve one another in love." Paul gives his friends some encouragement and an admonition.

Here are some guidelines in personified terms for us to think about today:

License says, "I'll do what I want without regard to others."

Freedom says, "I'll do what's best for everyone concerned."

Anarchy says, "It's nobody's business but mine how I live my life."

Freedom says, "I'm free to make good choices that benefit my teammates."

In today's game and in all of life, make your choices based on the freedom that comes from a renewed life. Don't fall into the trap of thinking that your life is yours alone and no one else is affected. As a team, each player has a direct affect on the others, on the floor and off it. Play in great freedom today. Make this the greatest effort of the year.

Bible Reading Plan:
Luke 1:67-80
Ephesians 3:14-21

June 26

WISE WORDS

Proverbs 25:11

Have you ever wanted to say something to a friend, but chickened out at the last minute because you thought it might seem silly or embarrassing? Did you later regret not saying it? What does God think about such situations?

In the book of Proverbs chapter 25 and verse 11 it says, "Like apples of gold in settings of silver is a word spoken in right circumstances." We all know the value of gold and silver, even if we can't afford to have any. We also know how sweet to the taste apples are. How valuable and how sweet to our souls would apples of gold be? Certainly they would have great value, especially when served to us on fine silver.

The point of this proverb is that our words, spoken in the right circumstances are of immeasurable value. Here's my challenge to you: speak with purpose to those in whom you'd like to invest. You probably have teammates who have followed you all this season and possibly for your whole career. Tell them what you want for them, challenge them to excellence, call them to be athletes of great character like yourself. Build a tradition through speaking carefully chosen words to those who follow you.

Choose others in your program who have been important to you and express your appreciation for them as well. The opportunity will soon be gone, don't miss your chance to serve some golden apples on a beautiful silver platter.

Bible Reading Plan:
Psalms 119:49-56
I Kings 12

June 27

LOVING GOD

It's important to have priorities and to know what's most important. These values give our lives direction and purpose.

In Matthew chapter 22 and verses 37 and 38, Jesus says, "Love the Lord your God with all your heart and with all your soul and with all your mind. This is the first and greatest commandment."

Jesus says that the number one priority in life is to love God. That's the big deal, to love God with all your life; heart, soul and mind.

Apply your heart - to loving God in deep devotion.

Apply your soul - love God emotionally, passionately, deeply.

Apply your mind - love God with thoughtful expression.

Let your love for God find expression today on the field of competition. Give Him your absolute best - heart, soul and mind. Make this contest a huge, gift-wrapped expression of love. He's worthy of your very best.

Bible Reading Plan:
Luke 4:1-12
Ephesians 6:1-9

June 28

THOUGHTS

How much thoughtful preparation goes into a single competition for you? If we were to total up the collective hours of thought, contemplation, analysis, dreaming, visualization and anticipation among your teammates and coaching staff, the sum would be staggering. How much do you believe God thinks about you? How often are you at the front of his mind? Who could calculate such a number?

We get a glimpse at how God thinks in Psalm 139 and verses 17 and 18. Here's how David described these ideas, "How precious concerning me are your thoughts, O God! How vast is the sum of them! Were I to count them, they would outnumber the grains of sand. When I awake, I am still with you."

David was overwhelmed with the concept that an all-powerful God would spend His time thinking of him. That's a little staggering for me too! He has a universe to run, but He's concerned with every detail of my life.

The largest number David can conceive of is the number of grains of sand on the earth, but that's a smaller number than the sum of God's thoughts concerning each one of us.

For me, that leads to a great deal of confidence. I draw great comfort from knowing that my life is not hidden in a corner out of God's view. Rather He's intimately aware of every facet of my life and my every concern.

As you compete today, let these words from the Psalms result in a great confidence and assurance that every moment of this day is in the center of God's attention for each one of us. His thoughts toward us are precious, innumerable and always loving.

Bible Reading Plan:
Psalm 119:97-104
II Kings 1-3

June 29

SECURITY

Isaiah 59:1

Have you ever felt like you were out of God's reach? Have you ever prayed on game day and wondered if God was hearing you? The Scripture is full of promises that assure us of His love and care.

In Isaiah's book of prophecy at chapter 59 and verse 1 it says, "Surely the arm of the Lord is not too short to save, nor his ear too dull to hear." We have a great privilege in being related to God through Christ. We have the assurance of His saving right arm of protection and we have His ear to hear our prayers.

The exciting thing to me is that the Lord is interested in every area of my life. His arm can reach into any area to save and to protect. His ear never grows dull from hearing my prayers. This is high privilege, to have the Creator of the universe listening to me and extending His arm to save.

Today as you pray and prepare, ask the Lord to extend His arm as you compete. He's plenty strong. Also thank Him for hearing your prayers, those of every sort in every area of life. Let's trust Him in all of our lives and He'll prove Himself faithful to each of us.

Bible Reading Plan:
Luke 5:17-26
Philippians 2:12-18

June 30

MOTIVATION

Hebrews 10:24

What is it that best motivates you to compete at your highest level? Some athletes are motivated by challenge. Others are moved by the thrill of winning. Others still are provoked to excellence by the fear of losing. What is it for you? We're certainly not all wired the same.

The writer of the letter to the Hebrews has some insight into motivation and writes about it at chapter 10 and verse 24. "And let us consider one another in order to stir up love and good works." How do your coaches and teammates stir you up to be your best?

There are three important parts of this simple sentence which have direct application to today's competition:

Let us consider one another. This implies that serious thought should be given to each member of the team. Where motivation is concerned, one size does not fit all. Let's give a real effort to understand each member of the team.

In order to stir up. What stirs up a great performance in you may not affect me at all and vice versa. One teammate may require a pat on the back while another may be better motivated by a kick in the pants. We must consider what will stir up each person most effectively.

Love and good deeds. We all know plenty of people who get stirred up and it's not always toward love and good deeds.
As you compete today, give careful attention to the motivational keys in each of your teammates. Find a way to press that button that stirs up the best performance possible in each one. That is part of being a great teammate, coach and competitor.

Bible Reading Plan:
Luke 7:11-17
I Chronicles 1-2

July 1

BONDAGE

John 11:44

Have you ever seen a teammate or friend who seems to be bound by something? It looks like they have something wrapped around their life, which is just choking the life out of them. How do we help the situation? What can be done to free them? Jesus did that very thing in today's letter.

We read about Jesus and Lazarus again at John chapter 11 and verse 44, "And he who had died came out bound hand and foot with grave-clothes, and his face was wrapped with a cloth. Jesus said to them, 'Loose him and let him go.'"

Lazarus was bound with grave-clothes and his face was covered with a cloth. He had been in the grave for four days, that's what dead men wear. But here he comes walking out and Jesus says to loose him and let him go. Living men don't wear grave-clothes.

Your teammate or friend may be bound with something equally unfitting. Bad relationships, drug addictions, defeated attitudes and despair don't fit this team. They're inappropriate for a group like this. Jesus says the same to us, "Let him loose and let him go."

Whatever it is that has your teammate or friend bound, find a way to set him free. We can help loose the bonds and restore freedom.

As you compete today, loose your teammates to play with greatness by freely encouraging and challenging each one. Let them go with unselfish team play and powerful focus on the game.

Bible Reading Plan:
Luke 7:18-35
Colossians 1:15-29
Psalms 125
I Chronicles 3-4

July 2

BOLDNESS

Proverbs 28:1

When you come into game day, are you confident or fearful? Do you run to the field with great expectation or run away with great anxiety? How do we put away our apprehension and take on boldness?

In the book of Proverbs at Chapter 28 and verse 1 it says, "The wicked flees though no one pursues, but the righteous are a bold as a lion." There are lots of teams that come to play in an opponent's home arena and tremble. Lots of players from other teams flee though no one is chasing them. We need not do so.

It says that the righteous are as bold as a lion. We'd all like to have that kind of courage and unshakable confidence. I want you to know that it's attainable through loving God. That's where being righteous comes from. Our relationship with God makes us righteous and that results in a quiet, strong confidence in any situation.

Let's compete with a quiet, strong confidence today. Let's be like lions prowling across the field of competition. Who knows, maybe the home folks will start running away?

Bible Reading Plan:
Luke 7:36-50
Colossians 2:1-7
Psalms 126
I Chronicles 5-6

July 3

RELATIONSHIPS

Matthew 22:39

How well do you get along with the people on your team? How well with the coaching staff? How well with your family? Our relationships with people are a life long set of joys, challenges, grief and love.

After Jesus spoke of loving God as the greatest commandment, he said this in Matthew 22 and verse 39, "The second is like it: Love your neighbor as yourself."

Second only to loving God is Jesus' command to love people as we love ourselves. That's a tall order!! To love anyone that strongly is a powerful thing. It's also rather rare.

Do this today... Express real love toward your teammates through unselfish play. Show love for your coaches through respect. Show love to your fans and the officials through honorable actions and speech. The power of this kind of love transforms people and makes for the best relationships.

Give it all you have today. Pursue the victory with your last drop of energy. Play with enthusiasm and vision. Be a champion.

Bible Reading Plan:
Colossians 2:8-15
Psalms 127
I Chronicles 7-9

July 4

FOCUS

Isaiah 26:3

How do you focus your mind on game day? How do you keep thinking about doing well and not about failure and loss? How do you keep worry and anxiety from crowding into your mind? The Bible has a lot to say about that.

In Isaiah's book of prophecy, at chapter 26 and verse 3 it says, "You will keep him in perfect peace whose mind is steadfast, because he trusts in You." What a great promise! Perfect peace for our minds through steadfast trust in God.

How do we accomplish that? It's simple really, trust God with all the affairs of your life. Talk to Him, that's prayer. Listen to Him, that's Bible reading. Commit the things that concern you to Him through loving conversation with your teammates.

When you compete today, rest in the promise that your mind can be at peace. You'll have the ability to block out the things that cloud your mind and to focus on the game. Focus and intensity on the floor come from a mind that's uncluttered and at peace. He keeps our minds in perfect peace through steadfast trust.

Bible Reading Plan:
Luke 8:16-25
Psalms 128
I Chronicles 10-11

July 5

THE GREATEST

Mark 10:42-44

Which of these would most people see as being greater, the driver of the team bus or the star player riding in the back? Which would appear to be more important, the star athlete or the trainer who hands her a bottle of water? Who would seem greater, the guest of honor at the team banquet or the person washing the dishes? We know what most would say, but what do you think? What would Jesus say?

We can read about Jesus' value system in the book of Mark at chapter 10 and verses 42 through 44, "You know that those who are regarded as rulers of the Gentiles lord it over them, and their high officials exercise authority over them. Not so with you. Instead, whoever wants to become great among you must be your servant, and whoever wants to be first must be slave of all."

While totally turning the value system of the world upside down, Jesus said that the great ones are those who serve and that the ones who want to be first must be slaves to the others. Ouch! That doesn't feel good at all.

The problem is that He's right. The bus driver is actually more important to the trip than the one riding in the back. The dishwasher is more important to the dinner than the guest of honor. The trainer is often more important to the life of a team than one star player. Each of these people takes on a servant's role and even resembles a slave at times, in order to further the process for everyone else.

As you compete today, keep in mind that being great will come as you serve your team and that being first is a direct result of putting everyone's needs ahead of your own.

Bible Reading Plan:
Luke 8:26-39
I Chronicles 12-14

July 6

REST

I John 3:19-20

Have there been moments in your sport career when you found yourself burdened by feelings of guilt or condemnation? How did you deal with those feelings? From where do those feelings come? Today's scripture offers some answers for how to deal with our hearts.

In John's first letter at chapter 3 and verses 19 and 20 we read, "This then is how we know that we belong to the truth, and how we set our hearts at rest in his presence whenever our hearts condemn us. For God is greater than our hearts, and he knows everything." John gives us invaluable counsel for handling our condemned hearts.

Those whose hearts have been renewed through relationship with Christ have the power of God at work in them. Even when their hearts feel condemned because of foolish choices or selfish actions, they can rest in His presence. He won't condemn them for their errors. God is greater than our hearts and knows everything about us.

It's a lot like a coach who so loves and trusts his/her players that he/she has full confidence that even if they play the worst game of their lives, they still have the favor and acceptance of their coach. They can rest in his/her presence. The coach is greater than their hearts and knows they gave their best.

As you prepare to compete today, let your commitment lead you to play your heart out. Trust your teammates, your coaches and your God to give you the freedom to be your best.

Bible Reading Plan:
Luke 8:40-56
Colossians 3:15-25
Psalms 130-131

July 7

INTIMIDATION

Numbers 13:30-33

Who was the most intimidating opponent you ever faced in competition? How did you perceive yourself in comparison with his/her abilities and stature? Did your opponent see you in that same light? Today's scripture tells a similar story.

In the Old Testament book of Numbers at chapter 13 and verses 30 through 33 we read, "Then Caleb silenced the people before Moses and said, 'We should go up and take possession of the land, for we can certainly do it.' But the men who had gone up with him said, 'We can't attack those people; they are stronger than we are.' And they spread among the Israelites a bad report about the land they had explored. They said, 'The land we explored devours those living in it. All the people there are of great size. We saw the Nephilim there. We seemed like grasshoppers in our own eyes, and we looked the same to them."

Caleb was about to lose his patience with his teammates. They had seen the greatest place they could ever imagine and he was ready to take possession of the place, but his teammates were all afraid.

Did you hear how they perceived themselves? They said they saw themselves as grasshoppers in comparison to their opponents. Worse still, they appeared to be grasshoppers in the eyes of their opponents.

As you compete today, will you see yourselves as Caleb did – fully able to compete with anyone and anywhere? Or will you see yourself as a grasshopper, one totally out of his league?

My challenge to you today is to look your opponent directly in the eye and when you see a reflection of yourself in his eyes, see the image of a champion and not that of a grasshopper.

Bible Reading Plan:
Luke 9:1-17

July 8

WISDOM

Proverbs 1:7

As we all know, the fundamentals of your sport are the beginning of success. How foolish would it look to compete at your level without knowledge of techniques and training?

In Proverbs chapter 1 and verse 7, the King writes, "The fear of the Lord is the beginning of knowledge, but fools despise wisdom and discipline." Just like the fundamentals of your sport lead to success, the fear of the Lord leads surely to knowledge. Not only knowledge of one's sport, but knowledge in the larger matters of life.

Fools despise wisdom and discipline, says the proverb. A fool is one who has the ability to learn, but refuses to do so. Fools turn up their noses at understanding and a well-ordered lifestyle. A life under control seems, to them, to be unthinkable.

In today's competition and through the rest of the season, apply every bit of knowledge you have concerning your sport. Be careful not to despise the coaching staff's wisdom and discipline, we don't want to be fools. Most of all pray and ask God's blessing on your life... a healthy respect for Him is the beginning of real knowledge for all of your life.

Bible Reading Plan:
Colossians 4:10-18
Psalms 133-134
I Chronicles 20-22

July 9

COMMANDMENTS

Have you ever competed in a domed stadium or seen a game in one? Do you fully understand what holds the roof up? How does that thing stay up there with snow on it? From what does the roof hang?

In Matthew chapter 22 and at verse 40, Jesus concludes His talk about the greatest commandments, "All the Law and the Prophets hang on these commandments."

Jesus is saying that all the Bible's wisdom and insight for living hang on the commands to love God and to love people. How much of your life hangs on these? How deeply have you committed yourself to loving God, then to appropriating His inexhaustible love toward others?

Let's make it our mission to abandon all in the pursuit of this kind of love. The whole of life hangs on loving God and people.

Let's also abandon all tonight in pursuit of today's victory. The whole of this season may hang on this ball game. We can best do that as we love God with every fiber of our beings and love others as we love ourselves.

Bible Reading Plan:
Luke 9:28-36
Psalms 135
I Chronicles 23-25

July 10

ATTITUDE

I Corinthians 13:4

How would you describe your attitude coming into today's game? How well are you getting along with your teammates and coaching staff? How about some thoughts on attitudes that transform people and teams? Let's talk about love in its purest form.

In Paul's first letter to his friends in Corinth at chapter 13 and verse 4 he says, "Love is patient, love is kind. It does not envy, it does not boast, it is not proud." This is God's kind of love, way beyond human emotions and based in deep commitment.

These are attitudes we can take into today's contest. Exercise patience and kindness with your teammates when they fail. Put away the envy that separates the players who play a lot from those who play much less. Put down your prideful boasting over your personal statistics and concentrate on the team's success. Love is the key for each of these characteristics to be found in us.

Bible Reading Plan:
Luke 9:37-50
I Thessalonians 2:1-9
I Chronicles 26-28

July 11

FEAR

Isaiah 41:13

What helps you to ward off fear when it comes? How do you find confidence to combat such an enemy? Who comes to your aid when you're gripped by fear? One of many great promises for overcoming fear from the Bible follows.

In Isaiah's book of prophecy at chapter 41 and verse 13 he says, "For I am the LORD, your God, who takes hold of your right hand and says to you, Do not fear; I will help you." I hope that's an encouraging idea, that God would take you each by the hand and help you. I don't know about you, but I need help every day.

If you can, imagine what it would look like for God to take you by the hand and help you in the work you have to do. He takes your right hand and leads you through the times of grief, stress, loneliness, depression, even through times of great success. He's really there for each of us, just like He was running up and down the floor, holding your hand and encouraging you with each step.

He says, "Do not fear, I will help you." Whatever produces fear for you, commit it to Him in prayer as you prepare and trust Him to help you.

Bible Reading Plan:
Luke 9:51-62
I Thessalonians 2:10-20
Psalms 137

July 12

SERVANT-LEADERSHIP

Mark 10:42-45

Who is someone from your sport, that if he was to walk in the room right now, we'd all feel compelled to give up our seats, to offer something to drink and to serve in any way possible? Who would be deserving of such respect and admiration?

Jesus was certainly such a person in His day, but He refused such treatment. Why? We can read about His reasoning in Mark chapter 10 and verses 42 through 45, "You know that those who are regarded as rulers of the Gentiles lord it over them, and their high officials exercise authority over them. Not so with you. Instead, whoever wants to become great among you must be your servant, and whoever wants to be first must be slave of all. For even the Son of Man did not come to be served, but to serve, and to give His life as a ransom for many."

With each sentence, Jesus raised the price tag for leadership.

He said that greatness comes through service of the team.

He said that being first comes as we subject ourselves to everyone else.

He now says that to be like Him, means self-sacrifice.

How does that happen in competition? When you put your team's success ahead of your personal achievement, that's self-sacrifice. When you prefer the team's goals to your personal goals, that's great leadership. When you sacrifice your privilege in order to free a teammate to achieve, you're leading like Jesus.

As you approach this day's competition, do so with a pre-determined will to lead through service and sacrifice. Pay whatever it costs to free your teammates to achieve at their highest level of the season. Be a team leader like Jesus and give your life as a ransom for many.

Bible Reading Plan:
Luke 10:1-16
I Thessalonians 3:1-6

July 13

LOVING DEEPLY

I Peter 1:22

Who is there in your life that you love deeply, from the heart? You're probably thinking of family members, your best friends, hopefully some teammates and coaches. Today's scripture encourages us to love that way.

In Peter's first letter at chapter 1 and verse 22 it says, "Now that you have purified yourselves by obeying the truth so that you have sincere love for your brothers, love one another deeply, from the heart."

Peter calls these people to love each other from the depths of their souls. Most of us love shallowly, from our self-interests.

My challenge to you is to love your teammates deeply, from the heart. Not shallowly from simple emotion or sentimentality. Love deeply, from the very center of your being. Not just on the surface or only when it's convenient.

Such love among teammates is built on commitment to each other. You have forged your team's commitment to each other on the field of competition and through countless of hours in practice and conditioning. Commit yourself to your teammates and your coaching staff and you will love deeply, from the heart.

As you prepare to compete today, make some commitments to your team in your hearts. Demonstrate those commitments by how you perform, lead and encourage.

Bible Reading Plan:
Luke 10:17-24
I Thessalonians 3:7-13
Psalms 139
II Chronicles 3-5

July 14

WISDOM

Proverbs 2:6

Who is the greatest source for wisdom in your life? Maybe you're thinking of your mom or dad. Maybe it's your coach. The Scripture speaks of someone who is the ultimate source for wisdom and understanding.

In Proverbs chapter 2 and verse 6, Solomon writes, "For the Lord gives wisdom, and from his mouth come knowledge and understanding."

He says that from the Lord's mouth come knowledge and understanding. God speaks through His Word daily and gives us knowledge that is pertinent information for daily living. He also shares his understanding with us, the ability to rightly apply knowledge.

As you prepare for competition today, listen for the Lord's voice. He's always speaking in ways to lead us to knowledge and understanding. He gives wisdom related to relationships on the team, for excellence in the classroom, and understanding for athletic achievement.

God's Word, the Bible is always open to us and He speaks loudly each time we're faithful to open its pages and to read.

Bible Reading Plan:
I Thessalonians 4:1-10
Psalms 140
II Chronicles 6-7

July 15

HUMILITY

Matthew 23:12

Have you ever seen the last place team, jump up and beat the previously undefeated, first place squad? How could that happen?

In Matthew's gospel at chapter 23 and verse 12, Jesus is recorded as saying, "Whoever exalts himself will be humbled and whoever humbles himself will be exalted." That happens a lot in competition.

Many times we see a team strut onto the floor, exalting themselves and believing themselves to be invincible. How quickly they can fall, often to teams with inferior talent. They are those who exalt themselves and are humbled.

Other teams have an honest estimate of their strengths and weaknesses. They are conscious of their abilities and those things they should not attempt. They approach the game with respect for opponents and quiet confidence in their teammates and coaches. These are the humble who are consequently exalted.

In this contest, have an attitude of quiet confidence. Know fully your team's strengths and weaknesses. Have an honest estimate of your abilities and a healthy respect for your opponents. If you will humble yourselves, it's God's job to exalt you, to lift you up at the appropriate time. Trust Him deeply and play with all your heart.

Bible Reading Plan:
Luke 10:38-42
Psalms 141
II Chronicles 8-9

July 16

RENEWED STRENGTH

Isaiah 40:30-31

When was the last time you were running in practice and your legs felt like spaghetti? Did you wish for wings so you could fly? Did you long for a new set of legs that didn't get tired? Where could one find new strength and vigor for the day's competition? The Bible has an answer.

In the prophet Isaiah's book at chapter 40 and verses 30 through 31 it says, "Even youths grow tired and young men stumble and fall; but those who hope in the Lord will renew their strength. They will soar on wings like eagles; they will run and not grow weary, they will walk and not be faint." Everybody gets tired, even the best of us get a little weary. The promise here is that we don't have to be overcome by fatigue, but can soar beyond our limits.

How does that work? He says here that those who wait on the Lord will renew their strength. This waiting is to trust, to see a source of power outside ourselves. Even when you're growing tired, out of breath, legs turning to rubber, trust and press on.

Trust God to put some spring back in your legs, some wind back in your lungs, some focus back in your vision, some power back in your arms. Most of all trust Him for some renewed faith, hope and love in your heart.

Play today with a sense that you've tapped into an inexhaustible source of power. Play with strength that's renewed minute by minute.

Bible Reading Plan:
Luke 11:1-13
I Thessalonians 5:1-11
II Chronicles 10-12

July 17

BAD ATTITUDES

I Corinthians 13:5

Do you know anyone who holds grudges or seems to have a recording of every wrong ever done to him or her? These are generally joyless, less than loving people who make for poor teammates and friends.

Paul wrote to his friends in Corinth some enlightening words about God's kind of love, at chapter 13 and verse 5 of his first letter he says, "It is not rude, it is not self-seeking, it is not easily angered, it keeps no record of wrongs."

These rather ugly characteristics don't fit in a heart filled with love. They're like oil and water, they don't mix. Keep these things away from your team and you'll find success as a strong, cohesive unit. Love is the key and it's born of a heart of commitment to family, friends, and teammates.

Bible Reading Plan:
Luke 11:14-28
I Thessalonians 5:12-28
Psalms 143

July 18

DISTRACTIONS

Mark 11:7-8

Can you recall the feelings of arriving home after winning a championship or a victory over your fiercest rival? Maybe there were crowds awaiting your return, a police escort with fire trucks and a motorcade of minivans painted with the names of your teammates and uniform numbers. How did you keep your mind focused on your sport and not get distracted by all the noise?

In Mark chapter 11 and verses 7 and 8 we can see how Jesus handled similar circumstances in his life. There we read, "When they brought the colt to Jesus and threw their cloaks over it, he sat on it. Many people spread their cloaks on the road, while others spread branches they had cut in the fields. Those who went ahead and those who followed shouted, 'Hosanna! Blessed is he who comes in the name of the Lord! Blessed is the coming kingdom of our father David! Hosanna in the highest!' Jesus entered Jerusalem and went to the temple."

When I read this I see a team bus coming back into town having just won a championship and crowds of fans waiting for the team on the edge of town. Everyone is excited, honking horns, screaming and shouting congratulations to the team. Imagine how Jesus and His followers must have felt.

Watch Jesus' reaction and gain some wisdom about how to handle success. Does He get caught up in all the excitement and lose His head in the adulation? No, rather He maintained His focus on His mission.

Let's learn from Jesus and keep our minds focused on our team goals even when we're surrounded by people telling us how great we are.

Bible Reading Plan:
Luke 11:29-36
Psalms 144

July 19

TRUST

Proverbs 3:5-6

In whom do you place your trust? How much do you trust that person? Could you trust him or her with your very life? Today's letter will encourage us to trust someone with every facet of life, even your sport.

In Proverbs chapter 3 and verses 5 and 6 we read, "Trust in the Lord with all your heart and lean not on your own understanding; in all your ways acknowledge Him, and He will make your paths straight."

To trust someone is to place you faith in that person, to give him or her a measure of control of your fate. That's scary for most of us. This verse says to trust God with all your heart. Not with 50% of your heart but 100% of it. We're not given the luxury of hedging our bets and leaving an easy escape route. This requires real commitment.

Even scarier is that it is our heart with which we're asked to trust Him. More valuable than your body or your mind is your heart. He wants you to trust Him with 100% of your inmost being.

The great thing for us is that God is also 100% trustworthy. He won't trick us or leave us hanging when we commit ourselves to His trust. He can be trusted in all matters of life to pursue our best interest with an unlimited amount of power, wisdom and love. What a deal!

In today's competition, trust the Lord to enable you to make the plays you dream about. Trust Him to help you be a team leader. Trust Him to help you battle injury, doubt and frustration. Remember trust Him 100% because He's 100% trustworthy. Have a great game!

Bible Reading Plan:
Luke 11:37-54
II Thessalonians 1:8-12

July 20

UNDERSTANDING

Proverbs 3:5-6

Who is the smartest person you know? Who knows more about your sport than anyone else does? How smart are you? How heavily do you rest on your limited understanding? Let's consider some wisdom in these matters.

In Solomon's writings of wisdom at Proverbs chapter 3 and verses 5 and 6, we read, "Trust in the Lord with all your heart and lean not on your own understanding; in all your ways acknowledge Him, and He will make your paths straight."

Most of us would have to admit that we have a limited understanding of our game. Even our coaches know that even with their extensive experience, they have not exhausted the available knowledge of the sport. That's the focus of that phrase, "lean not on your own understanding." Solomon is encouraging us to seek a source of wisdom and understanding outside ourselves.

In today's competition, look to your teammates and coaching staff for understanding of situations, opportunities and techniques. Look to family for encouragement and love. Look to God for understanding in the most important matters of life. You can lean on His understanding it's available and immense. Have a great day of competition.

Bible Reading Plan:
Luke 12:1-12
II Thessalonians 2:1-12
Psalms 146
II Chronicles 22-24

July 21

LOVE

Matthew 25:40

What kind of things do you do for people you love? How do you express your love for your family, friends, teammates and others? How do we express a love for God?

Jesus gives us an answer as to what He sees as loving action, in Matthew chapter 25 and verse 40. He says, "I tell you the truth, whatever you did for one of the least of these brothers of mine, you did for me." There are two big ideas in this text. Who are Jesus' brothers and what can we do for them?

Who are these Jesus calls the least of His brothers? In the context of this parable, they're people in jail, the sick, strangers, the hungry, the thirsty and the homeless. Jesus says that acts of love and mercy toward these people are equal to loving acts toward Him.

What can we do for people like these? What would you do for anyone whom you encounter daily? Show respect, compassion, mercy and love. If you encounter the least, as in the list above, love God through loving them. If you encounter your teammates, coaches, classmates, even professors; love God through loving them. Show them respect, compassion, mercy and love.

In today's game you have a marvelous opportunity to express love for God by treating people as you would Him. Imagine how you'd treat Him if He showed up here and you were face to face. Treat everyone that way tonight. Even the officials! Have a great game and thereby honor the Lord Jesus.

Bible Reading Plan:
Luke 12:13-21
II Thessalonians 2:13-17
Psalms 147
II Chronicles 25-27

July 22

COURAGE

Joshua 1:7

What are some essential qualities for an athlete to bring into competition? Make a list. I'm sure that your list will include strength and courage. The Bible speaks of these often and one such instance follows.

In Joshua chapter 1 and verse 7 it says, "Be strong and very courageous..." In times like these we need to bring a truckload of both strength and courage to the field of competition.

The people that Joshua was leading were about to try to take possession of hostile territory and could lose their lives in the effort. They were challenged to be strong and courageous. How much more should we be strong and courageous in our pursuits? The rewards for us are great and the risks are much less.

As you compete today, keep in the back of your mind Joshua's challenge to his players. Be strong and very courageous!! Bring strength and courage to every facet of today's competition. You can make this a day of greatness.

Bible Reading Plan:
Luke 12:22-34
II Thessalonians 3:1-5
Psalms 148
II Chronicles 28-29

July 23

BODY BUILDING

Jude 20-21

What makes up the daily workouts that you use to build your body? What is most effective in building up your mind? How do you build your heart? Today's scripture has an answer to that question.

In Jude's letter to believers at verses 20 and 21 it says, "But you, beloved, building yourselves up on your most holy faith, praying in the Holy Spirit. Keep yourselves in the love of God, looking for the mercy of our Lord Jesus Christ unto eternal life." Jude calls this group of men, "Beloved", as he deeply cares for them.

The big idea that Jude wants them to know is in verse 21. He says, "Keep yourselves in the love of God..." Remember this is written to a group, not to an individual. We keep ourselves in the love of God as a group through things like prayer as a group. Through day to day living as teammates and friends. Through caring enough about each other to encourage, admonish, confront, correct and to steer our teammates away from trouble. We experience the mercy of the Lord Jesus and His eternal life when we keep ourselves (as a group) in the love of God.

Let's begin today's competition with prayer as a group, building ourselves up on our most holy faith. Then let's keep ourselves, as a group, in the love of God as we look out for the interests of the team, more than just our individual interests. In doing so we'll experience the mercy of our Lord Jesus.

Bible Reading Plan:
Luke 12:35-48
II Thessalonians 3:6-13
Psalms 149
II Chronicles 30-33

July 24

HONOR

Proverbs 3:25

What would it be like to receive a great inheritance? Maybe there's one coming to you someday; real estate jewels, heirloom furniture, money, who knows? What would the most valuable inheritance be for someone of wisdom?

Proverbs chapter 3 and verse 25 states, "The wise inherit honor, but fools He holds up to shame."

It doesn't take long to figure out which side of this equation is better for us. He says that the wise inherit honor. They don't earn it, nor do they don't find it. They receive it like a gift from granddad. They inherit honor, which often looks like favor with coaches and teachers. Sometimes it looks like respect among teammates and opponents. It always looks like personal dignity.

On the other hand, it says that fools are held up to shame. Just holding them up to the light exposes their foolishness, thus bringing shame, disgrace and humiliation.

Which would you rather receive, honor or shame? You'll attain more wisdom and thus honor and will accumulate less shame as you choose to surround yourself with friends who are wise and not foolish.

In today's competition, display wisdom as you compete and you'll inherit honor. Act like a fool and you'll be the subject of ridicule and shame. Please be a credit to your team, coaches and your family by competing with greatness today.

Bible Reading Plan:
Luke 12:49-59
II Thessalonians 3:14-18
Psalms 150
II Chronicles 34-36

July 25

REPRESENTATION

Mark 12:17

How much of your personal success do you owe to your team? How many hours per week are reasonable for you to practice? Who determines the proper amount of preparation that is necessary for each competition? To whom are you responsible for the most important parts of your life?

Jesus spoke about such matters at Mark chapter 12 and verse 17, where it says, "Give to Caesar what is Caesar's and to God what is God's.' And they were amazed at him."

Let's think about this in athletic terms.

If you're wearing the uniform of your school – you must give your allegiance to the leadership they've appointed for your team.

If you've accepted a scholarship from a university – you must submit to your coaching staff.

While you're on your own time, away from team responsibilities – you must make your own choices about behavior.

When you're on your own – give God first priority as you direct your life.

As you compete today, be mindful that you represent a number of people beyond yourself. You certainly represent your teammates, your school, your family and friends, and many of you represent your God. Compete in such a way that they can each be proud of you and that displays your allegiance to each with pride.

Bible Reading Plan:
Luke 8:1-15
Colossians 2:16-23

July 26

MOTIVATION

Hebrews 10:24

What is it that best motivates you for competition? Is it the sight of your parents in the stands? The encouragement from your coach and teammates? Maybe it's the prospect of being a champion. The Bible speaks of another type of motivation.

In the Book of Hebrews at chapter 10 and verse 24 it says, "And let us consider how to stimulate one another toward love and good deeds."

A different translation of that verse says "to provoke," to love and good deeds. Many of us provoke one another when we compete, but it's not always toward love and good deeds. The important thing is not to stimulate, but to do so toward these two objects.

The remaining question for us is, how? We can certainly stimulate love and good deeds in our friends and teammates by showing them examples. We can do so by encouraging words. We can praise them when they're caught doing it right. We can correct them when they do it wrongly.

Take time to pray today and ask the Lord to use you to stimulate your teammates toward love and good deeds.

Bible Reading Plan:
Psalms 129
I Chronicles 15-16

July 27

OPPORTUNITY

Matthew 26:11

Have you ever heard people speak of "once in a lifetime opportunities?" Have you ever had one of those? Did you recognize it at the time?

In Matthew chapter 26 and verse 11, Jesus talks about taking advantage of opportunity. He says to his disciples, "The poor you will always have with you, but you will not always have me." This followed Judas' complaint about a woman who poured some very expensive perfume on Jesus' feet, an act he saw as very wasteful.

The perfume cost about one year's wages and this woman pours the whole thing on Jesus' feet. Why would Jesus not want it sold and the money given to the poor? He knew what Judas didn't, that His remaining days with them were very few. This woman had taken advantage of a great opportunity to honor Christ.

Jesus told them that the poor would always be around, but He would not. Their opportunity to be with Him was very short in duration. It would not be the same in a week.

You have much the same situation today. Tomorrow at this time your opportunity to play this game will be gone, forever. It can never be revisited. Competition will be around all season, but this game will be gone in about two hours. Do as this great woman of faith did. Take full advantage of your opportunity. Expend all that you have to maximize your opportunity. It won't be the same tomorrow.

Bible Reading Plan:
Luke 9:18-27
I Thessalonians 1

July 28

217

FAITHFULNESS

I Corinthians 13:6-7

Is there someone in your life you can count on to always be the same? Who do you know that you would describe as steady, faithful, and consistent?

In First Corinthians chapter 13 and verses 6 and 7, the Apostle Paul writes, "Love does not delight in evil, but rejoices with the truth. It always protects, always trusts, always hopes, always perseveres." This is descriptive of the kind of love God gives us and offers to us for sharing with others.

Love is something you can count on. More than a fleeting emotion, it's a conscious exercise of one's will, a commitment between people. That's how it can be always protecting, trusting, hoping and persevering.

Take these attitudes into competition today as you commit yourself again to your teammates and coaches. Love is the key, commitment makes it happen.

Bible Reading Plan:
Psalms 136
I Chronicles 29

July 29

PLANS

Jeremiah 29:11

Do you ever wonder if God has a real plan for your life? Maybe as you think about the future, you see it as being fully a matter of your choices and will. Is there ever a thought that maybe God has something in mind for you that would make you most fully satisfied and wholly fulfilled. He speaks to us in today's Scripture.

In Jeremiah's book of prophecy, at chapter 29 and verse 11 it says, "For I know the plans I have for you,' declares the Lord, 'plans to prosper you and not to harm you, plans to give you hope and a future." Surely the Lord has plans for each of us individually, and plans for us collectively.

He says that these plans are to prosper us. How would we be prospered in athletic terms? Obviously we think of wins, trophies, medals and titles. But how could we be prospered otherwise?

We are prospered by the Lord when we display His character on the floor or in relationships with teammates. We are prospered when our program signs new recruits and they come to aid us in our pursuit of excellence. We prosper when the program gains notoriety for having done well athletically and in the classroom. The Lord's hand is evident and his plan to prosper us is accomplished as we trust Him to work in our lives.

Lay it all on the line in today's competition and trust in the Lord's plans to prosper those who trust in Him.

Bible Reading Plan:
Luke 10:25-37
I Thessalonians 4:11-18

July 30

ADVERSITY

Jeremiah 29:11

Have you ever suffered an injury and wondered where the Lord was? Why did He allow me to get hurt? Could it be in God's plan for me to be injured? Why me, why now? Receive some assurance from the Lord in this scripture.

In Jeremiah's book of prophecy, at chapter 29 and verse 11 it says, "For I know the plans I have for you,' declares the Lord, 'plans to prosper you and not to harm you, plans to give you hope and a future." Surely the Lord has plans are not to harm us. Rather, His plans are for our good.

When we encounter adversity in any form; injury, illness, conflict, strife, bad calls, or any other thing, it's easy to think that the Lord's not looking out for us. Some even think that He's mad at us about something. Nothing could be farther from the truth. In this verse He says that His plans are not to harm us.

Let's trust in the Lord's plans. Let's trust His heart and His undying love to keep us from harm and to enjoy prosperity.

Bible Reading Plan:
Psalms 142
II Chronicles 13-16

July 31

HOPE

Jeremiah 29:11

Have you ever lost hope in doing well? Have you had a season where you dreaded competition because you expected to lose? How do you turn that around? How do we redeem our attitudes and expect the best? The Bible has some words of encouragement for us in relation to our future and our hopes.

In Jeremiah's book of prophecy, at chapter 29 and verse 11 it says, "For I know the plans I have for you,' declares the Lord, 'plans to prosper you and not to harm you, plans to give you hope and a future." The Lord's plans include some marvelous things, among them hope and a future.

Hope can best be defined as a confident expectation of good, based upon the promises of God. Rest in the confident expectation of the good things you've heard in God's promises from the Bible. Compete with an expectation of doing well. Expect to get the marginal call. Expect to get the rebound, to make the catch, to get the hit, to make the pass, to succeed in all facets of the game.

The Lord's plans may include a future of post-season competition for you and your team.

Bible Reading Plan:
Luke 13:1-9
I Timothy 1:1-11
Proverbs 1
Ezra 1-2

August 1

100%

If you were to pick out one principle for competing in your sport as the most important, which would it be? If there were one commandment for life that is primary, what would it be? Jesus spoke clearly about such and His words are recorded in Mark chapter 12 and verse 30.

There we read the most important commandment, "Love the Lord your God with all your heart and with all your soul and with all your mind and with all your strength."

Jesus said that the most important thing in life is to love God like this:

With all your heart – with strong emotional attachment. Love God passionately.

With all your soul – with purposeful, willful desire. Love God on purpose.

With all your mind – with intellectual understanding. Love God wisely.

With all your strength. – with strong physical performance. Love God actively.

Love God with 100% of your person, with integrity.

As you prepare today, fix your heart, soul, mind and strength toward competing passionately, purposefully, wisely and actively. That will lead you to a performance that will be pleasing to your teammates, your coaches, the fans and even to God.

Bible Reading Plan:
Luke 13:10-21
I Timothy 1:12-20
Proverbs 2
Ezra 3

August 2

ENCOURAGEMENT

Hebrews 3:13

What sorts of things do you need on a daily basis to compete well? You'd certainly say things like food, rest, training, water, are all physical, daily necessities for the competitor. What could be the things that feed your soul that are also needed daily? Today's scripture has an answer.

At chapter 3 and verse 13, the writer of the letter to the Hebrews says, "but exhort one another daily, while it is called Today, lest any of you be hardened through the deceitfulness of sin."

Nourishment, sleep, exercise and practice are certainly necessary to make prepare your body and mind for high level competition, but if you neglect to feed your soul with daily encouragement, you'll be spiritually and emotionally malnourished.

As you prepare for this day's competition, give your teammates some encouragement, share some with your coaches, and let the trainers and equipment managers have some also. Feed each other's souls with encouraging words and gestures of support. Daily encouragement will keep our hearts from becoming hardened through deceit and bitterness. Play like a champion today.

Bible Reading Plan:
I Timothy 2
Proverbs 3
Ezra 4-5

August 3

INSTRUCTION

Proverbs 4:13

Can you imagine how tightly you'd grip a rope if it were the only thing holding you from falling off a 500-foot cliff? Of course you'd hold on with all your strength… the rope is life to you. Today we'll talk about something else to hold on to with all your strength.

In Proverbs chapter 4 and verse 13, Solomon the king writes, "Hold on to instruction, do not let it go; guard it well, for it is your life."

Solomon says to hold tightly to instruction. Instruction is the knowledge you receive from parents, teachers, coaches, experiences and friends. It has to do with your sport, academics, with faith and life in general. He says hold on to it.

He also says, "Don't let it go." There are some things that could loosen your grip on instruction. Things like fatigue, distraction, and weakness could have us falling without ability to recover.

Solomon says to guard instruction well. Guard it from being stolen by a lack of discipline. It can be lost to inattention or wasted by disuse.

The reason for all these directives is that instruction is your life! It can help you avoid problems, find success and enjoy peace. Within your sport, instruction is the key to development of your skills and to execution of a successful game plan.

As you prepare for competition today, hold on to the instruction from this week's practices. Guard well the things you've been taught and you'll find that instruction is as valuable as life itself.

Bible Reading Plan:
Luke 14:1-14
Proverbs 4
Ezra 6

August 4

EXPRESSIONS OF HOPE

I Peter 3:15

How do you respond when you see a teammate who demonstrates strong commitment and devotion to his/her sport or to his/her team? Do you wonder why? Maybe you follow his/her example. Have you ever asked him/her why he/she's so committed?

In the book of First Peter at chapter 3 and verse 15 we read the following, "But in your hearts set apart Christ as Lord. Always be prepared to give an answer to everyone who asks you to give the reason for the hope that you have. But do this with gentleness and respect."

Peter's counsel is simple – a committed heart will be noticed by others. A committed heart will prompt questions. When people ask you about your commitment, give them an answer with gentleness and respect.

It's the same for us in sport. Your commitment to your sport and to your team will be noticed by many. Some of them will even ask you questions about it. Your committed heart is an enigma to them and most will not understand. When they do ask you about it, give them a simple answer gently and respectfully. Even if they still don't understand, you've answered them well.

As you approach today's competition, understand that your level of commitment may be out of the ordinary and others may not fully appreciate it. Expect such commitment to be noticed, to raise questions and even objections. Be prepared to answer all who ask with gentleness and respect.

Bible Reading Plan:
Luke 14:15-24
I Timothy 3:11-16
Ezra 7

August 5

ARROGANCE

Proverbs 6:16

What do you hate more than anything on earth? Is it spinach, sauerkraut, cough syrup, lies, or losing? Maybe it's coming in any place but first. In today's letter we'll hear about the first of 6 things that God hates, seven that he finds detestable.

In Proverbs chapter 6 and verse 16 we read, "There are six things the Lord hates, seven that are detestable to Him: haughty eyes..."

Have you ever seen the swagger of a returning champion? That's what haughty eyes look like. They're proud of themselves and they haven't even won anything yet!

Haughty eyes are proud, arrogant and filled with selfishness. They look down on others as they perceive everyone else as inferior. They wear their superior glasses as they look in the mirror of vanity.

Rather than being like those with haughty eyes, choose humility. Put away arrogance and pride and take on a humble attitude toward your teammates and opponents. Let your speed, strength and endurance speak for you and you won't have to run your mouth nearly as much.

Make this a great day of competition and choose to compete humbly. In doing so you will avoid displaying the haughty attitude God hates.

Bible Reading Plan:
Luke 14:25-35
I Timothy 4
Proverbs 6

August 6

LYING TONGUES

Proverbs 6:16-17

Have you ever had a teammate who lied to your coach or the team? How did you react? Don't you hate that? God does also...

In Proverbs chapter 6 and verses 16 and 17 we find more of the things God hates, "There are six things the Lord hates, seven that are detestable to Him: haughty eyes, a lying tongue..."

Your tongue usually betrays your real feelings and thoughts, even when you try to disguise them. Your tongue sometimes brings out speech like, gossip, trash talking, and excuses for missing class or practice. At other times it might deceive the trainer regarding the severity of an injury, or mislead the coach about your behavior away from the team. These are called lies and the Lord hates them.

Lying is purposeful deception, half-truths or empty flattery. In any case, it is detestable to God and to the victims of such speech.

Choose to speak truth. No one wins when we deceive and the best for everyone is always served when we speak the truth.

In today's competition, speak the truth in encouraging your teammates and coaches. Speak truthfully to the trainers and your opponents. Remember, God hates a lying tongue... I'd rather have Him on my side than against me.

Bible Reading Plan:
Luke 15:1-10
I Timothy 5:1-15
Proverbs 7
Ezra 9

August 7

VIOLENCE

Proverbs 6:16-17

Have you ever been the victim of a cheap shot in your sport? Some athletes take advantage of their opponents by using a compromising position to hurt or humiliate them. This is similar to another of the things God hates.

Proverbs chapter 6 and verses 16 and 17 says, "There are six things the Lord hates, seven that are detestable to Him: haughty eyes, a lying tongue, hands that shed innocent blood..."

A person's hands are symbolic of his deeds or actions and hands that shed innocent blood literally kill people. In our world of sports though, we would say that they injure or wound an opponent or teammate. I've seen many competitors undercut while making a lay up or viciously hit after a whistle on the football field. To maliciously injure a teammate, opponent, coach or friend is tantamount to shedding innocent blood. What then shall we do?

Choose to love. I don't know anyone who is more competitive than me. However we must make the conscious choice to subdue that old, win at any cost, mentality and choose to compete wisely. That kind of an attitude is driven by love, the thing God loves more than anything. Have a great day of competition.

Bible Reading Plan:
Luke 15:11-32
I Timothy 5:16-25
Proverbs 8
Ezra 10

August 8

WICKED SCHEMES

Proverbs 6:16-18

Do you remember hearing about some of the outrageous recruiting violations of recent years? How about the academic cheating at some institutions? Who dreams up that stuff? Why do they do such things?

Such scheming is another of the things God hates as we read in Proverbs chapter 6 and verses 16 through 18, "There are six things the Lord hates, seven that are detestable to Him: haughty eyes, a lying tongue, hands that shed innocent blood, a heart that devises wicked schemes…"

The proverb says it's the heart that drives these schemes. Your heart contains your passions, your affections and emotions that can sometimes override your mind. To devise a scheme is to conceive a plot, to carefully plan a course of action. A wicked scheme is one that illicitly profits from another's loss, it seeks to injure others, to cheat or defraud. Nasty stuff, huh? No wonder the Lord hates these.

Let's choose purity. Rather than devising wicked schemes, let's plot how to encourage and uplift one another. Rather than planning to cheat or steal, let's consider how we may embellish our teammates and coaches. Guard your heart and check your motives and you'll keep your heart turned toward purity. Compete with purity and passion today.

Bible Reading Plan:
I Timothy 6:1-10
Proverbs 9
Nehemiah 1-2

August 9

SUDDEN DESTRUCTION

Proverbs 6:16-18

Have you heard the story of Len Bias? He was the first round draft pick of the Boston Celtics in the 1986 NBA draft. During the evening that followed his selection, he overdosed on cocaine and died. His story serves to illustrate another of the things God hates.

In Proverbs chapter 6 and verses 16 through 18 we read, "There are six things the Lord hates, seven that are detestable to Him: haughty eyes, a lying tongue, hands that shed innocent blood, a heart that devises wicked schemes, feet that are quick to rush into evil..."

You may be wondering why God hates these things. It's simple really; all the things from this passage injure people. Some quickly, some slowly, but the end is inevitably the same, people die. That's why He hates these behaviors, He profoundly loves people.

Len Bias' feet were quick to rush into cocaine abuse and it cost him his life that same night. A thing that kills some people over the space of decades did him in with one stroke. His feet were quick to rush into evil and death was waiting for him there.

Let's choose to avoid evil. You probably already know where it lives and which of your friends hang out there. Avoid it at all costs! You could dodge it effectively for a while, or you could be like Len Bias and suffer immediately. The sure solution is to avoid the evil all together.

In today's competition, let your feet be quick to rush into first place!! Let them be quick to serve your team and to fulfill your goals. Have a great day of competition!

Bible Reading Plan:
Luke 16:10-18
Proverbs 10:1-16
Nehemiah 3

August 10

PRESS CONFERENCE

Proverbs 6:16-19

How well do you handle press conferences or newspaper and television interviews? How do you handle it when a coach resigns or is fired? What do you tell your friends when a teammate is suspended, benched, injured or dismissed? Do you tell the truth or do you concoct a story to cover the situation? Be careful...

In Proverbs chapter 6 and verses 16 through 19 we read about the things God hates, "There are six things the Lord hates, seven that are detestable to Him: haughty eyes, a lying tongue, hands that shed innocent blood, a heart that devises wicked schemes, feet that are quick to rush into evil, a false witness who pours out lies..."

A false witness is someone who knows the truth, but is unwilling to tell it. Rather than tell the truth or say nothing, the false witness makes up a story to cover his backside. Usually this takes place in public, like the courtroom or the press conference.

To pour out lies looks like a huge bucket being tipped over and spilling out its contents of deception, half-truth and perjury. The lies thus poured out are meant to obscure the truth like paint would cover a stain.

Choose to speak wisely in public. There are always situations that require us to protect information given us in confidence. We must protect the trust given us by teammates, coaches and friends and sometimes the best thing to say is nothing. Speak wisely and everyone will be pleased, with the possible exception of sportswriters.

Have a great day of competition and enjoy the interviews as you speak with tremendous wisdom!

Bible Reading Plan:
Luke 16:19-31
II Timothy 1:1-7

August 11

DISSENSION

Proverbs 6:16-19

Have you ever been on a team where someone is constantly stirring up trouble between teammates or with the coaching staff? It's not a pleasant place to be and that person is in a precarious position.

Here is the last of seven things the Lord finds detestable in Proverbs chapter 6 and verses 16 through 19, "There are six things the Lord hates, seven that are detestable to Him: haughty eyes, a lying tongue, hands that shed innocent blood, a heart that devises wicked schemes, feet that are quick to rush into evil, a false witness who pours out lies, and a man who stirs up dissension among brothers."

This is different that the other six in that this time it's the person the Lord finds detestable, not just his or her behavior. This kind of person dredges up the sediment of past hurts and divisions between people to divide them. Once settled arguments are fired up again by his whispering accusations or emphasis on contrary opinions.

People who should be the most natural allies, like teammates or brothers, are suddenly divided by this person's cutting words. Rather than do that, let's choose to preserve unity. Instead of dividing people, we can unify them through encouragement and by promoting quick resolution of problems. We can maintain tremendous attitudes on the team by seeking reconciliation at the first mention of conflict and division.

Preserve unity in this day's competition by making your best effort in every moment as you pursue a win for your teammates and coaching staff.

Bible Reading Plan:
Luke 17:1-10
II Timothy 1:8-18
Proverbs 11:1-15

August 12

CIRCUMSTANCES

Romans 8:28

What sorts of things get you down during the season? Bad performances during games? Ugly practices? Long road trips? Strained relationships on the team? Challenges in classes? Whatever the circumstance, we have a great promise related to God's will and His provision.

In Paul's letter to his friends in Rome at chapter 8 and verse 28, he tells them, "And we know that in all things God works for the good of those who love Him, who have been called according to his purpose." According to Paul, a guy who had decades of difficult days, God's at work in the whole process of our lives.

It says that He's at work in all things... good things, bad things, smart things, stupid things, fun things, painful things... all things. God is at work in all these things to bring about good for you. Even in the worst, most stupid and dreadfully painful situations of life, God is at work to bring good to you.

Whether it's a losing streak, a lost friendship, a broken family, a failing grade or whatever; God's promise to you is the same. He's seeking your good every day, all day. Rest in that promise today and trust Him as you compete in confidence and security.

Bible Reading Plan:
Luke 17:11-19
II Timothy 2:1-13
Proverbs 11:16-31
Nehemiah 7

August 13

LOVE YOUR...

Mark 12:31

We talked elsewhere about the most important principle of your sport and about the number one commandment for life. What might be principle and commandment number two?

Jesus voices this second commandment right on the heels of the first in Mark chapter 12 and verse 31, where we read, "The second is this: Love your neighbor as yourself. There is no commandment greater than these."

You've probably heard this for years, but I would like to have you substitute some sport-oriented words for the word "neighbor."

Give this a try... Love your teammate as yourself. Love your coach as yourself. Love your officials as yourself. Love your opponent as yourself. Love your athletic trainer, equipment manager, even your fans as yourself. That sounds easy, but how do we do this in practical terms?

Do you expect the best of yourself? Expect the same of your teammates. Love them as you do yourself. Do you believe your intentions are pure? Believe the same of others. Love them as you do yourself. Do you desire love and respect? Desire the same for all those around you. Love them as you do yourself.

As you compete in today's contest, extend the love you receive from God to the people who surround you. Whether coach, teammate, fan or official, give each one the love and respect that you desire for yourself.

Bible Reading Plan:
Luke 17:20-37
II Timothy 2:14-26
Proverbs 12:1-14
Nehemiah 8

August 14

GOALS

When do you feel conflicted, like your heart is divided? Sometimes we're caught between two sets of values. These moments of divided hearts and conflicting values happen more often that we'd like to admit.

In Paul's first letter to his young friend Timothy at chapter 1 and verse 5 he wrote, "The goal of this command is love, which comes from a pure heart and a good conscience and a sincere faith."

Paul was instructing Timothy to focus on God's work and to avoid foolish controversies. His goal for such instruction was love, purity of heart, a clear conscience and faith with integrity.

The goal of these simple thoughts is love. That you would love God and your teammates is my foremost aspiration. Such love comes from a heart that is pure, one that's been made clean and restored to wholeness. Such love comes from a good conscience, one that has been freed from guilt and despair. Such love comes form a sincere faith, one that simply trusts God with all the matters of life, especially sport.

As you prepare to compete today, take some time to examine your heart. Is it pure? Is you conscience good? Is your faith sincere? I trust that affirmative answers to such questions will enable you to compete freely and confidently.

Bible Reading Plan:
Luke 18:1-8
II Timothy 3:1-9
Proverbs 12:15-28
Nehemiah 9

August 15

PURITY

Matthew 5:8

With whom have you competed that had extraordinary vision for your sport? Who seemed to be able to see things on the field of competition that no one else could see? What would it be like to see things as God sees them? How can we begin to do so?

In Matthew's gospel at chapter 5 and verse 8 we read, "Blessed are the pure in heart, for they will see God." This is another of the verses from the Beatitudes.

To be blessed is to be contented and happy with one's lot in life. Jesus says we're blessed when we're pure in heart, that is pure in our motives and purposes. We all need to check out our motives and our purposes for the things we do. Am I being selfish or selfless? Am I seeking the best for others? Is my personal agenda being placed above that of the team? How pure am I in heart?

The exciting promise is this. When we are pure in heart we have an uncommon insight into God's view of the situation at hand. We can understand what would please Him and have the ability to choose wisely.

As you prepare for competition today, ask the Lord to cleanse and purify your heart. Ask Him for pure-hearted vision to see what He sees and to thereby be the ideal teammate and competitor.

Bible Reading Plan:
II Timothy 3:10-17
Proverbs 13:1-12
Nehemiah 10

August 16

EVALUATION

Jeremiah 12:5

When was the last time you did some honest evaluation of your abilities? When have you sized up your competition to see how well you've done?

In Jeremiah's book of prophesy he writes about this idea, "If you have raced with men on foot and they have worn you out, how can you compete with horses?"

Many times athletes who are doing very well get overly confident of their abilities. They are often simply competing against inferior opponents and receive a rude awakening when they face some better competition.

Jeremiah asks a hard question. He says that if these third string athletes are wearing us out, how well do we expect to compete with the first team players? What are we to do? Have an honest estimate of your abilities and work to improve. Don't boast about your successes, you may have been playing against inferior competition and you could be embarrassed by superior athletes later.

As you pray before today's competition, ask the Lord to help you compete well. You may be playing against athletes the level of men on foot or you may be up against athletes that seem to run like horses. Either way seek to honor the Lord with your life.

Bible Reading Plan:
Luke 18:18-30
Proverbs 13:13-25
Nehemiah 11

August 17

BOASTING

Psalm 20:7

Have you ever been a part of a great team? Have you noticed how people around the team tend to boast and brag about how good they are? They take great pride in the team and talk about championships. In whom do you boast? In whom do you take pride?

In Psalm 20 and verse 7 the writer says, "Some boast in chariots and some in horses, but we will boast in the name of the Lord, our God." This makes me question the things in which I make my boast. In what do you boast? What do you talk about most? Whom do you speak of most often?

Some players boast in their physical strength or their jumping ability or their quickness. Some teams boast in their coaches, or their records, or their winning traditions. Others, however boast in their relationship with the Lord Jesus. These people know that their relationship with God is the only thing that is truly permanent and eternally durable. They know that strength will wane and teams will dissolve, but the Lord is unchanging and He is always available to them.

Today when you pray, look to the Lord for real strength. Ask Him to give you opportunities to boast in His name. Examine your heart and see where your boasting resides. Is it in horses or chariots? In strength or quickness? In hoops or jump shots? Or is it in the name of the Lord?

Make your boast in the Lord, today and every day of your life.

Bible Reading Plan:
Luke 18:31-43
Titus 1:1-9
Nehemiah 12

August 18

EXPECTATIONS

Hebrews 10:23

What were your preseason expectations? Upon what were they based? Were they based on returning veteran players, on new players just joining the team, on a new game plan or some other intangible factor? Upon what do your expectations of God rest? Let's think together about how these fit in the life of a competitor.

The writer of the letter to the Hebrews writes at chapter 10 and verse 23, "Let us hold fast the confession of our hope without wavering, for He who promised is faithful."

It's normal and often helpful to have great expectations of your team through the preseason and into the first competitions of the year. We all start with great hopes for a successful season and dream of championships. We'd be less than true competitors if we did anything less. We are wise if we base these expectations on the people around us rather than on all the circumstances beyond our control. We can hold fast to our hope, as a team, by trusting each other and working together.

Another comforting thought from this scripture is that our hope for real life, now and throughout the future, is based on the nature of God. The writer says that "He who promised is faithful." The very faithful nature of God is the guarantee of the promises made by our Father to us in the Bible. That's worth holding onto with both hands!

As you compete today, hold fast to your expectations of your team and of yourself. Cling tightly to your hope for the team's success. Trust the Lord Jesus to be faithful and to keep his promises to you. Make this a day in which you exceed even your greatest expectations.

Bible Reading Plan:
Luke 19:1-10
Titus 1:10-16

August 19

239

DAILY WISDOM

When I was a young man and pursuing my girlfriend (now my wife of over 30 years), I knew exactly where she lived, when and where she went to class and every angle that made for an opportunity for me to know her. Today's scripture tells us to pursue wisdom just like that.

Proverbs chapter 8 and verse 34 says, "Blessed is the man who listens to me, watching daily at my doors, waiting at my doorway."

Wisdom is personified by the author as a lovely woman, full of life giving truth. It says the man who listens to her is blessed. The key to receiving the blessing is to listen, watch and wait for her.

We can hear wisdom as we listen to our coaches and other mentors. Further, we must listen daily; implying regularity and discipline. We hear most effectively when we listen at wisdom's doors… where she lives.

Wisdom lives in the minds of your coaching staff, your parents, your instructors and even in some teammates. Listen closely and you'll be blessed. Wisdom resides in the Bible and God speaks loudly and clearly daily through its words. Have a great competition today.

Bible Reading Plan:
Luke 19:11-27
Titus 2:1-10
Proverbs 15:1-17
Esther 1

August 20

LIVING SACRIFICES

Romans 12:1-2

What sort of sacrifices have you made for your athletic career? What have you given up to pursue a life of athletics? Sacrifice is something most people never even consider, let alone complete. In these next three letters we'll consider what it is to be a living sacrifice.

In Paul's letter to the Romans at chapter 12 and verses 1 and 2 it says, "Therefore, I urge you, brothers, in view of God's mercy, to offer your bodies as living sacrifices, holy and pleasing to God-this is your spiritual act of worship. Do not conform any longer to the pattern of the world, but be transformed by the renewing of your mind."

At the time of this writing by Paul, sacrifices were usually killed and laid upon an altar to be burned up. The problem with "living sacrifices" is that they tend to crawl off the altar when it gets a little hot. We start with good intentions of making a sacrifice for our teammates, our family or career, but when it gets uncomfortable we often snatch the sacrifice from the altar and lose the reward that comes from faithfulness.

The good news is that God's grace enables us to offer our very bodies in daily service to Him. He calls it holy, pleasing service that is a spiritual act of worship. Let God's grace move you to sacrifice whatever it takes to pursue a life that's holy and pleasing to the Lord. Further, make the sacrifices necessary to pursue the goals you and your team have established for this season.

Bible Reading Plan:
Luke 19:28-38
Titus 1:11-15
Proverbs 1518-33
Esther 2

August 21

TREASURE

Matthew 7:6

What sort of things do you value most highly? What are some treasures worthy of protection?

Jesus is recorded as saying these words in Matthew chapter 7 and verse 6, "Do not give to dogs what is sacred; do not throw your pearls to pigs. If you do, they may trample them under their feet, and then turn and tear you to pieces."

You are in possession of some of life's greatest commodities: vision, athletic ability, intelligence, friends and leadership skills. Don't throw these pearls in the mud with the pigs. Don't give these sacred gifts to dogs. There are people with whom you're acquainted who are not worthy of your devotion. They'd only trample your gifts and then turn to destroy you.

Choose your friends carefully. Judiciously think about with whom you'll spend your time. Invest your time in people with whom you can be influential for good and with people who bring out the best in you.

As you prepare to compete today, focus on the tremendous gifts you've been given by a loving God. Thank Him for your opportunities and ask Him for the wisdom to value and protect your pearls.

Bible Reading Plan:
Luke 19:39-48
Titus 3:1-8
Proverbs 16:1-16
Esther 3-4

August 22

FIERCE COMPETITORS

Psalm 104:21

Have you ever seen an athlete compete like he was stalking his opponent? When you compete do you do it with passion and ferocity? Is it possible that these kinds of ideas are in the Bible?

In Psalm 104 and verse 21 it says, "The young lions roar after their prey, and seek their food from God." I've read this at times and thought about how athletes sometimes "roar" after their opponents in competition. Often when I'm competing in athletics it seems like I'm stalking my opponent, preparing to make a kill.

As we compete, like a wild lion, we can fiercely pursue our goals, but ultimately we must seek our food from God. We must see the Lord as the only source of the kind of food that satisfies. Food for our souls.

Let's compete today in a way that is like a roaring, young lion. Let's doggedly pursue our quarry and let's not be satisfied until we've accomplished our goals. As you pray, ask the Lord to feed your soul with the food that only He can provide.

Bible Reading Plan:
Luke 20:1-8
Titus 3:9-15
Proverbs 16:17-33
Esther 5-6

August 23

FAITH, HOPE, LOVE

I Corinthians 13:13

What is the most durable thing you can think of? What is there in your life that will outlive you? I have some ideas from a powerful scripture.

In the first letter to the Corinthian church, Paul the Apostle writes at chapter 13 and verse 13, "And now these three remain: faith, hope and love. But the greatest of these is love." Here are three things that are eternally durable.

Two thousand years from today they will still be as vital and powerful as they are now. Of the three, love is preeminent because it provides the relationship that is the context for the faith and hope.

Today play with confident expectation of good - that's hope.

Play in faith - actively trusting your coaches, your teammates and your God. Play in the great freedom afforded by those who love you and are committed to you.

Bible Reading Plan:
Luke 20:9-19
Philemon 1-11
Proverbs 17:1-14
Esther 7-8

August 24

WISDOM

Where do you look for wisdom about how to do things? What is the source of ultimate truth? How do we find real life? The Bible answers these and many more questions with a one word answer...Jesus.

In the gospel of John chapter 14 and verse 6, Jesus says, "I am the way and the truth and the life, no one comes to the Father but through me." In pursuing our goals in life and in competition we must know the way to go, the truth to hold on to and the life that satisfies.

Christ is the way - He directs our paths to the right things, the right people, away from things that are harmful to us and toward things that bring us life. Look to Him for the way to win.

Christ is the truth - He speaks to us the truth about all matters of life. A life based on lies cannot be successful. Search God's Word to know real, timeless truth. Listen for the truth when making decisions moment by moment.

Christ is the life - He gives us life through relationship with Him. Life that is powerful, exciting, confident, secure, bigger than death and free of fear. Receive this kind of life and enjoy it!!

Compete today with the great confidence that comes from knowing the right way, the real truth and possessing real life.

Bible Reading Plan:
Luke 20:20-26
Philemon 12-25
Proverbs 17:15-28
Esther 9-10

August 25

LIFE AND FAVOR

Proverbs 8:35

What could you look for that upon its being found, pays the dividend of life itself? What could be so valuable that when it's attained brings the best stuff of life? The scriptures have the answer.

In Proverbs chapter 8 and verse 35 we read further about Wisdom personified, "For whoever finds me finds life and received favor from the Lord."

The proverb says that whoever finds me finds life. I would infer that not everyone is going to look... there are plenty of fools around... they can't even spell wisdom! The person who would be wise will have to search for wisdom and pursue it at all costs. When one does find it, the payoff is life itself... what a great reward!

Additionally, the one who finds wisdom also receives favor from the Lord. Favor is often entrance to a most exclusive place of influence...like being a college athlete. Sometimes it is gracious accommodation of you as a person...like when you get to fly first class when you paid coach fare. We receive such favor from the Lord as we pursue and attain wisdom.

In today's competition, find wisdom and find its rich rewards. Life and favor will be yours as you compete wisely and with all you hearts.

Bible Reading Plan:
Luke 13:22-35
I Timothy 3:1-10

August 26

COMMUNICATION

I Corinthians 6:11

Who are the best leaders among your teammates? Would you say that they communicate freely or rather grudgingly? Today, we'll all receive a leadership lesson in communication.

In his second letter to the Corinthian church at chapter 6 and verse 11, the Apostle Paul wrote these words, "We have spoken freely to you, Corinthians, and opened wide our hearts to you." This is the nature of good leadership – free and open communication.

In the first century and in the 21st century, good leadership comes from the open hearts of leaders. When leaders are open and honest with their teams, following is rather natural and productive. Good leadership speaks freely and from the heart. Such speech inspires and encourages teammates to be their best.

Take a moment to examine your personal leadership style, is it characterized by an open heart and free communication? Do your teammates believe you when you speak to them or do they wonder about what you're trying to get from them?

As you approach today's competition, open wide your hearts to each other and your communication will flourish. Let your open hearts lead you to a great victory.

Bible Reading Plan:
Proverbs 5
Ezra 8

August 27

RESPECT

John 1:26-27

What would happen if the greatest player you've ever heard of came to your practice and wanted to play with your team? How would you react? How much respect would he be given? A similar situation happened one day in Jesus' life.

In John's Gospel at chapter 1 and verses 26 and 27 we read, John answered them saying, "I baptize with water, but there stands One among you whom you do not know. It is He who, coming after me, is preferred before me, whose sandal strap I am not worthy to loose."

John the Baptist knew what no one else could grasp on that day. He knew who Jesus was and he knew the respect that was due Him. The people who stood there that day had no clue that this young man from Nazareth would in the space of three years die a sacrificial death on a cross in Jerusalem.

Had they been athletes, John might have said that he wasn't worthy of carrying Jesus' shoes to the gym. John knew the respect that Jesus was due, even when no one else recognized Him.

It may be that way with you and your team today. There could be in your midst, on the field of competition with you, one of the great players of the game. The important thing is to recognize and respect such greatness. Your coaching staff may prove to be among the most influential people in your life, give them the respect and honor they are due. Be like John the Baptist and recognize the wise and honorable people who cross your life's path. Have a great game today.

Bible Reading Plan:
Luke 16:1-9
I Timothy 6:11-21

August 28

FAITH

Hebrews 11:1

For what do you hope with a great confidence that it will be realized? A conference championship? A win in this competition? A date this weekend? Your mother's love? Of what are you certain without ever having seen it? Are you certain that the ball will come down after it goes up? Are you certain that your mother will be there when you go home for break? That's what faith looks like.

Faith is defined in the book of Hebrews at chapter 11 and verse 1, "Now faith is the substance of things hoped for, the evidence of things not seen." Obviously the things for which we hope are just out of reach or it wouldn't be hope. Faith is the substance of such things. Things which we can't see are often hard to believe, but faith is the evidence that they are real.

As competitors we'd be terribly weakened if we had no hopes, no aspirations, and no expectations of success. Through faith, active trust, in our teammates and coaching staff we can experience the substance of those things hoped for. We can touch those achievements that are often months in the future.

We all need faith, active trust, to continue to believe that we can achieve like champions on the days when we fail like losers. To see the untapped potential in a teammate is the stuff of faith. To see yourselves as winners during a frustrating practice session is to have evidence of things not seen. Faith = active trust.

Exercise faith in today's competition and so achieve like never before.

Bible Reading Plan:
Proverbs 10:17-32
Nehemiah 6

August 29

HATE WISDOM – LOVE DEATH

Proverbs 8:36

When does failure sting the most sharply? Immediately or after a year or two? What kind of failure results in personal loss? Have you ever had a teammate who seemed addicted to failure? Today's scripture talks about people who seem to love death.

We again find Wisdom personified in Proverbs 8 and verse 36, "But whoever fails to find me harms himself; all who hate me love death."

In direct contrast to verse 35's encouragement about finding wisdom, life and favor; those who fail to find wisdom suffer harm at their own hands. They could fail because of lack of effort, through being undisciplined or simply by quitting. You probably know someone who suffered great loss by giving up too easily.

It says that all who hate wisdom, love death. If we receive life as we attain wisdom, then when we despise it we reveal our bent toward death and destruction.

In today's competition, be careful to act wisely. Don't miss wisdom's instructions when they come from your coaches or teammates. Don't despise the words of wisdom and so embrace the destruction of your team's goals and aspirations. Make this a day of life-filled victory!

Bible Reading Plan:
Luke 18:9-17
II Timothy 4

August 30

THE COMPLETE PLAYER

II Peter 1:3

What one thing could be added to your game that would make you the competitor that you've always dreamed of being? I'm sure you have a short list of things that you dream about having that would make you more complete. What do you really need to be the most complete person you could be?

Peter wrote about these ideas at chapter 1 and verse 3 of his second letter, "…as His divine power has given to us all things that pertain to life and godliness, through the knowledge of Him who called us by glory and virtue." All things? Really?

Yes, really. God has given us everything that we need… pertaining to life and godliness. We certainly may be missing some facets of the game that would make us more complete players, but we have been given everything we need to be the people He's called us to be.

That's great news. I can practice, learn, train and compete to become a more complete athlete, but it's tremendous to know that God has supplied all I need to honor Him with my life through godly living.

As you prepare for competition, remember the great gifts you've been given and employ them all in pursuit of a victory. Remember also the great investment that God has made in you to be the person He has created you to be.

Bible Reading Plan:
Proverbs 14:1-18
Nehemiah 13

August 31

CONFORMITY

Romans 12:1-2

When you were a child, did you play with Play-doh modeling clay? Do you remember how it was soft and moldable? You could form it with a mold or use you hands to squeeze it into most any shape you could imagine. How much are you like Play-doh? What pressures in your life squeeze you into strange shapes?

Paul writes to his friends in Rome about being molded by pressures in Romans chapter 12 and verses 1 and 2. "Therefore, I urge you, brothers, in view of God's mercy, to offer your bodies as living sacrifices, holy and pleasing to God-this is your spiritual act of worship. Do not conform any longer to the pattern of the world, but be transformed by the renewing of your mind."

Paul tells his friends that the world has a pattern and it will work to make you conform. We've all seen this in what's called "peer pressure." There is an unseen pressure that comes from our friends, our culture, just the way the world does things, that tries to make us conform. The problem is that many times the way of the world is directly contrary to the ways of God. That's why Paul says, "Do not conform." His call is for us to be less like Play-doh and more like a rock.

If the world says, "That's good enough for them..." Reject that thought, be a rock. If the world says, "Go ahead, nobody's watching." Reject the notion, be a rock. When the world says, "Look out for number one." Reject that attitude, be a rock. Don't be squeezed any more by the world's Play-doh mold. Be a rock that resembles God and His pattern for life.

Bible Reading Plan:
Luke 20:27-40
Hebrews 1:1-9
Proverbs 18
Isaiah 1-2

September 1

TRANSFORMATION

Romans 12:1-2

Metamorphosis is the process of transformation from a caterpillar into a butterfly. What a marvelous, mysterious thing. We can see it in insects, but can we see a similar thing in people?

Paul writes to his friends in Rome about metamorphosis in Romans chapter 12 and verses 1 and 2. "Therefore, I urge you, brothers, in view of God's mercy, to offer your bodies as living sacrifices, holy and pleasing to God-this is your spiritual act of worship. Do not conform any longer to the pattern of the world, but be transformed by the renewing of your mind."

How can people undergo metamorphosis? Paul says that it comes by the renewing of one's mind. Like a caterpillar inside a cocoon, it's a process that works from the inside out. With people, we don't build cocoons, but our minds are changed as a part of a long process. We begin as unlovely as caterpillars, we offer our bodies as living sacrifices, we resist the conforming nature of the world and we're transformed in our thinking, suddenly we emerge as beautiful as butterflies. We've undergone metamorphosis as people.

Let's look to God for the transforming power of His grace to change us, from the inside out. Let's ask Him to make us ready for this day's competition, for great teamwork and for lives that honor Him every day.

Bible Reading Plan:
Luke 20:41-47
Hebrews 1:10-14
Proverbs 19:1-14
Isaiah 3-5

September 2

EXPECTATIONS

Romans 12:3

Do you wonder from time to time how you'll match up with your competition over the season? How good a player are you in relation to others on your team or on your opposing teams? The older I get the better athlete I was. The Bible calls us to have sober judgment about ourselves.

In Paul's letter to the church at Rome, at chapter 12 and verse 3, he writes, "For by the grace given me I say to everyone of you: Do not think of yourself more highly than you ought, but rather think of yourself with sober judgment, in accordance with the measure of faith God has given you."

To have sober judgment is to think clear-mindedly about our abilities, skills, and our team's potential. As we approach this season's games, let's not flatter ourselves and live in self-deceit regarding our team. Conversely, let's not have expectations of ourselves that are too low. Let's think clearly and set goals for our team and for each member that challenge us to achieve greatly with reasonable chances of success.

Compete today with clear-minded expectations. Achieve greatly as you exercise sober judgment in evaluating your opponents. Be champions today.

Bible Reading Plan:
Luke 21:1-19
Hebrews 2:1-9
Proverbs 19:15-29
Isaiah 6-8

September 3

DISSENSION

Proverbs 10:12

Does your team seem divided at times? Is strife at work to tear your teammates apart and to cause disharmony? How do we bring about the healing of relationships and the restoration of teamwork?

In Proverbs chapter 10 and verse 12 it says, "Hatred stirs up dissension, but love covers all wrongs." Hatred seems like such a harsh word for the things that we see dividing our team. Most people wouldn't admit to hating anyone. Look at what causes the strife on your team and you'd probably say it's selfishness, which is simply a soft word for hate.

The good news is that there's a solution. According to the scripture, love covers all wrongs. Not just a few wrongs all of them. What a powerful thing love is! What's more, it's proven in the life of Christ. His love for us has covered our transgressions for all time and has ushered us into an eternal relationship with God.

Love is the key to good relationships on your team. Let love, selfless giving to each other, counter the strife born of selfishness. Let love rule your conduct in practice, on the field of competition and in the classroom. Cover your teammates' shortcomings by loving them and seeking their best, even when it comes at your cost.

Let the love flow and compete like a champion today!

Bible Reading Plan:
Luke 21:20-28
Hebrews 2:10-18
Proverbs 20:1-15
Isaiah 9-10

September 4

PRIVILEGE

Matthew 7:13-14

As an athlete, yours is a special privilege into which only a few people can enter. Don't lose sight of that privilege or its responsibilities.

In Matthew chapter 7 at verses 13 and 14 we read Jesus' words, "Enter through the narrow gate. For wide is the gate and broad is the road that leads to destruction, and many enter through it. But small is the gate and narrow the road that leads to life, and only a few find it."

Achievement of greatness is rare thing. It only requires a small gate to accommodate those who go that way. The road is also straight for them because they have direction, purpose and goals. This is the path that leads to life in its fullest sense.

Mediocrity requires a very wide gate, as there are so many flooding through. The road of the mediocre meanders broadly as its travelers lack vision, foresight and leadership.

Let's choose to enter through the narrow gate and walk the straight road of greatness. Let's have purpose, direction and vision. Let's walk the path that leads to life.

Come to think of it, lots of teams approach competition and walk through the gate of mediocrity. Don't be one. Enter through the narrow gate and compete like a champion.

Bible Reading Plan:
Hebrews 3
Proverbs 20:16-30
Isaiah 11-13

September 5

STANDARDS

I Corinthians 3:18

What is your standard for greatness, for intelligence, for wisdom? How are these things measured in the world? Real wisdom is measured differently.

In the Apostle Paul's first letter to his friends in Corinth at chapter 3 and verse 18, he writes, "Do not deceive yourselves. If any one of you thinks he is wise by the standards of this age, he should become a 'fool' so that he may become wise." Paul calls us to change the standards by which we measure things.

No one would look at former N.B.A. star Spud Webb and think that he would be a Slam Dunk Champion. He's 5'-7" tall. By normal measures only a fool would say he could succeed in such a venture. But there was more to Spud than could be measured with a tape.

It's the same with us and how we approach our competition. If one was to measure our team just in terms of years of experience, national championships and other standards of this age, we wouldn't seem to have a chance. Today we can confound the wise with our foolish ways and beat the experienced and talented at their own game. Let's pull a Spud Webb and set the world on its ear with a day of greatness.

Bible Reading Plan:
Luke 22:1-13
Proverbs 21:1-16
Isaiah 14-16

September 6

DISCIPLINE

Proverbs 10:17

Who among us likes to get his or her ear chewed off by the coach? Who enjoys correction? Obviously everyone wants to think that he or she competes at the highest level of his or her ability each time on the track. The problem is, most of us never approach that level of competence and thus need correction.

In Proverbs chapter 10 at verse 17 we read, "He who heeds discipline shows the way to life, but whoever ignores correction leads others astray."

We've probably had teammates who ignore the correction that the coaching staff gives them. They give verbal agreement when the coach is speaking, but go on doing everything the way they were before. This scripture says that in doing that they do a great disservice to not only themselves, but to the whole team. Here it says they lead others astray by their actions.

The promise of this verse is that if we listen closely to discipline, or correction, we will show others the way to life. When we make adjustments as corrected by our coaches, parents, pastors, friends or teammates, we provide a rich example of humility and grace to those around us.

Pray and ask the Lord for a gracious attitude that accepts correction and shows the way to life for your team. Compete greatly today!

Bible Reading Plan:
Luke 22:14-23
Hebrews 4:12-16
Isaiah 17-20

September 7

SINCERITY

Romans 12:9

Who is there in your life who loves sincerely? Your parents? Your teammates? Your best friend? How is sincere love expressed? The Apostle Paul has some ideas in today's scripture.

In Romans chapter 12 and verse 9, Paul writes to his friends saying, "Love must be sincere. Hate what is evil; cling to what is good." In this passage Paul gives us an idea of the nature of real, sincere love.

Paul says that a sincere or pure hearted love will lead us to hate what is evil, that is things that harm people. There are plenty of evil things that surround an athletic team, just think about everything that could creep into your team and harm various ones.

He also says that a pure hearted love will lead us to hold tightly to things that improve our lives and the lives of those we love. That's what it means to cling to good. What are some things to which you can cling that will enhance the lives of your team?

In today's contest: Hate what is evil - things that will hurt your team. Cling to good - attitudes and behavior that leads to victory and teamwork. Let these values lead you to excellence today.

Bible Reading Plan:
Luke 22:24-30
Hebrews 5
Proverbs 22:1-16

September 8

FAVOR

Psalm 90:17

In Psalm 90 we read the prayer of Moses. At verse 17 we read, "May the favor of the Lord our God rest upon us; establish for us the work of our hands- yes, establish the work of our hands." This is the prayer of one of history's greatest leaders.

He asks for God's favor to be upon him, what would that be? How do we see God's favor in our lives? What makes an official give you a call in a charge / block situation? Why does the football bounce to you, rather than away from you sometimes? Why does your instructor give you a break in class when he doesn't have to? Sometimes it's the favor of God upon you.

How would God establish the work of our hands? What do you do with your hands that God should care to establish? How many hours have you spent in the weight room? How many miles have you run this year? How many free throws have you shot during practices? It's God's way to establish the hard work and effort we make by bringing them to full fruition.

Let's join Moses in praying for God's favor and for His power to establish the work of our hands.

Bible Reading Plan:
Luke 22:31-38
Hebrews 6:1-12
Proverbs 22:17-29
Isaiah 24-26

September 9

TRUST

John 2:5

In whom do you most strongly trust? Your parents? Your coaches? Your closest friends? If you were Mary, how much would you trust Jesus? Let's see how much she trusts Him.

In the Gospel of John at chapter 2 and verse 5 we read, His mother said to the servants, "Whatever He says to you, do it."

While at a wedding with friends, the host had run out of wine and Mary was asking Jesus to do something special to lessen the host's embarrassment. He asks her to back off a little bit, then her trust of her Son shows in her instructions to the servants.

How much do you trust your coaching staff? As much as Mary trusted Jesus? You are probably thinking that Jesus is not our coach! True, but the principle is the same. This kind of trust rests in the knowledge of the trusted one's love, respectability and competence.

You can have that kind of trust in your coaches. They do care for you deeply. They are fully respectable. They are completely competent. You can also trust your teammates for the same reasons.

In today's competition, trust completely in your coaches and teammates. Then when they give instructions and call plays, whatever they say to you, do it. Have a tremendous game today.

Bible Reading Plan:
Hebrews 6:13-20
Proverbs 23:1-18
Isaiah 27-28

September 10

TRASH TALKING

Proverbs 10:19

How much trash talking do you hear on the field of competition? I can't help but believe there are some players who run their mouths all the time. How should we think about such speech? The Bible is full of wisdom related to this and one such verse follows.

In Proverbs chapter 10 and verse 19 it says, "When words are many, sin is not absent, but he who holds his tongue is wise."

As we speak more and more words, our chances of speaking foolishly certainly increase. You probably know someone who talks too much and in doing so speaks in ways that can cause harm to her or to others. That is what is meant by "sin is not absent." Talk long enough and the best of us will sin with our tongues.

The other side of this is that when we remain silent in certain discussions, we display an uncommon wisdom. Some people talk when there is nothing to say. We would do well to speak only when it's appropriate and when the situation is enhanced by our comments. "He who holds his tongue is wise."

As you pray in preparation for competition, ask the Lord to give you control of your speech. Ask Him to fill your mouth with encouragement and wisdom, not criticism and foolishness.

Bible Reading Plan:
Luke 22:47-53
Proverbs 23:19-35
Isaiah 29-30

September 11

ACHIEVEMENT

Hebrews 11:39-40

How many Hall of Fame members or All Americans end their athletic careers without the ultimate championship for which they had hoped and competed? Certainly the number is staggering, just think of the great competitors from your sport who never won a championship. They and many others had stellar careers, but had one achievement left undone. The Bible speaks of such hope unfulfilled.

Hebrews 11 and verses 39 and 40 says, "And all these, having obtained a good testimony through faith, did not receive the promise, God having provided some thing better for us, that they should not be made perfect apart from us." These melancholy words follow 38 verses that list the names and accomplishments of the Bible's Hall of Fame.

There is a key element for a life of achievement that we can draw from this passage. Though these great people had their lives come to a close without the fulfillment of their hopes and dreams, they were faithful and now enjoy rich, fulfilling life with us in Christ.

Similarly, when you consider the Hall of Famers and All Americans from your sport, many of them finished with goals unachieved and aspirations unattained. Like the Bible's Hall of Famers, they too join in our achievements and our successes. They find great satisfaction in watching you compete and seeing you succeed.

As you compete today, give your absolute best effort and you'll be a great part of fulfilling the unrealized portions of your predecessors' careers.

Bible Reading Plan:
Luke 22:54-62
Hebrews 7:11-28
Isaiah 31-33

September 12

FOUNDATIONS

Matthew 7:26-27

What are the foundational principles upon which your sport is built? Do they appear to be wise or foolish? How enduring will the lessons you learn from sport be? Today's scripture contrasts foundations, foolishness and wisdom.

In Matthew chapter 7 and verses 26 and 27 it reads, "But everyone who hears these words of mine and does not put them into practice is like a foolish man who built his house on sand. The rain came down, the streams rose, and the winds blew and beat against that house, and it fell with a great crash."

When you were on the beach last summer, did it seem like a safe place to build a house? Of course not. The tide alone would wash it away. Throw in an occasional hurricane and you'd have to be a fool to build there. That's Jesus' picture here. The house has no foundation to withstand the wind, rain or floods.

A house or a team built on sand is one that has awareness of the principles for success, but doesn't employ them. Knowledge without application is empty and leads to destruction. In the story the house and all its inhabitants would be swept away in the great crash.

We probably all know athletes and coaches whose foundations crumbled and they suffered a tremendous crash. If we're fortunate we also know people who have wisely built their athletic careers on strong foundations. Which will you be?

In your time of prayer today, ask the Lord to lead you to wisdom and away from foolishness. Ask him to help you build wisely upon the solid foundations of faith, hope and love.

Bible Reading Plan:
Luke 11:63-71
Hebrews 8:1-6
Proverbs 24:23-34

September 13

BELONGING

II Corinthians 1:21-22

What is there in your sport that gives you a sense of belonging? What makes you feel like you belong to the team or the organization? Maybe your uniform does that or signing a letter of intent. These are simply a foreshadowing of good things to come. Today's scripture speaks of similar ideas.

In Paul's second letter to the Corinthians at chapter 1 and verses 21 and 22 we read, "Now it is God who makes both us and you stand firm in Christ. He anointed us, set his seal of ownership on us, and put his Spirit in our hearts as a deposit, guaranteeing what is to come."

When a person is in relationship with Christ Jesus all these things happen in our hearts. We're enabled to stand firmly; he marks us as his own and puts a portion of his own Spirit in our hearts.

That's similar to what happens on sport teams. We have coaches and teammates who enable us to stand firmly and to compete well. We wear uniforms that declare our allegiance to a team. We even begin to experience the best things of our sport during practices and early season games, each of them small deposits of what we trust will be postseason successes.

As you compete today, rest in the assurance that comes with being chosen for this team. You have and will continue to experience in your hearts the best parts of sport as you stand firmly with your teammates.

Bible Reading Plan:
Luke 23:1-12
Hebrews 8:7-13
Proverbs 25:1-14
Isaiah 37-39

September 14

SPORT

Proverbs 10:23

What do you do for sport? I know guys who go fishing for sport, some hunt for sport, and some play golf. What do you do? Sport is the active pursuit of pleasure and fulfillment.

In the book of Proverbs at chapter 10 and verse 23 we read, "Doing wickedness is like sport to a fool; and so is wisdom to a man of understanding."

How could doing wickedness be like a sport? Have you known any fools? Lots of people I know seem to find great pleasure and fulfillment in activities that leave them with hangovers and social diseases. They brag about doing foolish things in the same way you might boast about a career day of personal records and championships. Fools find pleasure and fulfillment in things that dishonor God and ruin their lives.

The powerful message of this verse is that living wisely is equally pleasurable and fulfilling to the person of wisdom. Doing things that honor God and serve others is like a sport to those who display wisdom. A life of wisdom is not boring and passive; rather it's full of power, activity and adventure, like a sport!

As you pray today, ask God to make you a person of wisdom and to make your life rich with pleasure and fulfillment.

Bible Reading Plan:
Luke 23:13-25
Hebrews 9:1-10
Proverbs 25:15-28
Isaiah 40-41

September 15

HONOR

Romans 12:10

What sort of person would be worthy of honor if he/she walked into this room right now? A Hall of Fame player or coach? The President? The Pope? How much do you honor your teammates? How devoted are you to your team?

Paul writes about this idea to his friends in Rome at chapter 12 and verse 10, "Be devoted to one another in brotherly love. Honor one another above yourselves." Paul challenged his friends with these words and I will do similarly today.

Here we're challenged to be devoted to our teammates like we're family. Further, we're challenged to honor each other above ourselves. Let's give the same level of honor to our teammates that we would to people of position and authority. Let's sacrifice our preferences for the greater good of the team, the family.

In today's competition, devotion and preferential honor will lead to a great performance by our team.

Bible Reading Plan:
Hebrews 9:11-28
Proverbs 26:1-16
Isaiah 42-43

September 16

COMMITMENT

John 2:24-25

With whom are you more likely to spend some time in conversation after a hard fought game, the first-time spectator or the friends and family who have invested years of life and love into your career? Seem like a silly question? Many athletes act like they don't know the answer.

Jesus knew very well how to answer and in John chapter 2 at verses 24 and 25 we hear how He sees people. "But Jesus did not commit Himself to them, because He knew all men, and had no need that anyone should testify of man, for He knew what was in man."

This simply means that Jesus stayed aloof from the uncommitted and shallow. He would not commit Himself to those who just wanted a show. He wouldn't give the same time to the first-time ticket buyer at a game as He would those among the family who had committed themselves long ago.

It should be the same with us. Don't commit yourself to the first clown to come around wearing your team's colors and screaming at ball games. Be a little discerning. Look around to see who is paying the dues of commitment, investing the years, driving the miles and shedding the tears for your life. Those are the ones in whom you can deeply trust and to whom you'd be wise to commit your own life.

Make some commitments on the field of competition today. Invest in your team, your coaches and your family.

Bible Reading Plan:
Luke 23:32-37
Proverbs 26:17-28
Isaiah 44-45

September 17

INFLUENCE

I Corinthians 3:6

Who has been the strongest influence on your athletic career? Has there been more than one person who has made a significant impact in making you the player you've become? Today's scripture speaks about compounded influence.

In Paul's first letter to his friends in Corinth at chapter 3 and verse 6, he writes, "I planted the seed, Apollos watered it, but God made it grow." Paul wrote in farming terms, we'll talk in athletic language.

Growing an athlete is like farming. In the growth process of a crop, there's the obvious collaboration between those who plant, cultivate, irrigate and harvest. In athletics it's equally true. In the growing of a champion, we see the compounding influences of parents, high school coaches, coaches from camps, teammates, opponents, college coaches and so on.

This is also true in the building of one's character spiritually. Parents, teachers, pastors, priests and friends all walk beside us on the way to a rich life in Christ.

Let's honor our eternal architect in this day's competition. Let's make each of our mentors and contributors proud through a great performance and outstanding character.

Bible Reading Plan:
Luke 23:38-43
Hebrews 10:19-39
Proverbs 27:1-14
Isaiah 46-48

September 18

INTIMIDATION

Deuteronomy 28:10

Have you ever seen an athlete compete who seemed to be completely in his or her own league? No one else in the game seemed to be 1/2 the player in comparison. That happens at times on the field of competition, but sometimes it's not just about athletic abilities. Sometimes we meet a person like Moses writes about.

In Moses' book called Deuteronomy at chapter 28 and verse 10 it says, "Then all the peoples on the earth will see that you are called by the name of the Lord, and they will fear you." Moses knew that when these people honored God by their obedient attitudes and actions, they would be honored by God.

It's God's way to have people who honor Him to be noticed and revered by those around them. In some cases the identification with God's name even causes fear in people. Don't be surprised if your team is now intimidating to some of your opponents... that's what Moses said would happen.

Compete with confidence and power. You may even see some people being awestruck by the way your team plays. Play with great heart and let the world watch in amazement!

Bible Reading Plan:
Luke 23:44-49
Hebrews 11:1-16
Proverbs 27:15-27
Isaiah 49-50

September 19

ANXIETY

Proverbs 12:23

As we approach competition, anxiety and worry often burden us. I'm sure you wonder how you'll perform, how good your opponents are, how well we know the game plan and more. While these are legitimate concerns, they can serve to hinder our performance as athletes.

In Proverbs chapter 12 and verse 23 we read, "An anxious heart weighs a man down, but a kind word cheers him up."

Anxiety seems to coat our hearts with lead and turns our legs to limp spaghetti. Suddenly, doubt, confusion and frustration weigh us down. All these lead to a performance on the court that's far less than our best.

There is also a great promise in this verse. It says that a kind word cheers one up. Encouragement is a powerful tool for the athlete. A simple word, a kind expression, a well-timed compliment can put a charge into a teammate or a coach, thus lifting the weight he'd been carrying.

As you pray and prepare tonight, ask the Lord to help you see just the right moment to encourage your teammate who's being assaulted by frustration, doubt or discouragement. Your kind word could cheer him up and make a great difference in the competition.

Bible Reading Plan:
Luke 23:50-56
Hebrews 11:17-31
Proverbs 28:1-14
Isaiah 51-53

September 20

LEGACY

II Corinthians 3:2-3

Who are the coaches and players in your team's history that are still impacting your lives today? Take a moment to recall their names, their faces, their unique gifts and abilities. They are a heritage for you, like a letter written to each of you to challenge and to encourage.

The Apostle Paul wrote these words in his second letter to his friends in Corinth, Greece at chapter 3 and verses 2 and 3, "You yourselves are our letter, written on our hearts, known and read by everybody. You show that you are a letter from Christ, the result of our ministry, written not with ink but with the Spirit of the living God, not on tablets of stone but on tablets of human hearts." Paul's friends were the living evidence of his passion for people and his love for God. It's similar for us.

Players are the evidence of a coach's skill, passion and commitment. They are the coach's legacy, like a letter written on human hearts and bearing his/her signature. Coaches love to tell the stories of their favorite players from the past. They are letters known and read by everybody. The players who come through this program behind you will be your legacy. Your lives, your commitment to sport, the stories shared about you will be a letter written to them. It's up to each of us to determine the content of that letter.

The stationery for these letters is most remarkable. It's far more durable than paper or even granite, it's written on the hearts of players and coaches. Their hearts are immortal and will permanently carry the legacy we leave with them.

As you prepare to compete today, I pray that this passage will encourage you to write the best lines of your legacy on the field of competition.

Bible Reading Plan:
Luke 24:1-12

September 21

LITTLE FAITH

Matthew 8:26

Of what are you sometimes afraid? Are there some things that bring you fear and rob you of courage? Jesus' friends also had some fears.

In Matthew's gospel at chapter 8 and verse 26 he records the words of Jesus, "You of little faith, why are you so afraid?"

He said this to his disciples as they were on a boat in the middle of the sea, being tossed around by the wind in a furious storm. The answer seems obvious, "We're about to drown here!" Jesus seems to be looking deeper, though.

He points to their lack of faith as the source of their fear. Faith is an active trust in someone. The disciples had a less than great trust in Jesus or they wouldn't have been so fearful of the storm.

In whom do you have an active trust? The disciples had a less than great trust in Jesus or they wouldn't have been so fearful of the storm. Who do you trust when your team is in turmoil and nothing is working?

Continue to build your trust for your coaches and for your teammates. They're committed to you. Even more so, build your trust for the Lord Jesus. He will care for you on your worst day when you're overcome with fear. Actively trust the Lord with today's competition. He's worthy of your faith.

Bible Reading Plan:
Luke 24:13-27
Hebrews 12:1-13
Proverbs 19:1-14
Isaiah 56-58

September 22

ATTITUDES

I Peter 5:5-6

How would you describe the attitudes on your team as the youngest players relate to the eldest and to the coaching staff? Are they respectful and honorable or arrogant and rebellious? What value does humility have among you?

Peter wrote about these dynamics in his first letter at chapter 5 and verses 5 and 6, "Likewise you younger people, submit yourselves to your elders. Yes, all of you be submissive to one another and be clothed with humility, for 'God resists the proud, but gives grace to the humble.' Therefore humble yourselves under the mighty hand of God that He may exalt you in due time."

It's very common for a young, talented player to come into a program with intentions to take over and to be the leader from day one. The problem with that is obvious. That player often discounts the years of investment made by the veteran players. That kind of arrogance can cause the team's total collapse.

A healthier attitude is for the younger teammates to keep themselves in respectful relationship to the veterans and to let their play win them the playing time and the positions to which they aspire. Remember, "God resists the proud, but gives grace to the humble."

Make this a day of great competition. Compete with humility and grace. Ask God to put down any arrogance or prideful attitudes in your heart and to replace them with the grace and wisdom that leads to great teamwork.

Bible Reading Plan:
Luke 24:28-35
Hebrews 12:14-29
Proverbs 29:15-27
Isaiah 59-61

September 23

GIFTS

What would it be like to be a record holder in your sport, right at the top of your game, only to watch someone else come along and immediately break all your records with apparent ease? John the Baptist experienced just such a dynamic, but with a lot more poise than most of us could manage.

We read about it in John chapter 3 and verse 27, "John answered and said, 'A man can receive nothing unless it has been given to him from heaven.'"

You may say, "But I earned every point I've scored." You certainly have, but John knew that the real stuff of life, the things that have the greatest value are gifts from God in heaven.

In John's case, he is the first man in 400 years to speak with authority from God. That's impressive, but along comes his younger cousin and immediately eclipses his whole life. As the people who watched expected jealousy, John exhibited joy and acknowledged God as the giver of every good gift.

Your gifts are much the same. Much of the grace given to you is nothing you could ever earn. It's a gift, not a merit badge. The ability to play and the opportunity to compete is a gift to be treasured and for which to be thankful.

As you approach today's competition, appreciate such gifts, revel in them, and enjoy them to the fullest with a grateful heart.

Bible Reading Plan:
Luke 24:36-44
Hebrews 13:1-8
Proverbs 30
Isaiah 62-64

September 24

FOCUS

Philippians 3:13

Every athlete I've ever known needed a powerful focus upon his goals in order to achieve his highest performance. How do we appropriate our faith in Christ toward our life as athletes? Today's Scripture speaks of these ideas.

In Paul's letter to the Philippians at chapter 3 and verse 13 it says, "But one thing I do: Forgetting what is behind and straining toward what is ahead, I press on toward the goal to win the prize for which God has called me heavenward in Christ Jesus." This is a dynamic principal about the pursuit of goals.

It's obviously hard to focus on your goals as a person or a team if your constantly looking backward. That's why he says he forgets what is behind. Let go of the things that have hurt you in the past. Forgive the people and forget the hurts. Don't focus too much on your past successes either. We can't be successful if we answer today's problems with yesterday's solutions.

He said to strain toward what's ahead. The short term objectives that we set should be in line with our ultimate goal and should be kept fully in sight. You can't play a whole season of games in one day, but you can work to win the one game you have to play today. The short term objective is immediately ahead of you on the road to achieving your ultimate goals.

He also said to press on toward the goal. You have a great opportunity to do that today. Focus clearly on the goals you've established as a team and pursue them with great vigor. Do as he said and strain toward what is ahead. A clear vision of your team goals will add to team unity, teamwork, success and even increase the fun in playing. Press on toward the goal!

Bible Reading Plan:
Luke 24:45-53
Hebrews 13:9-25

September 25

FAVOR

Do you enjoy a good relationship with your coaches? Do you have favor with them or do they seem to be angry with you a lot? We read about some probable causes for both cases in the Bible.

In the book of Proverbs at chapter 14 and verse 35 it says, "The king's favor is toward a servant who acts wisely, but his anger is toward him who acts shamefully." Don't let the king and servant language throw you, just think coach and athlete.

One good reason for a coach to favor a player is that he's acting wisely. That player is working hard, responding to correction, being respectful, and working with his teammates, in short acting with wisdom. This kind of behavior often results in a player having favor with his coach or teacher or supervisor.

One good reason for a coach to be angry with a player is that he's acting shamefully. This person seems to do all the things that displease the coach. No wonder he's angry! Players who skip class, break curfew, engage in foolish activities and disrespect their coaches and teammates are acting shamefully. They deserve and get their coach's anger.

As you prepare for competition in prayer today, ask the Lord for favor with your coaching staff. Ask Him to lead you to act wisely, not shamefully.

Bible Reading Plan:
Luke 21:29-38
Hebrews 4:1-11

September 26

THREE GREAT ATTITUDES

Romans 12:12

Some arenas have an atmosphere in which it seems almost impossible for visiting teams to win. This is a tough place to play for every team that comes in here. Let's talk about some attitudes that overcome atmospheres.

In Paul's letter to the Romans at chapter 12 and verse 12 he writes, "Be joyful in hope, patient in affliction, faithful in prayer." Here we have three attitudes; joy, patience and faithfulness that work in three atmospheres; hope, affliction and prayer.

Here's how this works for us today:

A joyful attitude helps you press on while waiting for the things hoped for.

Patience helps you endure afflictions like muscle pulls, sprained ankles and such.

Faithfulness in prayer provides confidence and assurance in any atmosphere.

Let these three attitudes: joy, patience and faithfulness lead you into greatness in today's competition.

Bible Reading Plan:
Proverbs 21:17-31
Isaiah 21-23

September 27

REVELATION

Matthew 11:25

Are there things to be learned by playing sports that cannot be learned through books, seminars and lectures? I think so.

In Matthew's gospel at chapter 11 and verse 25 we read, "I praise you Father, Lord of heaven and earth, because you have hidden these things from the wise and learned, and revealed them to little children."

Could you as athletes, playing little children's games, be privy to knowledge that escapes those in the philosophy department? Yes!! You know things about discipline, determination, teamwork and loyalty that can only be learned through competition. The great thing is that those concepts are revealed to us from above. Our Lord uncovers truth for us to observe and to grasp, then to implement in the life of our team.

Play today with great confidence, knowing that you're among the highly privileged people of sport. God has chosen to reveal things to you that most other people will never discover.

Bible Reading Plan:
Luke 22:39-46
Hebrews 7:1-10

September 28

SUFFERING

I Peter 4:12

When have you most recently suffered as a result of competition? Was that suffering physical, emotional or mental in nature? Did it seem like you were alone in your suffering? That's a very common feeling, but I have good news for those in the midst of trials.

Peter wrote to his friends who were themselves undergoing intense suffering at chapter 4 and verse 12 of his first letter, "Beloved, do not think it strange concerning the fiery trial which is to try you, as though some strange thing happened to you..." Peter calls his friends to be mindful that they're in good company when they suffer.

In the middle of suffering, whether from an injury or a disappointing loss, there is often a profound loneliness that comes to us. We feel alienated when injury or illness sends us to the sideline and we're unable to contribute to the team as we're accustomed. The whole situation seems very strange.

Peter's encouragement is that we are not the victims of some strange misfortune. He says that these trials can even make us better than we were. What's more, if we'll listen closely, we can sense the Lord Jesus right there with us in the middle of the trial and working for our good. We can have the assurance of his presence as we suffer any misfortune.

Play this day's game with courage and great passion. Play with full confidence in the Lord's presence and His great love for you.

Bible Reading Plan:
Proverbs 24:1-22
Isaiah 34-36

September 29

HUMILITY

John 3:30

What does true humility look like? Is it that, "Aw, shucks, it weren't nothing," kick the dirt with your head down and slumping shoulders look? Maybe it's the quiet, "Thank you," when you've been complimented. Maybe it's something even greater.

In John's Gospel at chapter 3 and verse 30 we read, "He must increase, but I must decrease." These are the words of John the Baptist as his younger cousin, Jesus of Nazareth, is being criticized.

Please bear in mind that this man, John, is the first one in 400 years to do the job he's doing. HE'S THE MAN!! There's nobody else in his league. Up comes Jesus and John immediately deflects the praise and honor to Him. Even more, he says that Jesus must increase and John must decrease.

This is true humility. John knew who was greater, it was Jesus. He knew that Jesus was God and thus gave Him the respect and honor He was due.

A similar dynamic works on good teams. We all know who the most talented players are and who is best to have the ball in the most crucial moments. Let's defer to them like John did to Jesus. For the good of the team, let's give proper respect and honor to our teammates. In exercising proper humility, we will find ourselves to be winners of another sort, the godly sort. Have a great game today.

Bible Reading Plan:
Luke 23:26-31
Hebrews 10:1-18

September 30

WORRY

Philippians 4:6

What are the keys to overcoming anxiety and worry? What can we do that will lead to an active trust in God? How can we approach the Lord and overcome our fears? The Bible verse for today answers these questions.

In Paul's letter to his friends in Phillipi at chapter 4 and verse 6 he says, "Be anxious for nothing, but in everything by prayer and supplication with thanksgiving let your requests be made known to God." Today, don't be overcome by the anxiety that sometimes accompanies a big game, rather take your needs and concerns to God in prayer.

God knows just what you need, He just likes to talk with you. That's what the Lord wants in prayer, a relationship with the people He loves.

As you prepare for today's competition, be confident that the Lord is hearing your prayers and He is working out the best for you. You can be confident in praying for the Lord's purposes to be accomplished in your life. Pray with thanksgiving in your heart and bring the Lord of love your requests.

Bible Reading Plan:
John 1:1-18
James 1:1-11
Ecclesiastes 1
Jeremiah 1-2

October 1

HUMILITY

Proverbs 15:33

Everyone likes to win awards, especially things like championship medals and trophies. It's easy to assume that the person who wins such awards is just lucky or got a break of some sort. However the Bible tells plainly how these things tend to work.

In Proverbs chapter 15 and verse 33, Solomon writes, "The fear of the Lord teaches a man wisdom, and humility comes before honor."

Not everyone who wins awards is serving God, but many are living by this proverb's principles. Most who win these awards have spent hours, months and years in practice and working on their skills. Many spend years toiling in obscurity, out of the spotlight, then all of a sudden... Champion!! They worked in humility for a long time and were rewarded with honor.

Ultimately the best honor springs from humility. That humility is born of a relationship with Christ Jesus. That is what he means when he says "The fear of the Lord."

As you prepare for today's competition, pray and ask God to honor your years of hard work and humility. Watch for him to teach you wisdom and wait patiently for the honors to roll down.

Bible Reading Plan:
John 1:19-28
James 1:12-18
Ecclesiastes 2:1-16
Jeremiah 3-4

October 2

A DAILY DEBT

Romans 13:8

How many bills have you had come due this week? I've had my share too. Today, I want us to think about a debt that is always due.

As Paul the Apostle wrote to his dear friends in Rome, at chapter 13 and verse 8, he said, "Let no debt remain outstanding, except the continuing debt to love one another, for he who loves his fellow-man has fulfilled the law." It seems the one debt that is always due is our obligation to love people.

We'll always have bills to pay, the grocery bill, utility bills, car payments, etc... This is a debt we can't pay with money; it costs us our blood, sweat and tears.

Our daily debt to our team is paid in our best effort, its payable in today's competition. Our daily debt to our families, friends and team is to love sacrificially, it's payable today. It's always due. Make your payment on the field of competition today.

Bible Reading Plan:
James 1:19-27
Ecclesiastes 2:17-26
Jeremiah 5-6

October 3

SOUL FOOD

John 4:32

We all know that we need to eat well for our bodies to perform well on the field of competition. How many of us know what feeds our souls well? What keeps your soul from starvation and running strongly? Jesus knew about soul food.

In the Gospel of John at chapter 4 and verse 32 we read, "But He said to them, 'I have food to eat of which you do not know.'"

Jesus' disciples were thinking with their stomachs, but Jesus knew how to feed His soul with something even better than pizza. He knew that doing what God wants for us is even more satisfying than your favorite meal at home. That's the food the others didn't know about.

In your life, don't simply feed your stomach and let your soul shrivel up from starvation. Feed it with rich relationships, with sweet music and literature. Dine on satisfying study and wash it all down with generous floods of prayer. This diet will satisfy your soul and will endure long after you're dreaming about a milkshake from the Dairy Queen.

Have a great game today, and then celebrate with food for the body and the soul.

Bible Reading Plan:
John 1:35-42
James 2:1-13
Ecclesiastes 3:1-15
Jeremiah 7-9

October 4

DISCIPLINE AND KNOWLEDGE

Proverbs 23:12

What are the keys to success as an athlete? What brings about the best life for us as Christians? It seems that these ideas overlap a great deal.

In Proverbs chapter 23 and at verse 12 it says, "Apply your heart to discipline and your ears to words of knowledge." As you press through your season of competition it is imperative that you apply your heart to discipline.

The first part means you must involve your mind, your will, even your emotions in a life of disciple or self-control. It's easy to let your imagination and your emotions get out of control and to thus see your hard work go to waste.

It says to apply our ears to words of knowledge. That's what the coaching staff is for. Apply your ears to those who have invested years in learning their craft. Listen to the words of wisdom that come from your coaches, teachers, parents, ministers, teammates and others.

Lives lived with discipline and knowledge are of great worth and lead to profound success. In today's competition, apply your heart to the discipline of your game with all your heart, soul and mind. Pursue the goals you have set as an individual and as a team. Apply your ears to working out the wise game plan as outlined by your coaches.

Bible Reading Plan:
John 1:43-51
Ecclesiastes 3:16-22
Jeremiah 10-11

October 5

SOUL FOOD

John 4:34

What is most pleasing to your soul? Setting a new personal record? Maybe it's a new scoring record? Perhaps a solid friendship is most pleasing? Beautiful music? Today, we'll see what was pleasing to Jesus' soul.

In John chapter 4 and verse 34 we read, "Jesus said to them, 'My food is to do the will of Him who sent me, and to finish His work.'"

Jesus says that doing God's will and finishing His life's work is more satisfying to Him than the biggest steak dinner. Pleasing His Father in heaven was what fed his soul.

Think about it:

Food for your body will only satisfy you for a short time, and soon you'll be hungry again.

Soul food like Jesus mentions will last for years.

Pleasing God with all of your life yields satisfaction that endures throughout eternity.

Step up to the Soul Food Cafeteria line and satisfy your heart's deepest longings. Take as much as you like, the bill has been paid. Jesus is picking up the check.

As you play today, invest your soul, your mind and your body in this season's best endeavor. Playing with your best effort will encourage your teammates and will feed your soul.

Bible Reading Plan:
John 2:1-11
James 3:1-12
Ecclesiastes 4
Jeremiah 12-13

October 6

GIFTS

I Peter 4:10

Which of your athletic gifts is most important to you as a competitor? Is it strength, speed, hand-eye coordination, your competitive nature? Who is the giver of that gift? What would be a proper response to your benefactor?

Peter mentions giftedness in his first letter at chapter 4 and verse 10 where we read, "As each one has received a gift, serve one another as good stewards of the manifold grace of God." How do we thank the giver of our gifts, by serving our teammates.

Peter takes it as a given that each one of us is gifted. Probably no group on the planet understands this like an athletic team. The issue for us is not whether or not we're gifted, but who gives the gifts and how shall we respond to him?

Our gifts are described as being part of the manifold grace of God. In other words, God's grace has been parceled out to each one of us in a unique way. Our best response to a gracious giver is to employ our giftedness in the service of those around us.

As you compete today, drain every drop of benefit from your gifts for the good of your team. Be a great steward of God's grace as you serve your teammates in the pursuit of a great victory.

Bible Reading Plan:
John 2:12-25
James 3:13-18
Ecclesiastes 5
Jeremiah 14-15

October 7

PLANNING

Proverbs 16:3

What are the keys to seeing your goals achieved? How would one go about the pursuit of athletic achievement? I have some ideas.

In Proverbs chapter 16 at verse 3 it says, "Commit to the Lord whatever you do, and your plans will succeed."

How does one commit to the Lord everything that he does? Simply put, that would be to approach all of life's activities and pursuits with prayer and attention to doing things God's way. Commit all of your life to pursuing God's will and His ways in class, in practice, in competition, in family life, in coaching, in all of life. Commit it all to Him.

The promise is that when we do this, He works in us to see that our plans succeed. That assumes that you have a plan. Make a plan that will honor God, and then commit everything about yourself to Him. The Lord is faithful and His promise is that He'll work to see our plans succeed.

Pray and prepare for a great performance today... you can do it!!!

Bible Reading Plan:
John 3:1-15
James 4:1-10
Jeremiah 16-18

October 8

TEAMWORK

Romans 14:19

Sometimes keeping the peace and building teamwork is easy, sometimes though it requires great effort. Today's scripture speaks of this dynamic in the life of a team.

Paul's letter to his friends in Rome reads like this at chapter 14 and verse 19, "Let us therefore make every effort to do what leads to peace and to mutual edification." Paul calls his friends to make every effort to improve their teamwork.

There are lots of things that fight against a team's peace and work to destroy their teamwork. In these times we must make every effort to promote peace (harmony in relationships) and mutual edification (building each other up).

In today's competition, make every effort to promote peace on the team. Let's also give our best to each other in building up our teammates in a day of greatness.

Bible Reading Plan:
John 3:16-21
James 4:11-17
Ecclesiastes 7:1-14
Jeremiah 19-22

October 9

GREAT COACHING

John 21:17

What is the hallmark of a truly great coach? What characterizes the best of team leaders? They deeply love their teammates and pay the price to seek their best.

In John chapter 21 and verse 17 we can read what Jesus says to His teammates related to leadership. It says, "He said to him the third time, 'Simon, son of Jonah, do you love Me?' Peter was grieved because He said to him the third time, 'Do you love Me?' And he said to Him, 'Lord, You know all things; You know that I love You.' Jesus said to him, 'Feed My sheep.'"

Jesus simply tells Peter that to love Him is to nourish and care for those that He cares for. It's that simple.

It's similar for us on this team. Do you love your coaches and teammates? Then the thing to do is to nurture the people on your team. To develop the younger players is the most appropriate thing the veteran players can do. To lead them well is to seek their best, even at personal cost.

On a deeper level, do you love Jesus? If so, do the same. Seek the best things in life for your teammates and coaches. Appropriate the Lord's love for you in loving others. Compete like this and we'll all sense the Lord's love in you.

Bible Reading Plan:
John 3:22-36
James 5:1-6
Ecclesiastes 7:15-29
Jeremiah 23-25

October 10

INJURY

I Peter 4:1

Who has more confidence about recovery from injury, the one who's never been hurt or the player who has come through the pain and has found renewed strength? If the answer seems obvious, you may have never been injured. Suffering is tough, even after recovery.

Peter makes mention of suffering and its results in his first letter at chapter 4 and verse 1, "Therefore since Christ suffered for us in the flesh, arm yourselves also with the same mind, for he who has suffered in the flesh has ceased from sin..." He's not saying that after we've suffered that we're somehow exempt from making moral mistakes, rather suffering changes our mind-set and leads us to live for more than physical gratification.

Before we've suffered any significant injury, many of us play a little tentatively in dangerous situations. There is a latent fear that if we risk a possible injury, we can never recover or play the same again.

However, in the player who has suffered and recovered, that indecision and fear is overcome by the assurance that even if this daring play leads to pain, he can come through it to compete even more strongly.

As you compete today, play with strength, courage and daring. Don't be intimidated by the potential injury that you may imagine could wreck your playing career. Those of you who have come through injury, who have suffered in the flesh, loan some courage to your teammates and play with great passion.

Bible Reading Plan:
John 4:1-14
James 5:7-12
Ecclesiastes 8

October 11

DIRECTION

Proverbs 16:9

Have you ever wondered why your path through life has zigzagged sometimes? Does it seem that your path to a championship has been sidetracked? How did I wind up here? Lots of athletes ask those kinds of questions in their pursuit of excellence.

In Proverbs chapter 16 and verse 9 we read, "In his heart a man plans his course, but the Lord determines his steps."

Every athlete I know sometimes lies on his bed and dreams about what he'd like to achieve, the awards that he'd like to win, the career that he'd like to pursue. In his mind he plans his way.

But somewhere along the way to those dreams becoming reality, he gets sidetracked and before long he's not sure how he got here. Here's the comforting word in this verse. It's the Lord's way to direct our steps along the way to fulfilling His purposes in our lives. The Lord can see very clearly the best path for us and everything we need in preparation for our ultimate place of serving Him.

It's good to make our plans, but it the Lord's place to direct our steps along the way.

You've made your plans... a championship. Now pursue it with all you have and don't be frustrated if that wanders through a long stretch of practices, injuries and disappointments. Compete greatly today!

Bible Reading Plan:
James 5:13-20
Ecclesiastes 9
Jeremiah 30-31

October 12

GLORY

Romans 8:18

Some people say that difficult times develop character. However, I believe that hard times reveal the character that's already in a person or in a team.

In Romans chapter 8 and verse 18, the Apostle Paul writes to his friends, "I consider that our present sufferings are not worth comparing with the glory that will be revealed in us." In times of suffering we have a strong assurance that better things are on the way.

Paul seems to say that the overwhelming greatness of the good to come far surpasses our present, momentary suffering. Take that kind of attitude when you're competing and your legs ache. Think that way when you've been in the training room all week recovering from the last game. When anything assaults your attitude and tempts you to quit or to simply give up, focus your mind on the glory that awaits the completion of the task and the attaining of the goal.

When you pray, ask for the power to press through the suffering and into the glorious reward of achievement.

Bible Reading Plan:
John 4:27-42
Ecclesiastes 10
Jeremiah32-34

October 13

THE IDEAL TEAMMATE

I John 3:16

Who is your model for the ideal teammate? What does he/she do that makes him/her such a great teammate? For me, that person is Jesus Christ. Let's consider him as a model today.

In John's first letter at chapter 3 and verse 16, we read, "By this we know love, because He laid down His life for us. And we also ought to lay down our lives for the brethren."

That's what a great teammate looks like, one who lays his life down for the others! Certainly we can see that vividly in the life of Jesus. He died a real death in our places.

How can we, in less drastic and bloody ways, lay down our lives for our teammates? Think about it. We do this when we give up playing time to help develop younger players. We do it when we sacrifice personal records or accomplishments for the good of the team. We do it when we change positions to fill a weakness that has appeared due to an injury or illness. A great teammate is one who lays down his life for his friends.

As you compete today, lay down your life for your team. Give your 100% best effort throughout the competition. Sacrifice your personal goals for those of the team and you'll be a teammate like the Lord Jesus.

Bible Reading Plan:
John 4:43-54
I Peter 1:10-16
Jeremiah 35-38

October 14

HEALING

John 5:8-9

When do you sense the real healing in a once injured knee, in the training room or while chasing a loose ball? When does the confidence return, while looking at an x-ray or after making the difficult cut toward the basket? I think you know. So did Jesus.

In John's Gospel at chapter 5 and verses 8 and 9 we read, "Jesus said to him, 'Rise, take up your bed and walk.' And immediately the man was made well, took up his bed, and walked."

This man had been afflicted with his infirmity for 38 years! Along comes Jesus and he says to get up. Say what!? He's been lying here for 38 years!

I wonder when his healing took place...while lying on the mat or when he made the effort to stand and walk? I believe the latter. That's why Jesus said what He did. It's always a heart-check when we hear someone give us a command to do the seemingly impossible. Do we trust or do we not?

In today's game you must trust the Lord and your coaching staff when they say, "Rise, take up your sport, and compete like a champion." Whether you feel like one or not, you're called to make the play. That's my challenge to you as well. Play like a champion today!

Bible Reading Plan:
John 5:15-26
I Peter 1:17-25
Ecclesiastes 12

October 15

PATIENCE

Proverbs 16:32

How well do you control your emotions during competition? Do you get easily distracted or do you stay under control? Might the Bible have anything to say about these matters?

Proverbs chapter 16 and verse 32 states, "Better a patient man than a warrior, a man who controls his temper than one who takes a city." Sometimes the greatest battles we fight take place between our ears.

It's often the struggle over who controls our minds and emotions that is the foremost factor in our success or failure. In this verse, patience and self-control are valued even more highly than physical strength or military power.

As you compete today, ask the Lord to enable you to master your mind and emotions. Ask Him to take control of them for His purposes. Compete with patience and in full control of your mental and emotional focus. As the proverb says, these qualities make us better than the mighty warrior and even stronger than the one who can overthrow a city. Compete like a champion today!

Bible Reading Plan:
John 5:16-30
I Peter 2:1-8
Song of Solomon 1
Jeremiah 44-46

October 16

SUFFERING

Romans 5:3

Somewhere in the course of every season, suffering and pain come along to meet us. Whether it's in the form of a losing streak, an injury, academic challenges or family tragedy, suffering is inevitable. What makes the difference in people is how one reacts to suffering.

In Paul's letter to his friends in Rome, at chapter 5 and verse 3, he writes, "Not only so, but we also rejoice in our sufferings because we know that suffering produces perseverance; perseverance, character; and character, hope. And hope does not disappoint us because God has poured out his love into our hearts by the Holy Spirit, whom He has given us."

If our lives are without suffering, we just skate along and remain unprepared for life's big crises to come. Paul says that suffering produces perseverance. The small aches and pains of life prepare us for dealing with the big hurts and teach us how to press through them in pursuit of excellence. Let's let suffering produce in us the desired result... perseverance. When we're possessed of that great quality, we can press through any difficulty and come out the other side as victors.

Bible Reading Plan:
John 5:31-47
I Peter 2:9-17
Song of Solomon 2
Jeremiah 47-48

October 17

AFFECTION

Who is your dearest friend? For whom do you care deeply, family, friends, teammates, coaches? What is the source of those affections? How durable are those relationships? The Scripture points to a source of love that will endure forever.

In Paul's letter to his friends in Philippi, at chapter 1 and verse 8 he says, "For God is my witness, how I long for you all with the affection of Christ Jesus." More than anything else, with these letters I want to communicate the love I have for you. I want you to know furthermore that the source of this love is my relationship with God. His love for you leads me to do the same.

There is a security and a power that comes from being loved. As I know with certainty that I'm loved by my wife, son, mom and dad, my friends and most importantly, loved by God; I'm free and empowered to love others also.

This same security and power is a great source for competition and all sorts of pursuits. In sports, business, family life, all the areas of life, you are free to love and to pursue excellence because you're loved and greatly valued.

Take that confidence onto the floor tonight. Play with passion, confidence, heart, power and perseverance because you're loved. If not by anyone else in the world, you're each loved by me. I'm for you in all of life.

Bible Reading Plan:
James 2:18-25
Song of Solomon 3
Jeremiah 49

October 18

TALK OR PLAY?

I John 3:18

Whom do you respect more, the player who talks a good game or the one who shows his game on the field of competition? I'm sure your answer would be the same as mine. Actions speak more loudly and clearly than any mouthy wannabe.

The Apostle John talks about this at chapter 3 and verse 18 of his first letter, there we read, "My little children, let us not love in word or in tongue, but in deed and in truth."

I'm sure we all get a little tired of the people who make themselves out to be experts in the game, but when questioned a little further, turn out to be novices at best. We've all known people who talk an "A" game, but can't play up to a low "D." Their sport experience is in word and tongue only.

We must be players who live in deed and in truth. A friend of mine is fond of saying, "Say less, do more." That should characterize our competition. Let's let our performance on the field of competition do our talking for us. That's how we compete in deed and in truth.

As you compete today, take seriously John's admonition to love in deed and in truth. Love your teammates and coaching staff by giving your best effort to secure a win. That will speak volumes about your game and your character.

Bible Reading Plan:
John 6:16-24
Song of Solomon 4:1-7
Jeremiah 50

October 19

LEADERSHIP

John 5:19

From whom have you taken instruction in the game? Certainly your coaches at each level of your sport have taught you well. Who else provides wise guidance? Who would have done this for Jesus? He tells us in today's letter.

In John chapter 5 at verse 19 we read, "Then Jesus answered and said to them, 'Most assuredly, I say to you, the Son can do nothing of Himself, but what He sees the Father do; for whatever He does, the Son also does in like manner.'"

There it is, Jesus' key to wise living. Do whatever your leader does. He saw what His heavenly Father would do and simply copied his actions.

In like manner, we can emulate the best models we've gathered from our coaches, teammates and opponents to bring about the best game of our lives. Remember the lessons of life and the game taught you through years of practices and hours of video study. Remember the models for great play, and then simply walk in the footsteps of those who have gone before you.

Bible Reading Plan:
John 6:25-40
I Peter 3:8-12
Jeremiah 51

October 20

CHARACTER

Romans 5:3-4

All of us have things in our lives that require perseverance. Whether it's suffering, pain from injuries, broken relationships or other pains; when we persevere through these things we find a great product. Character is the result of a life of perseverance.

The Apostle Paul writes to his friends in Rome at chapter 5 and verse 4, "Not only so, but we also rejoice in our sufferings because we know that suffering produces perseverance; perseverance, character; and character, hope. And hope does not disappoint us because God has poured out his love into our hearts by the Holy Spirit, whom He has given us."

Persevering through tough times is like a precious metal being refined by fire. The fire purifies the metal as impurities are liquefied and skimmed off. Perseverance removes the impurities, the excess baggage, the junk from our lives, producing character as its reward. Paul tells us that perseverance produces character. Persevere in today's competition and reap the reward of outstanding character.

Bible Reading Plan:
John 6:41-59
I Peter 3:13-22
Song of Solomon 5

October 21

MERCY

II Corinthians 4:1

What could happen during a practice or a competition that would cause you to lose heart? From where would you draw the power to press through such circumstances? In today's scripture we'll investigate a limitless source of power and courage for our hearts.

In the second letter to the Corinthian church at chapter 4 and verse 1, Paul wrote, "Therefore, since through God's mercy we have this ministry, we do not lose heart." In spite of some terribly harsh times, this man writes to his friends that his heart is not lost and that God's mercy has sustained his service of them.

The best source of perseverance in the world is the mercy of God. On our worst days, He does not give us what we deserve, He gives us the best. On our best days, it's still a matter of mercy that we receive the joys of life.

If we received what we deserve in relation to sport, most of us would be forever riding the bench. We'd be running for the next millennium to pay for our foolishness. Thankfully our coaches are merciful as well.

Since you have your position on this team as a result of God's mercy, and maybe your coach's as well, do not lose heart. Be encouraged that there must be a strong and vital role for you to fill with this team. Seek it and fulfill it with all your heart.

Bible Reading Plan:
John 6:60-71
I Peter 4:1-11
Song of Solomon 6
Lamentations 1

October 22

303

PEACE OF MIND

Philippians 4:7

How do you get your mind to calm down when worries and fear come your way? How do we trust God when everything we can see points to failure and despair? Take heart in the words of today's scripture verse.

In Paul's letter to his friends in Philippi he writes at chapter 4 and verse 7, "And the peace of God, which surpasses all comprehension shall guard your heart and mind in Christ Jesus."

Trust the Lord to continue to give you peace of mind and confidence of heart when you pray. Look to Him for what you need in all areas of your life.

Look to the Lord for wisdom in relationships, for knowledge in class, for abilities and courage in competition. He has everything we need to be people that honor Him.

Be assured that when we look to our Lord for these matters, we will be met with a peace that is far beyond what the human mind can comprehend. We will be carried along by the Lord's peace as a dove carries a flower.

The peace that the Lord gives serves to guard our hearts and our minds. It guards our hearts from pain and despair. It guards our minds from confusion and frustration.

As you pray today, rest in the peace of God and trust Him to guard your heart and mind through your relationship with Christ Jesus.

Bible Reading Plan:
John 7:1-13
I Peter 4:12-19
Song of Solomon 7
Lamentations 2

October 23

MIRACLES

John 5:20

What's the most miraculous thing you've ever seen on a basketball floor? A court-length desperation shot that went in? Maybe it was an incredibly athletic move by a player in the paint. Maybe it was a sacrificial act by a player to lead her team to an important victory. Jesus tells us why miracles happen in today's letter.

While talking with His disciples in John chapter 5 and verse 20 we read the words of Jesus, "For the Father loves the Son, and shows Him all the things that He Himself does; and He will show Him greater works than these that you may marvel."

Jesus did exactly what He saw His Father in heaven doing, and those were some miraculous things! Healing people, raising the dead, walking on water... that's not everyday stuff for people like you and me. The key is that those things came from their relationship. He says, "The Father loves the Son..."

The exciting thing to me is that the Father also loves me! That gives me confidence that He'll show me what He's doing and watch out! When I see that and act in like manner, some miraculous stuff is about to happen.

In today's competition, trust in the relationships you've developed on your team. See what your coaches and leaders are doing, and then join them in the excitement of great play. Some miraculous stuff happens when we join together in unified effort. Watch how people marvel when you play like champions!

Bible Reading Plan:
John 7:14-24
I Peter 5:1-7
Song of Solomon 8:1-7
Lamentations 3

October 24

TARNISHED TROPHIES

I Peter 1:3-4

Have you noticed the trophies in the school's trophy case which have been won over the past decades of competition? How is it that they so soon fade, tarnish and gather dust? Have they somehow lost their luster since the days of championships won? What kind of trophy would never grow old?

We read about such rewards in Peter's first letter to his friends at chapter 1 and verses 3-4. There it says, "Blessed be the God and Father of our Lord Jesus Christ, who according to His abundant mercy has begotten us again to a living hope through the resurrection from the dead, to an inheritance incorruptible and undefiled and that does not fade away, reserved in heaven for you."

Every medal, ribbon or trophy I've ever won has slowly faded, tarnished or been lost in the closet. How great an inheritance is ours through knowing God?! Here Peter says that this inheritance is incorruptible, that it will never decay. He also says that it's undefiled, that is it cannot be lessened by any outside force. He says that it will not fade away, like the ink on certificates does or the shine on a trophy does, or even like the memories of thrilling championships eventually do.

Best of all, the inheritance is kept for us in heaven. That's way more secure than anyone's trophy case! The security for our glorious inheritance is in God's hands. There is nowhere in the universe more secure for our treasures.

Play this day's game like there was an incorruptible, undefiled, never-to-fade trophy on the line and it's kept in heaven for you.

Bible Reading Plan:
John 7:25-36
I Peter 5:8-14
Song of Solomon 8:8-14

October 25

FOCUS

Philippians 3:13

Focus your mind for your best performance of the season. The Apostle Paul has some words from Scripture to help us do that.

In his letter to the Philippian church at chapter 3 and verse 13 he says, "But one thing I do: Forgetting what is behind and straining toward what is ahead, I press on toward the goal to win the prize for which God has called me heavenward in Christ Jesus."

Paul's first injunction is to forget what is in the past. That goes for both wins and losses. The great thing about having a post-season tournament is that even the last team to qualify has the same chance to be champion as the front runner. The team that just gets in can forget their whole season of challenges and make a three contest sprint for the title!

Forget the stuff of the past; team quarrels, ugly losses, easy victories, bad practices, all of it. Focus your mind on the present game to be played. Further, keep your attention forever on the next play, the next pitch, the next rebound. Be in the now and be a champion today.

Bible Reading Plan:
John 1:29-34
James 2:14-26

October 26

STRAIN

Philippians 3:13

Every competition involves strain. As we compete we strain our muscles, our minds and even our emotions. The following scripture contains even more encouragement for the pursuit of victory.

In his letter to the Philippian church at chapter 3 and verse 13 he says, "But one thing I do: Forgetting what is behind and straining toward what is ahead, I press on toward the goal to win the prize for which God has called me heavenward in Christ Jesus." Today we'll talk about straining toward what is ahead.

I believe he uses the word strain purposefully. Athletic achievement always involves strain. We strain to make the perfect shot, to run faster, to make a big play. It often involves strain to keep teammate relationships on the right track. It's sometimes a strain just to focus our minds enough to compete well.

The point is to strain toward what is ahead. Don't strain toward the past, it's over. Strain toward today's competition and the goal of being a champion. Strain toward doing the best to further your team and its goals. Make this the best game of your career. Strain like a champion today.

Bible Reading Plan:
Ecclesiastes 6
Jeremiah 26-29

October 27

GOALS

Philippians 3:13

The goal before you is the same with every contest: to win and to honor God in the process. Today, Paul has more words of challenge for you.

In his letter to the Philippian church at chapter 3 and verse 13 he says, "But one thing I do: Forgetting what is behind and straining toward what is ahead, I press on toward the goal to win the prize for which God has called me heavenward in Christ Jesus." Today we'll talk about pressing on toward the goal.

The goal is in sight. This day's win is at hand. Your part is to press on toward the goal of achieving it. Your opponent will not lie down and let you just walk off with it. You must win it.

Let's make it our task to press on toward that goal. Press on through momentary set backs. Press on through momentum swings. Press on through injuries. Press on through mental lapses. Press on through the excitement.... press on! You must compete right down to the final second with no thought of resignation. Give every ounce of courage and passion to today's game and you'll be a champion, regardless of the final score.

Bible Reading Plan:
John 4:15-26
I Peter 1:1-9

October 28

CHARACTER TESTS

I Peter 1:6

What do you find to be a trial while competing in your sport? What parts of your character are tried in that process? Does it test your will, your body, your attitudes, your emotions, maybe all the above? How deeply are you affected by those trials?

In Peter's first letter to his friends in what is now Turkey, at chapter 1 and verse 6 we read, "In this you greatly rejoice, though now for a little while, if need be, you have been grieved by various trials."

While we all find great enjoyment and fulfillment through playing the game, while many of us seemingly live for competition, the trying parts of the process often wear us down. The grief that comes with sore muscles, painful joints, disappointing losses and strained relationships are all trials for all of us.

We greatly rejoice in the best parts of our game, but we also, for a little while, may have to undergo plenty of grief through the more difficult parts of competition, practice, travel and study.

As you approach this day's competition, focus your mind on your favorite part of this game. Put the grief and the trying parts of it behind you. Keep clearly in view your team's goals and press on toward a great finish and a tremendous victory.

Bible Reading Plan:
Ecclesiastes 11
Jeremiah 39-43

October 29

TIMING

John 6:15

Have you ever heard your coaches talk about the rhythm of the game or not hitting your peak too soon in a season? How important is timing in the life of an athletic team? How important is it to life in general? We can see it in Jesus' life in today's letter.

In John's gospel at chapter 6 and verse 15 we read, "Therefore when Jesus perceived that they were about to come and take Him by force to make Him king, He departed again to a mountain by Himself alone."

How hard must it have been for Jesus to know that ultimately He would be the King of Israel, but this was not the proper time? How hard is it for a player who knows he will ultimately be a hall-of-famer to not act like the most arrogant person on the planet? It's hard, but important.

There is a rhythm to an athletic contest and even to a season. There are emotional peaks and valleys, swings of momentum and shifts of confidence from player to player and team to team. How we manage the timing of these swings of momentum and emotion are as critical as this day was for Jesus and His life.

Do all that you can to be at your absolute best at game time. Work hard to manage your emotions and focus your concentration in order to best contribute to a winning effort for your team today. That's exactly what Jesus would do.

Bible Reading Plan:
John 6:1-15
I Peter 3:1-7

October 30

RENEWAL

II Corinthians 4:16

When do you feel like your body is wasting away and your strength is drying up? Maybe that's at the end of practice, halfway through preseason or with one week to go in a long, difficult season. How can we have our hearts renewed and find the strength to press through such feelings? Today's scripture gives us such encouragement.

In the second letter to the church at Corinth at chapter 4 and verse 16 we read, "Therefore we do not lose heart. Though outwardly we are wasting away, yet inwardly we are being renewed day by day." Paul was aware of his friends' perilous times and the physical toll it was taking on them. He identified with their plight.

It's the nature of competition and long seasons to wear down our bodies. We can identify with these people and the outward wasting away of their bodies. The wisest among us also know how to be inwardly strengthened, day by day in our hearts.

Here's the challenge for us. Can we trust our hearts to lead us to do the right thing, even when our bodies are crying out for us to quit? Can we continue to find new strength through renewed hearts and press through the hard times?

As you prepare to compete today, trust your heart to the one who gives strength without measure. Ask Him to fill your heart with courage and to enable you to compete strongly. You will be amazed at how your mind and your body will respond to your heart's lead.

Bible Reading Plan:
Song of Solomon 4:8-16
Jeremiah 52

October 31

RENEWED POWER

John 5:21

How do we find power and renewed life for our bodies and emotions after the long months of a season? What can give us renewed vigor and an injection of energy? Jesus knows where this stuff comes from and He tells us today.

At John chapter 5 and verse 21 we hear His words, "For as the Father raises the dead and gives life to them, even so the Son gives life to whom He will."

While none of us are dead, technically, I'm sure some of us feel less than 100%. Who wouldn't like to have our legs restored to the way they were in pre-season? We could all use some resurrection of our energies for this championship game.

Here's the good news, Jesus says here that just like His Father in heaven can raise the dead, so can He. Let's trust Him to breathe life back into our tired lungs, to re-ignite the fire in our souls, to strengthen our formerly lifeless legs. If He can raise the dead, surely He can empower us to play this game with power, enthusiasm and passion. Let's go after this championship like we've just been raised from the dead. We'll show the crowd a life like they've never seen before!

Bible Reading Plan:
John 7:37-44
2 Peter 1:1-11
Job 1
Ezekiel 1-3

November 1

FINISHING

Philippians 1:6

Have you ever noticed how graduate students approach their papers, like a master's thesis? Even at the beginning of the program they know it must be done and it seems for some it's like giving birth to a baby....labor pains and all. We see a similar idea in Paul's letter to the Philippians.

In the letter to the church in a town called Philippi, at chapter 1 and verse 6 Paul writes, "...being confident of this, that he who began a good work in you will carry it on to completion until the day of Christ Jesus." Paul has confidence that his friends are in the process of being completed.

Like the master's degree student, God has a work to do and it began at your birth. His work continues in us until the day we die. The exciting thing to me is that He's faithful to complete everything He starts.

Bible Reading Plan:
John 7:45-53
II Peter 1:12-21
Job 2
Ezekiel 4-8

November 2

PREPARATION

I Peter 1:13

What kinds of things do you do in the process of preparing for competition? Surely you study film, practice, visualize your performance, warm up your muscles and more. We all know the value of physical preparation, but how important is it to prepare your mind?

Peter mentions this to his friends in his first letter at chapter 1 and verse 13, "Therefore prepare your minds for action, be self controlled and rest your hope fully upon the grace that is to be brought to you at the revelation of Jesus Christ."

Today we'll focus on the first part of that sentence. Prepare your minds for action. We'll think together about the three key words.

Prepare – At this level of play, one can no longer just show up and play. To succeed we will need to prepare. The good news is that by game day the preparation is done and we're ready.

Minds – There is more required than just physical preparation. We must be fully ready to compete, physically, mentally, emotionally and even spiritually. Come to competition 100% prepared and bring your brain with you.

Action – Even if your participation in this competition is rather doubtful, your team needs to have you fully engaged in it. Your teammates need your encouragement, your insight and your enthusiasm for them to compete at their best. Everyone must be ready for action, not half for action and the other half for passivity.

Let's prepare our minds for action and give this competition our best effort of the year.

Bible Reading Plan:
II Peter 2:1-9
Job 3

November 3

SELF-CONTROL

I Peter 1:13

What happens when one competes in an out-of-control way? That person commits foolish fouls, is assessed a technical foul, draws an unsportsmanlike conduct penalty or even gets disqualified. The value of competing under control is obvious and the penalty for not doing so is immediate. What value might self control have beyond competition?

Peter wrote to his friends about self control in his first letter at chapter 1 and verse 13 where we read, "Therefore prepare your minds for action, be self controlled and rest your hope fully upon the grace that is to be brought to you at the revelation of Jesus Christ."

After we have done the mental preparation for competition, we must exercise self control in order to execute the game plan and to play at an optimum level. If we lose control emotionally or lose our focus on the task at hand, we'll be distracted from the goal and failure will track us down.

In today's competition and throughout the season, prepare your minds for action and be self controlled. This will be the key to victory, on and off the field of competition.

Bible Reading Plan:
John 8:12-20
Job 4
Ezekiel 13-15

November 4

EXPECTATIONS

I Peter 1:13

Upon what are your confident expectations for this season and today's competition built? In whom or what do you fully place your hope for something? Are those people or things fully trustworthy?

Today's scripture tells us of someone who is completely worthy of our trust. Peter writes about this at chapter 1 and verse 13 of his first letter, "Therefore prepare your minds for action, be self controlled and rest your hope fully upon the grace that is to be brought to you at the revelation of Jesus Christ."

Our athletic hopes are usually resting upon the team's talent, the coaching staff's wisdom and insight, and the maturity and teamwork with which we compete. Those are sometimes very secure, but at other times less than reliable objects of our expectation. Things like injuries, illness, discouragement, staff transitions and even fear can tear at our hope for success.

A much more secure object of hope is the grace that we receive in Jesus. Trust the work that he's doing in you individually and collectively. Trust Him to do the very best in you everyday. He's 100% trustworthy and He will always work to bring about the best in you. As you pray in preparation to compete, ask the Lord to give you everything you need to fully contribute to your team's effort today. You can trust Him to be a consistent, faithful source of hope.

Bible Reading Plan:
John 8:21-30
II Peter 2:17-22
Ezekiel 16

November 5

PEACE

John 6:20-21

Who is the one person in your life that can calm the most fearful situation? Is it your mom or dad? Your best friend? Who is it? In today's letter we'll see who it was for the disciples of Christ.

John records this story in his gospel at chapter 6 and verses 20 and 21, "But He said to them, 'It is I; do not be afraid.' Then they willing received Him into the boat, and immediately the boat was at the land where it was going."

The disciples had been rowing across the Sea of Galilee for three or four hours, in the dark, against very strong winds when they see someone walking across the water toward their boat. They were scared to death... wouldn't you be? When they heard Jesus' voice and recognized Him, their fear disappeared, they gladly received Him and the situation was immediately resolved.

Jesus' presence calms fears. Just hearing His voice brought peace to a fearful situation. His presence in our lives will bring peace to us as well, if we will do as the disciples did. They heard His voice and then received Him to themselves.

Your teammates and coaches can likewise calm a chaotic situation or solve a thorny problem for your team. A calm question or a gentle word of encouragement can be as powerful as Jesus walking onto your storm-tossed boat. Receive the counsel and encouragement of your teammates and coaching staff in today's competition. They are keys to victory. Make this a day of greatness.

Bible Reading Plan:
John 8:31-47
II Peter 3:1-9
Job 6
Ezekiel 17-19

November 6

HALL OF FAME

Hebrews 12:1

What is the largest crowd before which you've competed? Was it nearer one hundred, one thousand or ten thousand? How did that crowd affect you? Were you inspired or intimidated by it? There's a similar picture in the pages of your Bible.

That picture is in Hebrews chapter 12 and verse 1 where it says, "Therefore we also, since we are surrounded by so great a cloud of witnesses, let us lay aside every weight, and the sin which so easily ensnares us, and let us run with endurance the race that is set before us." Can you see it? To me, this looks like a great stadium on the day of competition.

The great cloud of witnesses to which the writer refers is the Hall of Famers from the previous chapter. This stadium is filled with the great heroes of faith throughout history. The writer's intention is that such a crowd of spectators serve to inspire and to encourage us, the competitors in the race.

In a similar way, the great competitors that have preceded you in this game and at this institution should serve to inspire, to motivate and to encourage greatness in you. The crowd observing today's competition can be your greatest source of strength and inspiration. Let your vision of them be like the one we read above. See the seats as being full of Hall of Fame competitors and that each one of them is there to encourage and to cheer you on to success. Compete like Hall of Famers today.

Bible Reading Plan:
John 8:48-59
II Peter 3:10-18
Job 7

November 7

HINDRANCES

Hebrews 12:1

What is the single greatest hindrance to you as you compete? Is it a lack of concentration? Maybe it's a physical limitation? Could it be a nagging fear of failure? How can these things be overcome? Let's consider an idea from the Bible.

The writer of Hebrews had certainly seen the competitions of his day and he writes with reference to them in chapter 12 and verse 1, "Therefore we also, since we are surrounded by so great a cloud of witnesses, let us lay aside every weight, and the sin which so easily ensnares us, and let us run with endurance the race that is set before us."

The writer would have seen the athletes of the ancient world strip off all their clothes in order to compete unencumbered by the robes common to Greek culture. That's what he means when he says to lay aside every weight. He encourages us to lay aside the things which weigh us down as we compete.

For us, it's not usually clothes that weigh us down. More often it's a bad habit, a foolish attitude, a selfish lifestyle or an unhealthy relationship that hinders us as we compete. The solution to the hindrance is still the same, lay it aside.

You wouldn't dream of competing in a wet, heavy overcoat. So why be weighed down by other things which are equally detrimental to your personal and corporate goals? Lay it aside! You and your team will be better because of your good choices. Let that kind of selfless attitude characterize today's competition.

Bible Reading Plan:
John 9:1-12
I John 1:1-4
Job 8
Ezekiel 22-23

November 8

DISTRACTIONS

Hebrews 12:1

Do you remember watching Michael Johnson, the Olympic 200 and 400 meter gold medalist competing in oversized, baggy sweats with those big, fancy shoestrings and floppy socks? Of course not, that would be absurd! That stuff is too easily entangled with one's arms and legs. Rather you saw him in the most streamlined clothing and shoes that he could get. We can learn from such strategy.

Hebrews chapter 12 and verse 1 speaks of the same concept, "Therefore we also, since we are surrounded by so great a cloud of witnesses, let us lay aside every weight, and the sin which so easily ensnares us, and let us run with endurance the race that is set before us."

For the runner, he or she streamlines as much as possible so as to not become entangled and thus trip and fall. For us as competitors, on a deeper level, we must watch out for the things in our lives that could entangle or ensnare us. Sometimes we can become ensnared by foolish relationships or addictive behaviors and we can be tripped up by the things we wrap around our own lives.

In today's competition, run free from the things that would entangle or ensnare you. Lay aside those clumsy, useless things that would trip you up and keep you from being successful. Run freely and well like the champion you are.

Bible Reading Plan:
I John 1:5-10
Job 9:1-20
Ezekiel 24-26

November 9

ENDURANCE

Hebrews 12:1

How would you characterize your season of competition, more like a sprint or a marathon? Which one requires more perseverance, the ten second race or the two hour race? Those answers are obvious, but the keys to such perseverance and endurance are a little more elusive.

The letter to the Hebrews mentions such values in chapter 12 and verse 1, "Therefore we also, since we are surrounded by so great a cloud of witnesses, let us lay aside every weight, and the sin which so easily ensnares us, and let us run with endurance the race that is set before us."

I have a friend who is an 8 time winner of the Boston Marathon, in a wheelchair! Jean Driscoll knows what endurance is. To win that race requires going 26.2 miles in a wheelchair, in just over 1 and ? hours. That's fast and fast for a long time. That's what endurance looks like.

Your course is set before you this season, it's called a schedule. We can all see it, but can we all finish it with endurance? We certainly can if we'll heed the instructions from the earlier parts of the verse. We must keep our predecessors in mind for inspiration and encouragement. We must lay aside those things which weigh us down and ensnare our lives. Lastly, we must compete every day with the end of the season in mind. Let's compete for a championship and approach every day of practice and each competition like champions.

Bible Reading Plan:
John 9:26-41
Job 9:21-35
Ezekiel 27-28

November 10

PERSEVERANCE

James 1:12

Have you ever met someone who seems to glow with enthusiasm and zest for life? Have you ever talked with that person and asked from where that glow comes? In the Bible we are given a good idea about the source of life that comes with a crown.

In the apostle James' letter at chapter 1 and verse 12 he writes, "Blessed is a man who perseveres under trial; for once he has been proven he will receive the crown of life, which the Lord has promised to those who love Him." Most of us have experienced some kind of trial. Trials like sitting too many minutes on the bench, the death of a friend or family member, watching our parents' marriage crumble, or battling with cancer just to stay alive.

James says that when we persevere under trial we will receive something called the crown of life and it will make us blessed. To be blessed is to be contentedly happy, that would be nice, huh?

What might the crown of life look like? Have you ever seen anyone who has been through the fires of life and has come out the other side with grace and enthusiasm for life? You probably know someone who wears the crown of life every day. That same crown has been promised to us if we persevere under our trials.

Let's press on, through the hard times, through feeling unappreciated and under utilized, through broken relationships and physical pains. There is a crown waiting for us at the finish line. Press on toward the crown and toward being blessed of the Lord.

Bible Reading Plan:
John 10:1-10
I John 2:12-17

November 11

WISDOM

Proverbs 3:3-14

Do you have some precious metals at home in your jewelry box? How valuable are your rings, watches or necklaces? What could be worth more than silver, gold, or platinum?

In Proverbs chapter 3 and verses 13 and 14, Solomon (a very rich guy) tells about something with surpassing value, "Blessed is the man who finds wisdom, the man who gains understanding, for she is more profitable than silver and yields better returns than gold."

We would feel blessed if we had pounds of gold necklaces around our necks and looked like Mr. T. Solomon says a person is really blessed if he finds wisdom and gains understanding. To be blessed is to be contentedly happy with life. Silver and gold can't buy that.

Wisdom is something to be found. It won't sneak up on you. It takes pursuit and tenacity to find. Understanding is a commodity to be gained, like strength gained in the weight room. The exciting thing is that wisdom and understanding pay greater dividends and yield more benefits than silver and gold could ever do.

In preparing for today's competition, seek wisdom from every source available and gain understanding with every passing moment of the event. In the end, you'll be blessed with the greatest returns possible in athletic competition.

Bible Reading Plan:
John 10:11-21
I John 2:18-23
Job 11

November 12

HOPE

Romans 5:3-5

How does one maintain a good attitude in the midst of difficult times? How does one's character affect these situations? The character of a person, the true nature of his or her heart is a continual source of either hope or despair.

The Apostle Paul continues his letter to his friends in Rome with these words in Romans 5 and verses 3 through 5, "Not only so, but we also rejoice in our sufferings because we know that suffering produces perseverance; perseverance, character; and character, hope. And hope does not disappoint us because God has poured out his love into our hearts by the Holy Spirit, whom He has given us."

Hope is a confident expectation of good, based on the promises of God. That comes from a changed character that was born of persevering through suffering. Character has taught you to be confident and to have proper expectations. Paul says that character produces hope and that hope doesn't disappoint because He has put an every day reminder of His love in our hearts. The Spirit of God is alive in us to remind us of His love and promises. That's what real hope looks like.

Let hope spring from your character today and prepare you for a great day of competition.

Bible Reading Plan:
John 10:22-42
I John 2:24-29
Job 12
Ezekiel 33-34

November 13

325

FOCUS

Hebrews 12:2

When I was a high school athlete I ran the 110 meter hurdles. I can remember like it was yesterday being in the starting blocks and looking down the track through the tunnel of hurdles toward the finish line. Hurdlers and sprinters have a great advantage over longer distance runners in that they can see the finish line right out of the blocks. I see that same dynamic in today's scripture.

In the letter to the Hebrews at chapter 12 and verse 2 we read, "…looking unto Jesus, the author and finisher of our faith, who for the joy that was set before Him endured the cross, despising the shame, and has sat down at the right hand of the throne of God."

Like the hurdler, it seems that Jesus could see the finish line for His life right from the beginning. The clear vision of the destination and the rewards waiting at the finish line kept his life in perfect focus.

Every January, I watch the Super Bowl and am fully confident that all the players and coaches from both teams sneak peeks at the Lombardi Trophy sitting there waiting for the championship to be won. They all have the trophy in clear view and compete strongly to the final gun.

Let's emulate these champions and the Lord Jesus by keeping our goals clearly in focus and by putting away all the distractions that would keep them from being realized. If we all compete that way, we'll be a championship team.

Bible Reading Plan:
John 11:1-16
I John 3:1-10
Job 13
Ezekiel 35-37

November 14

AUTHORITY

I Peter 2:13-14

Who are the people with authority in your world of sport? You probably thought of coaches, officials, professors, conference administrators, parents, the University president or others. What is your attitude toward such authorities, is it one of submission or defiance? Is it more like obedience or rebellion? Why should that matter to us?

Peter shares some insight into these thoughts in his first letter at chapter 2 and verses 13 and 14 where he writes, "Therefore submit yourselves to every ordinance of man for the Lord's sake, whether to the king as supreme, or to governors, as to those who are sent by Him for the punishment of evildoers and for the praise of those who do good."

Some of the people who have authority over us we like and respect, that makes it a little easier to submit to their leadership. Others are a little tougher to follow.

Whether easy or difficult, the real motivation for submitting to proper authority is in Peter's words, "...for the Lord's sake..." We can exercise self control and submit to our leadership even when they're having their worst days. We can do the right thing and model proper behavior even in the face of poor character and bad leadership.

Let's all have a great competition today and so show the best of character. Let's model for the world and for our leaders a submissive attitude and proper respect for all those in authority.

Bible Reading Plan:
I John 3:11-18
Job 14
Ezekiel 38-39

November 15

DIVINE MOMENTS

John 7:6

Have you ever been in a competition and had the awareness that this might be a once-in-a-lifetime experience? Can you look back and see such occasions? Jesus has some wisdom for us related to these kinds of events.

In John's gospel at chapter 7 and verse 6 we read, "Then Jesus said to them, 'My time has not yet come, but your time is always ready.'"

Jesus knew that divine moments come rarely. Common opportunities come to us every day. Be ready daily and watch for the divine moment. Watch for the divine moment when you can make "The Play." These are the moments that define a player, a team or a season. Football players remember "The Catch" by Dwight Clark that put the San Francisco Forty-niners in the Super Bowl. Basketball players remember "The Shot" that Michael Jordan made at the end of his career to win the championship over the Utah Jazz. Those were the athletic equivalents to divine moments.

Only once a year is there a conference championship game. Rarely is there a play that could make or break a game or even a season. Each play of the game is important, but like Jesus knew, we must also be ready for the divine moment and bring our very best to make "The play." Let's have a great day of competition, make the best of the common opportunities and watch for the divine moment and make the play.

Bible Reading Plan:
John 11:38-44
Job 15:1-16
Ezekiel 40-41

November 16

UNDERSTANDING

Romans 11:33-36

Who do you suppose has the greatest knowledge and the most skill of anyone in your sport? Could it be the world's best player? Maybe it's the premier coach or possibly someone from the Hall of Fame? Whoever that is, how would your grasp of the sport compare with his or hers?

Who do you suppose has the greatest understanding about all of life? How strong is your grasp on life's big questions relative to His? The Bible has a very clear expression of God's immeasurable superiority to mankind. It's found at Romans chapter 11 and verses 33 through 36, "Oh, the depth of the riches of the wisdom and knowledge of God! How unsearchable his judgments, and his paths beyond tracing out! Who has known the mind of the the Lord? Or who has been his counselor? Who has ever given to God that God should repay him? For from him and through him and to him are all things. To him be the glory forever! Amen."

Much like the novice athlete's understanding of the sport pales in comparison with the veteran coach's, our grasp of the real stuff of life seems as nothing when compared to God's wisdom.

Young players often think the whole game revolves around them, but they soon learn otherwise. This scripture reminds us that all things in the Universe are from God, they come through God, they go to God and all glory is due God for all time.

As you compete today, keep in mind how your understanding of the sport compares to your coach's and team leaders'. Also remember the unsearchable depth of God's wisdom for life.

Bible Reading Plan:
John 11:45-57
Ezekiel 42-44

November 17

JUDGMENT

John 7:24

Do you remember your first impression of your coach? How about the first time you met your teammates? Now that you know them better, are they what they appeared to be at first glance? Jesus knew something about this and speaks about it today.

He is quoted by the John at chapter 7 and verse 24 as saying, "Do not judge according to appearance, but judge with righteous judgment."

First glances seldom produce a wise assessment of the truth about people. Your first impressions of your teammates were probably proven to be false by hours of interaction and weeks of competition. That's why Jesus says to not judge by appearances. Appearances only deal with the surface level of people. Jesus wants us to focus on the heart.

Righteous judgment is better because it can see past the appearances and facades, penetrating to the heart of the matter. Righteous judgment gets to motivation, to desires, to heart-felt qualities like compassion and love.

Let's employ this wisdom in today's competition. Let's not be ruled by what we see on the surface. Let's look deeper to the issues of the heart among our teammates and strive to call out the best in each other. Let's exercise righteous judgment and watch our team excel.

Bible Reading Plan:
John 12:1-11
I John 4:7-21
Job 16
Ezekiel 45-47

November 18

CORRECTION

Hebrews 12:7

What's the toughest part of your training as an athlete? Is it the running, the weight training, the diet, video tape study or maybe injury rehabilitation? Why do your coaches have you continue to do something that is so difficult? Do they hate you? I doubt it and today's scripture will help us see more clearly.

At chapter 12 and verse 7 the writer of the letter to the Hebrews speaks of such difficult training, "If you endure chastening, God deals with you as with sons; for what son is there whom a father does not chasten?"

Chastening equals discipline which equals loving training. When we experience the chastening or discipline of our coaches, our parents or even our God, it's a sign of love not hate. Just as the best parents both encourage and admonish their children, the best coaches both praise and correct their players.

I would begin to worry when the coaches stop correcting and challenging you. It probably means that they've given up on you or have lowered their expectations to where you really don't want them.

If we are wise, we'll listen closely to the leadership given us by our coaches, our parents, our teammates and our God. Such leadership is an assuring reminder of the loving relationship we have with them. Play strongly today and reward them all.

Bible Reading Plan:
John 12:12-19
I John 5:1-12
Job 17
Ezekiel 48

November 19

CRITICISM

John 8:7

How do you handle people who criticize your team or your coaching staff? Who are your strongest critics and how should we respond to them? Let's watch how Jesus deals with His critics.

In John's gospel at chapter 8 and verse 7 we read, "So when they continued asking Him, He raised Himself up and said to them, 'He who is without sin among you, let him throw a stone at her first.'"

Jesus is a very smart guy. The situation was that a woman was caught in the act of adultery (an offense punishable by death) and they tried to trick Jesus into either condemning her to death or excusing her sin. He showed great wisdom in doing neither. He simply reflected their judgments back at them and thereby silenced their accusations.

We all get tired of sports writers, radio commentators and critical spectators, making their accusations and second guessing athletes and coaching staffs. But how can we handle their criticisms well and wisely? Let's learn from Jesus' example.

Those who criticize and complain can be often silenced by simply reflecting their judgments back at them. There's no need to make excuses or to join in the criticism. Rather than that, simply show the same inconsistencies and errors in the accusers and they'll walk away in frustration.

As you compete today, give the accusers no chance for criticism by making this the best effort of the season. Play at the highest level of your capacity and there will be no room for criticism or complaint.

Bible Reading Plan:
John 12:20-36
I John 5:13-21
Job 18

November 20

STRENGTH

Hebrews 12:12

How has strength and flexibility training improved your game? In what ways is your team better with it than you would be without it? Could the Bible have anything to say about such things? Let's see.

In Hebrews chapter 12 and verses 12 and 13, we read, "Therefore strengthen the hands which hang down, and the feeble knees, and make straight paths for your feet, so that what is lame may not be dislocated, but rather be healed."

Certainly each player is better able to compete when he or she is stronger and more able to withstand injury than when weak. Thus we hear the admonition to strengthen the hands which hang down and the feeble knees.

Metaphorically, if we see our team as a body, we must all work together to strengthen our teammates who are tired and those who are diminished by injury. We all have a role in strengthening them and in making straight paths for their feet. That means to help them gain strength and health, rather than to put them in situations which will worsen their conditions.

Let's work together to strengthen our team. Let's work together as a well-coordinated body to compete in a strong, unified way.

Bible Reading Plan:
John 12:37-50
II John 1-13
Job 19
Daniel 3-4

November 21

FREEDOM

John 11:43

When was the last time you challenged your teammates to do something spectacular? How would you speak to a teammate who seems to be trapped in something that has boxed him in? What words would you use to call your teammate or friend to freedom? We'll watch Jesus do just that in today's letter.

In John chapter 11 and verse 43 we read, "Now when He had said these things, He cried with a loud voice, 'Lazarus, come forth!'"

We might use different words, but Jesus seemed rather effective. His friend, who had been in the grave for four days, comes walking out. Jesus called to His friend and Lazarus stepped into a life of freedom.

You can call your teammates out of their graves of despair, injury, illness and defeat. Many times they're just like Lazarus, trapped in a hole with no way out on their own. You may just be the person who can call out that teammate's name and have him respond in freedom and with renewed vigor.

Call your teammates out with a challenge. Call to them with compassion and strength. Our team is lessened when players are displaced, injured or unavailable. Call them back into active service and help them fill their roles with the team.

Bible Reading Plan:
John 13:1-11
III John 1-14
Job 20
Daniel 5-6

November 22

TEAM LEADERSHIP

Hebrews 13:7

How strongly do you value your team's leadership? Is their behavior, on and off the field of competition, something that you would imitate? Let's think together about team leadership.

A great lesson in leadership comes to us in Hebrews chapter 13 and verse 7 where we read, "Remember those who rule over you, who have spoken the word of God to you, whose faith follow, considering the outcome of their conduct."

The way to think clearly about your leaders' conduct is to consider the outcome of that conduct. What is the natural outcome of their lives? If he or she continues along the same line, how will his or her life turn out? That may help you determine those whom you should imitate.

If you're a team leader, give some careful consideration to your own life. Is your life one that you'd like to have the younger players to imitate? If you're one of those younger players, give careful consideration to those with whom you'll spend your time and whose lifestyles you'd be well served to emulate.

Let's give our teammates great examples to follow on the field of competition today. Great plays and courageous effort are contagious.

Bible Reading Plan:
John 13:12-17
Jude 1-7
Job 21:1-21
Daniel 7-8

November 23

PRODUCTIVITY

John 12:24-25

Which would seem to be more productive: strength and self-sufficiency or sacrifice and interdependence? That looks easy to the natural eye, but Jesus speaks about supernatural productivity.

In John chapter 12 at verses 24 and 25 we read, "Most assuredly, I say to you, unless a grain of wheat falls into the ground and dies, it remains alone; but if it dies, it produces much grain. He who loves his life will lose it, and he who hates his life in this world will keep it for eternal life."

Jesus knows something that the selfish and self-sufficient don't have a clue about. He knows that protecting one's self leads to isolation and loneliness. He also knows that self-sacrifice leads to new life and multiplication of effort.

It's the same with your team. If it's always "my ball, my position, my possession, my minutes," you will isolate your teammates quickly. However, if you give yourself away, sacrifice your preferences and serve everyone else, that will result in a rich life and tremendous influence.

Great team leaders and coaches constantly give their lives away through self-sacrifice and service of their teams. In doing so they reap a great harvest of team unity and a multiplicity of play makers. Let's all be such leaders and play makers today.

Bible Reading Plan:
John 13:18-30
Jude 8-16
Job 21:22-34
Daniel 9

November 24

AUTHORITY

Who has more authority on your team, the wet-behind-the-ears freshman walk-on or the Head Coach? Well that should be obvious… How about between the new graduate assistant and the fifth year captain of the team? That's a little tougher. Let's consider this matter by thinking about this scripture.

In Hebrews chapter 13 and verse 17 we read, "Obey those who rule over you, and be submissive, for they watch out for our souls, as those who must give account. Let them do so with joy and not with grief, for that would be unprofitable for you."

The writer uses two words which are very tough for competitors who are rather independent and strong-willed. Obey and be submissive.

Obey – why? Because our coaches and team leaders are not only responsible for their own actions and attitudes, but for those of the whole team as well. We owe them obedience because of their incredible investment in us and the great responsibility they carry.

Submissive – why? Because they have to give an account to people like the administration, to parents, to alumni, to the press and everyone who thinks himself an expert on the game. They need us to fit in and to keep ourselves in line so that their lives are full of joy rather than grief.

Let's work together in today's competition and bring joy to our team's leadership. That will be most profitable for us all.

Bible Reading Plan:
John 13:31-38
Jude 17-25
Job 22
Daniel 10-12

November 25

EXAMPLES

John 13:13-15

As you learned the basics of your game, how important was it to have an example to watch? How valuable is it to you to have videotape to watch of well-executed plays? What is the value of having experienced players on your team to demonstrate the proper techniques and skills for excellent play? These concepts are not new to athletics nor to life in general. Jesus speaks about such in today's letter.

We can hear Him in John chapter 13 and verses 13 through 15, "You call me Teacher and Lord, and you say well, for so I am. If I then, your Lord and Teacher, have washed your feet, you also ought to wash one another's feet. For I have given you an example that you should do as I have done to you."

Jesus' disciples had just experienced His washing their feet, one by one. More than just talking about service and humility, Jesus lived it out and provided an example for them.

This is also the best way for coaches and team leaders to teach the values that will guide their team. To lead with one's actions speaks more loudly than a thousand hours of talk.

In today's competition, lead with your actions, even more than your speech. If you want strong play, play strongly. If you want encouragement from the bench, you be the one to lead it. If you want an all out performance from your teammates, you give that for them. They will learn best when they experience the idea.

Bible Reading Plan:
John 8:1-11
II Peter 2:10-16

November 26

TROPHIES

I John 2:17

What's the most enduring part of this game? Is it the awards won, the championship titles, the trophies or medals? Probably not. How about the friendships, the memories and the tests of character that come with competition? Lots of stuff about the game passes away quickly.

The Apostle John wrote about the passing nature of the world in his first letter at chapter 2 and verse 17, it says, "And the world is passing away, and the lust with it; but he who does the will of God abides forever."

Even championship rings and trophies tarnish and lose their luster over time. As John says, the world is passing away. He also says that the lust, or strong desire for those things, passes away with it. That's true also. Even the desires for those things eventually wane.

Like the person who does the will of God, the more noble and wise parts of the game pay dividends in our lives for decades and even beyond the grave. The tests of character and the committed friendships that we develop in the course of athletic struggle shape our whole lives.

Give this day's competition every ounce of your heart. Commit yourself fully to your teammates and coaching staff, that's the will of God for you today. In doing so, you'll make an enduring mark in your soul and an abiding investment in each teammate.

Bible Reading Plan:
Job 5
Ezekiel 20-21

November 27

EXECUTION

John 13:17

Which is better: to know your team's playbook inside and out, or the flawless execution of one of those plays? I think you know and today we'll hear Jesus talk about how doing is better than knowing.

We can hear Him when we read John chapter 13 and verse 17, "If you know these things, happy are you if you do them."

This statement comes from Jesus on the heels of His washing the disciples' feet. They certainly thought that was a good idea, but now He says that it's more important to do it than to just know it as a fact.

It's the same with your team. The happiness of great team play comes with the doing of it, not just with knowing the playbook. You have to score to win. You have to execute the play to have a chance to score. Knowing the playbook alone will never result in a score, the game is not played on paper. You and your teammates have to actually make the play. Doing it is the key.

In this day's competition, take your knowledge of the playbook and put it into action. Make some plays. Execute each play with discipline and passion. These make for teamwork, victory and fun.

Bible Reading Plan:
John 9:13-25
I John 2:1-11

November 28

RESPECT

I Peter 2:17

What do players regularly do that is a genuine gesture of respect? I've seen you make complimentary comments after a good play. Some will point to their teammate after making a good pass. Maybe it's a nod or a tip of the cap. How can we show proper respect for our teammates, coaches, opponents and even the officials? Why should we even care about that?

Peter understood the value of showing proper honor and respect to people and he wrote about it at chapter 2 and verse 17 of his first letter. There it says, "Honor all people. Love the brotherhood. Fear God. Honor the king."

When you hear the word, honor, substitute the phrase, show proper respect. There are certainly many ways to show proper respect to your teammates during the course of the game. Peter challenges us to take full advantage of them.

When Peter says that we should honor the king, we think of showing proper respect to those with authority related to our team. Thus we honor the coaching staff, the game officials and our parents. Beneath the other statements is the one that fuels all the others. To fear God is to have a reverential awe and respect for Him. When we show proper respect for the Creator of the universe, it's a little easier to honor those with lesser provinces of authority in our worlds.

As you compete today, honor all people. That will include spectators and the other team's last reserve players. Love the brotherhood, your teammates with all your heart. Fear God, show him the proper respect. Honor the king, keep yourselves in order and show respect to those who must give an account for your attitudes and actions.

Bible Reading Plan:
Job 10
Ezekiel 31-32

November 29

FINISHING

John 19:30

Who is the best player you've ever seen at finishing a play? Who is best at finishing the season with strength and charging into the playoffs? Jesus knew some things about finishing well also.

We read about it in John's Gospel at chapter 19 and verse 30. It says, "So when Jesus had received the sour wine, He said, 'It is finished!' And bowing His head, He gave up His spirit."

Here's a list of good finishers: Joe Montana with the football and less than 2 minutes to play… he could finish. Michael Jordan taking a shot for the Bulls at he buzzer… he could finish. Michael Johnson sprinting to the line in the Olympic 400 meters… he could finish. Jesus was a better finisher than any of these.

He's about to die on the cross and He loudly exclaims, "It is finished!" He had accomplished all that He had come to do. He had finished 100% of His life goals.

Let's be like Jesus and finish well in today's competition. Let's not let up or give in until the absolute last play of the game is complete. We will honor both our team and the Lord with such play.

Bible Reading Plan:
John 11:17-37
I John 3:19-24

November 30

COMPETITION

John 8:31-32

What are the keys to playing the game naturally, freely and in a relaxed way? How do we prepare for game day in such a way as to allow us to play with great freedom? Jesus knows about such things.

In John's Gospel at chapter 8 and the 31st and 32nd verses we read, "Then Jesus said to those who believed Him, 'If you abide in My word, you are My disciples indeed. And you shall know the truth and the truth will make you free.'"

The key to freedom in competition is to abide in the elemental disciplines of the game. That's why coaches insist on drills and repetition. Those things build in the fundamentals that are the building blocks of successful game days. Abide in, live daily in things like practice, video study, team meetings, training... Live in the game.

In life on a broader scale, Jesus is saying that the key to freedom is to abide in, to live in His word. Disciplines like daily devotional reading of the Bible, daily prayer and meditation are the keys to a life of freedom. It's the abiding that precedes the knowledge of the truth, then the truth sets us free.

Let's watch in today's game for the hours, days, weeks, months and years of living in the game to result in a strong knowledge of the game. I'm very confident that with that kind of knowledge, a great performance is awaiting you today.

Bible Reading Plan:
John 14:1-14
Revelation 1:1-8
Job 23
Hosea 1-3

December 1

RESPONSIBILITY

James 3:1

Who is judged more strictly by the press for your team's standing in the conference, the head coach or the freshman walk-on? Who gets fired if the team doesn't meet the expectations of the administration, the coaching staff or the starting line up? Those answers are obvious, but why are they true? Today's scripture speaks about such matters.

In James' letter at chapter 3 and verse 1, we read, "My brethren, let not many of you become teachers, knowing that we shall receive a stricter judgment."

Coaching, like teaching comes with a very large price tag – responsibility. No matter whose fault it is when a team under-achieves, it's those who coach who are ultimately responsible. Certainly the leaders among the players can share some of that load, but the bottom line of responsibility rests squarely on the shoulders of the coaching staff.

Therefore we must commit even more highly to our coaches because of the incredible weight of responsibility that they carry daily. We must also carefully weigh the costs of becoming a coach or a teacher or even a team leader.

Make today's competition be one that will fulfill rather than frustrate your coaching staff as you give your absolute best effort.

Bible Reading Plan:
John 14:15-21
Revelation 1:9-20
Job 24
Hosea 4-6

December 2

THE DOOR

John 10:2

Do you have to sneak into the practice facility to practice? What kind of people would have to sneak in and would always worry about being found and kicked out? Do you come in through the door, or do you have to crawl in through a window? What allows you such easy entrance? Jesus knows…

In John chapter 10 and verse 2 He speaks about access through relationship. There we read, "But he who enters by the door is the shepherd of the sheep." He had just described those who don't come in through the door as thieves and robbers.

You don't need to sneak in, you're on the team. The security people know your face. Outsiders have to buy a ticket on game day, but you just stride right on in. If they're caught without a ticket, they're thrown out. Your relationship with the team is what gives you entrance. After a while, even those close to you become known and are at home with your team. Those with real relationships to the team can come right on in… the "wannabes" have to sneak in some other way.

It's the same in life; those with real relationship to Jesus can come right on in and speak with Him through prayer and study. The spiritual "wannabes" seem out of place and even foreign to His presence.

In this day of competition, watch for those you recognize on the bench and in the crowd of spectators. They are the ones with relationships that are worthy of your love and respect. Give them the access to your heart and your passion for the game that they've earned. Give this game and your team all you have.

Bible Reading Plan:
Revelation 2:1-17
Job 25-26
Hosea 7-8

December 3

WISDOM

James 3:13

Who among your teammates is the best student of the game? Whose knowledge of strategy and fundamentals can help shape the outcome of a contest? How is that wisdom evident to the rest of the team? Today's scripture tells us how to recognize real wisdom.

In the letter from James at chapter 3 and verse 13 we read, "Who is wise among you? Let him show by good conduct that his works are done in the meekness of wisdom." Just like real players show their stuff during competition, real people of wisdom show their true colors by their conduct.

The world is crowded with people who can "talk a good game." Those who can really play are much rarer.

The same is true when we look for people with real wisdom. Myriads of folks talk about their intelligence, their academic degrees and their grasp of athletic dynamics, but to find someone whose conduct speaks more loudly than his mouth is a rare thing.

In today's competition, let's be players of real wisdom who show their true colors by playing wisely, by serving our teammates and following the instructions of our coaches. That's what the author means by good conduct...done in the meekness of wisdom. Make this a great day of competition.

Bible Reading Plan:
John 15:1-8
Job 27
Hosea 9-12

December 4

TEAM LEADERS

John 10:11

What does it cost to be a good coach or a teammate? How much more does it cost to be a head coach or a team captain? You may not be aware of it, but those positions cost a good deal more. Jesus clues us in on the cost in today's letter.

Jesus says at John 10 and verse 11, "I am the good shepherd. The good shepherd gives His life for the sheep."

He who would be a team leader or a coach should count the costs associated with such responsibilities. It's just like flying on airplanes, the best seats cost the most. The cost of such leadership is sacrifice. It requires laying down one's life for the people he's leading. That comes in terms of time, convenience, preferences, and personal desires, all set aside in order to serve the team.

Jesus knows that love and leadership lead to sacrifice. His love led Him to die in our place. That's real sacrifice! That is what a good shepherd does.

Will you be a good shepherd for your team? What will it cost you? How will you lay down your life for your team today? How many times will you prefer your team's best over your own? This is the price tag for leadership. Pay it in full in today's competition and you'll be like Jesus. Play like champions today.

Bible Reading Plan:
John 15:9-17
Revelation 3:1-13
Hosea 13-14

December 5

HUMILITY

Psalm 131:1

How do you react when teammates or fans criticize your coaches' decisions? Sometimes you might nod in agreement or even voice your displeasure. At other times you might simply remain silent or vigorously defend the staff's strategy. What attitudes might be revealed by those various reactions?

In Psalm number 131 and verse 1 we read David's view on important attitudes. There we read, "My heart is not proud, O Lord, my eyes are not haughty; I do not concern myself with great matters or things too wonderful for me." Here's one of history's great leaders and he said that he had to guard his attitude from arrogant pride.

We've all seen haughty eyes that look down on everyone else. The arrogant heart has an opinion on everything and is fully convinced of his superiority.

Let's guard our attitudes and put on humility like David. Let's not be so proud or foolish to suppose that our few years of competition make us wiser than our coaches whose decades of experience far surpass our own. Let's not concern ourselves with the great matters of the sport, nor with things beyond our ability to understand.

In today's competition, be the competitor you were made to be. Do so with great humility and relax under the leadership of your wise, talented coaching staff.

Bible Reading Plan:
John 15:8-27
Revelation 3:14-22
Job 29

December 6

COMMITMENT

I Kings 19:19&21

Who is the greatest example of total commitment in your sport? Who has really committed him/herself 100% to your team and to excellence in competition? How would you rate your level of commitment? In today's scripture we see a striking picture of radical commitment.

In the first book of Kings at chapter 19 and in verses 19 and 21 we read, "So Elijah went from there and found Elisha son of Shapat. He was plowing with 12 yoke of oxen and he himself was driving the twelfth pair. Elijah went up to him and threw his cloak around him…. So Elisha left him and went back. He took his yoke of oxen and slaughtered them. He burned the plowing equipment to cook the meat and gave it to the people, and they ate. Then he set out to follow Elijah and to be his attendant."

Elisha was a wealthy farmer plowing his ground until Elijah the prophet came to town. By throwing his cloak around him, Elijah was inviting Elisha to join him in his work. This sounds a lot like a recruiting visit. At that point things changed radically for Elisha. He committed everything to the pursuit God's will.

Elisha slaughtered his oxen and cooked them over a fire made from the plow. That's like a modern farmer blowing up his tractors. The end result is the same; neither is going back to farming. That is what total commitment looks like. Elisha eliminated everything that would hinder his whole-hearted commitment to Elijah and to God.

My challenge to you today is to similarly commit to an absolute, whole-hearted, 100% effort in this competition.

Bible Reading Plan:
John 16:1-11
Revelation 4

December 7

REAL POWER

Psalm 147:10-11

In which part of your sport do you have the greatest sense of strength or power? Maybe it's in the weight room, maybe during drills in practice, or even on game day when it's all on the line. How central is that feeling to your enjoyment of the sport?

In Psalm 147 and verses 10 and 11 we read about where God senses power and strength. It reads, "His pleasure is not in the strength of the horse, nor His delight in the legs of a man; the Lord delights in those who fear Him, who put their hope in His unfailing love."

It seems that God is impressed with neither the normal measurements of strength nor the usual vessels for power. Neither the strongest horse nor the fittest athlete really brings him pleasure. Rather He is deeply pleased by those who respect and trust Him.

Most coaches are like this too. They might seem impressed at first with the very talented player, the powerful athlete with strength and speed, but if you hang around with them you'll hear stories about their real favorites. They are the ones who "bought in" and trusted their coaches. They are the ones who built unity among their teammates and gave themselves up to make the team better.

Good coaches, like the Lord Himself, find pleasure and take delight in the players who show respect and display trust. Make that your aim in today's competition and you'll be exhibiting real power and strength.

Bible Reading Plan:
Revelation 5
Job 31:1-23
Amos 1-2

December 8

APPEARANCE VS. HEART

I Samuel 16:7

How do you judge your teammates' performance on game day, by their appearance during pre-game or by their play during the competition? I wish the answer was as obvious to everyone as it is to you and to God. In fact the Bible shares a story of the vast difference between outward appearances and matters of the heart.

In the First Book of Samuel at chapter 16 and verse 7 we read, "But the Lord said to Samuel, 'Do not consider his appearance or his height, for I have rejected him. The Lord does not look at the things man looks at. Man looks at the outward appearance, but the Lord looks at the heart.'"

Samuel had come to a man's house knowing that the next king of Israel would be there. He was all set to look for the tallest, strongest and brightest of the sons. The Lord stopped him short in his search and clarified His values. Samuel was to see beyond the outward and to look for the heart of a leader.

People are often fascinated by the flashy player who puts on a great show in pre-game, only to wonder why that one never sees any playing time. They're looking at the outward appearance and can't see what the coach sees every day in practice.

As we compete today, let's not fall into the trap of judging by outward appearances. Rather, let's look into the hearts of our teammates and coaches. Let's see clearly and make wise decisions regarding this game and all of life.

Bible Reading Plan:
John 16:25-33
Amos 3-4

December 9

CORRECTION

Proverbs 3:11-12

Does it seem sometimes like the coach is getting on you more than some of the other players? Does it seem like your parents expect more from you than you can give? Ever feel like you're being overly disciplined or treated unfairly? This could be a blessing in disguise.

In the book of Proverbs at chapter 3 and verses 11 and 12 it says, "My son, do not reject the discipline of the Lord, or loathe His reproof, for whom the Lord loves He reproves, even as a father, the son in whom he delights."

It seems that the discipline we find ourselves under is more often the indicator of a loving relationship than some sort of benign disfavor with a coach or parent. The Lord will give us correction and training in what's right when we're in error, not because He's mean or cruel, but because He loves us and is committed to us.

Many times this same dynamic works with your coaches and other authorities. Sometimes they develop a relationship with you in which they invest themselves and their expectations grow. This relationship of respect and love leads them to correct, to discipline, to reprove. Heed this scripture's advice and don't despise their words, they're driven by love and commitment for you.

In your prayers today, thank God for those who love you and are committed to you. Thank Him for those who care enough to correct and discipline.

Bible Reading Plan:
John 17:6-19
Revelation 7
Job 32
Amos 5-6

December 10

SPORT

Proverbs 10:23

What do you do for sport? You've probably heard of people hunting for sport, fishing for sport and obviously athletic competitions are called sports. Sport is the active pursuit of pleasure and fulfillment.

In the book of Proverbs at chapter 10 and verse 23 it says, "Doing wickedness is like sport to a fool; and so is wisdom to a man of understanding."

How could doing wickedness be like a sport? Have you known any fools? Lots of people I know seem to find great pleasure and fulfillment in activities that leave them with hangovers and diseases. They brag about foolish things like you might boast about your batting average or slam dunks. Fools find pleasure and fulfillment in things that dishonor the Lord and ruin their lives.

The powerful message of this verse is that living wisely is equally pleasurable and fulfilling to the wise person. Doing things that honor God and serve others is like a sport to those who display wisdom. A life of wisdom is not boring and passive, rather it's full of power, activity and adventure, like a sport!

As you pray today, ask the Lord to make you a person of wisdom. Ask Him for the grace to find pleasure and fulfillment in the pursuit of wisdom.

Bible Reading Plan:
John 17:6-19
Revelation 8
Job 33:1-11

December 11

TEAMMATES

Proverbs 13:20

How have you chosen your friends? With whom do you hang out? What kind of people do you spend the most time with? The Bible has a lot to say about what makes for good friends and what kind of people we become as a result. One such passage follows.

In the Proverbs chapter 13 and verse 20 it says, "He who walks with the wise grows wise, but a companion of fools suffers harm."

You probably know someone who has chosen to make fools his constant companions. He hangs out with people who continually make bad choices. The warning of this verse is that people who choose fools for friends will suffer for it. They sometimes suffer financially, sometimes physically, often with great heartache.

The promise contained here is that if we choose to spend time with people who display wisdom, we too will become wise. We must be purposeful about with whom we spend our time and invest our lives. When we walk with someone we're obviously going the same direction and have the same destination in mind. Let's choose our friends, mentors and teammates with this in mind and I'm sure we'll grow wise together.

Pray for wisdom in choosing friends and in choices about how to use your time.

Bible Reading Plan:
John 17:20-26
Revelation 9
Job 33:12-33
Obadiah 1-21

December 12

HUMILITY

Proverbs 15:33

Everyone likes to win awards, especially things like MVP trophies. It's easy to assume that the person who wins such awards is just lucky or got a break of some sort. However the Bible tells plainly how these things tend to work.

In Proverbs chapter 15 at verse 33 it says, "The fear of the Lord teaches a man wisdom, and humility comes before honor."

Not everyone who wins awards is following the Lord, but many are living by this proverb's principles. Most who win these awards have spent hours, months and years in practice and perfecting their skills. Many spend years toiling in obscurity, out of the spotlight, then all of a sudden.... MVP!! They worked in humility for a long time and were rewarded with honor.

Ultimately, the best honor springs from humility. That humility is born of a relationship with Christ Jesus. That's what he means by the fear of the Lord. Fear of this sort is a reverential awe for the Lord God and that is best accomplished while in a daily, living, love relationship with Christ.

As you prepare for competition, ask the Lord to be honored by your humility. Ask Him to work in your life as you humbly serve the Lord and your team. Be assured as you do, He honors those who fear Him and humility comes before honor.

Bible Reading Plan:
John 18:1-18
Revelation 10
Job 34:1-20
Jonah 1-4

December 13

HOPE

Isaiah 40:30-31

Which is more draining to your heart for competition, physical fatigue or a sense of hopelessness and despair? Many times, these two thieves arrive at the same time.

Isaiah writes about the solution to both fatigue and despair in chapter 40 and verses 30 and 31. There we read, "Even youths grow tired and weary, and young men stumble and fall; but those who hope in the Lord will renew their strength."

In every season, each of us will certainly encounter a time when we're absolutely worn out. Our minds and bodies are just drained of strength and even our spirits are devoid of enthusiasm. These are the toughest moments in sport, because the season will continue with or without us.

This scripture breathes hope into our deflated chests as it points directly to the Lord as the one who renews the body, the soul and the spirit. This happens as we trust God with our lives. It comes to us as we place our hope in His love for us. We're energized as He renews our strength through daily communion with Him.

As you compete today and you find your legs weary, trust God for a renewal of strength. Breathe a silent prayer for help when it seems your team is stumbling. Ask the Lord to meet you at every moment of the competition and you'll experience His presence and strength.

Bible Reading Plan:
Revelation 11
Job 34:21-37
Micah 1-3

December 14

356

CONTROVERSY

John 7:1

What kinds of situations are there among your teammates, which if mentioned, immediately stir up controversy and dissension? Which issues in your family can most easily provoke a fight? How do we handle such hot potatoes? Let's watch how Jesus does it.

In John's gospel we can read about this at chapter 7 and verse 1. It says, "After these things Jesus walked in Galilee; for He did not want to walk in Judea, because the Jews sought to kill Him."

You might think this is rather simple, they want to kill Him in Judea, so don't go there! The problem is that much of what He needed to accomplish could only be done in Judea. It would be like knowing that the people who want to kill you are at the gym, but you have to go there for practice and competition. You're stuck in a tough spot.

The wisdom in this is that Jesus didn't kick sleeping dogs. He didn't awaken controversy or animosity without cause. He gave those who were most opposed to Him a little room.

We can do similarly with controversial situations and issues among our teammates and families. Don't provoke your coach with that look, gesture or tone of voice that you know will annoy him. Exercise some wisdom with officials and don't needlessly provoke a penalty against your team. Let's be as wise as Jesus in today's competition and give the sleeping dogs a little space. Our whole team will benefit from the applied wisdom of God.

Bible Reading Plan:
John 18:28-40
Revelation 12
Job 35
Micah 4-5

December 15

TRUST

Whom do you trust when you're being overcome by anxiety? Who is trustworthy when your life is in distress? How can you trust anyone when you're full of doubt? Today's scripture gives us some insight and direction.

In John chapter 14 and verse 1 we read these words from Jesus, "Do not let your hearts be troubled. Trust in God; trust also in me." In the middle of the most trying time of their lives, Jesus asked his followers to trust him just like they trusted God. He said that trust would calm their troubled hearts.

That same principle can work on your team. We trust people who have proven themselves in the past. As people show themselves trustworthy, we will take risks with and for them. Their trustworthiness calms our hearts and gives us confidence.

Jesus said, "Trust in God, trust also in me." I am saying, "Trust in God, trust also in your coaches. Trust in God, trust also in your teammates." They've proven themselves to be trustworthy, so take some risks with them. Give yourselves to them in total abandon. I promise that as you trust yourselves to those who are trustworthy, you'll find that your confidence will grow and your once troubled hearts will experience new peace.

Let today's competition be filled with trust, confidence and peace.

Bible Reading Plan:
John 19:1-16
Job 36:1-15
Micah 6-7

December 16

358

HOPE

Romans 5:5

Can you recall a time when you felt like your whole store of energy was poured out in competition? You surely experienced total exhaustion and fully depleted your energy resources. Who pours new life into your heart when you've been totally poured out?

The Apostle Paul wrote these words in Romans chapter 5 and verse 5, "And hope does not disappoint us, because God has poured out his love into our hearts by the Holy Spirit, whom he has given us." Here we find a source of energy and hope which will never run dry.

Many of us hope for things with little basis for believing they will actually happen. The good news here is that our hope in God is made more tangible by the love we feel in our hearts. That heartfelt love overcomes disappointment and breeds an unshakeable confidence.

As you compete today, recall the hope that does not disappoint. When you feel fatigue and pain pouring out of you, remember that God is pouring out his love into your heart, moment by moment. Let the assurance of an inexhaustible source of hope and power fuel your heart, your mind and your body.

Bible Reading Plan:
John 19:17-27
Revelation 14
Job 36:16-33
Nahum 1-3

December 17

TREASURES

Luke 2:19

What are some of the most treasured moments from your sport career? Are there some souvenirs or mementos from those events? Where do you keep them? When you anticipate the coming competitions, how eager are you for their arrival? Where do you keep your dreams and aspirations? Today's scripture reveals the best possible place for safe keeping of such treasures.

In Luke chapter 2 and verse 19 we read about where Mary kept hers, "But Mary treasured up all these things and pondered them in her heart." Mary kept her fond memories and her dreams of the future in her heart. She pondered upon their meaning and significance. We would do well to do the same.

Every athlete I've ever known has a collection of memorabilia from important competitions. Your room is probably decorated with trophies, medals, ribbons, championship photos and such. Your real treasures however are kept in your heart. It is the repository for memories, friendship and joy.

If you're the competitors that I believe you are, you also have a treasure chest of dreams for the future. You look ahead into the future and imagine what the coming season will hold. That's good and proper. Ponder what will be and let your heart lead you to be the best you can be. Lean into the path of excellence and strength that your coaches have outlined for you.

As you ponder today's contest. Imagine, in your heart, how you will compete and how you will achieve a new set of memories to be treasured.

Bible Reading Plan:
John 19:28-37
Revelation 15
Job 37
Habakkuk 1-3

December 18

PEACE

Philippians 4:7

What are the situations in your sport that bring fear, doubt, pain or disappointment? Is there anything that could guard your hearts from the onslaught of these thieves? Today's scripture points directly to a powerful force for your good.

In the letter to the Philippians at chapter 4 and verse 7 Paul wrote, "And the peace of God, which transcends all understanding, will guard your hearts and your minds in Christ Jesus." That's very simple, but incredibly powerful. The peace of God can guard both your heart and your mind.

As competitors there is a constant barrage of factors that assault our hearts and minds. It seems the more we dwell on them the larger they become and we spin down toward anxiety and even depression.

The great news here is that God gives a peace to our hearts that is well beyond what we can even understand. In the midst of painful loss and disappointment, we can be at peace and confident of the future. The peace of God is accessed through prayer, simple conversation with God in which you express your heart to Him and listen for His heart's response to your concerns.

As you prepare to compete today, take some time for a quiet, reflective conversation with God. Trust Him with your heart's concerns and you'll experience a new level of peace that even surpasses your understanding of the situation.

Bible Reading Plan:
John 19:38-42
Revelation 16
Job 38:1-21
Zephaniah 1-2

December 19

TREASURE

Luke 2:51

To whom are you a treasure? Who recalls the events of your life as a precious commodity? Probably you're thinking of your parents or maybe an old coach of yours, maybe even your best friend. How strongly do you think they hold to those memories? Today's scripture may give us some insight into the value we hold for those closest to us.

In Luke chapter 2 and verse 51 we read, "Then he went down to Nazareth with them and was obedient to them. But his mother treasured all these things in her heart." Even when he was just 12 years old, Jesus was an amazing young man. Daily he did and said things that astounded his mother. You see her attitude in the last sentence, "But his mother treasured all these things in her heart."

Neither you nor I are just like Jesus, but we are treasured in much the same way by those close to us. You are a treasure of infinite value to many. You may be aware of how much you're loved by some, but your influence with others may escape your notice. There may be some at today's competition or tomorrow's practice who treasure every word and event of your life.

As you prepare to compete today, please be fully aware of your value to the team, to your family and friends and to me. We're as proud of you as Mary was of Jesus and we treasure each day with you in our hearts. Compete today with all the confidence and joy that comes from heartfelt love and devotion.

Bible Reading Plan:
John 20:1-9
Revelation 17
Job 38:22-41
Zephaniah 3

December 20

SHARING

Teammates daily share such marvelous things as sweat and pain, meals and physical therapy, anguish and exhilaration. Sometimes they even share trophies and championships. Thus it's only natural to develop strong feelings of affection for the people with whom you share such things. Today's scripture hammers this point home.

In Paul's letter to the Philippians at chapter 1 and verse 7 he wrote, "It is right for me to feel this way about all of you, since I have you in my heart; for whether I am in chains or defending and confirming the gospel, all of you share in God's grace with me." Paul felt this way for these people because of their mutual sharing in God's grace. We in sport share a number of other things as well.

We all share the pain of losing and the joy of winning. We all experience the aches and pains of competition as well as the exhilaration of record setting performances. These shared experiences build a special bond in our hearts for our teammates and coaches. This bond is a mystery to those outside the team, but it's a most valuable part of life for us who have our teammates in our hearts.

As you prepare for today's competition, hold your teammates in your heart and fully grasp your affection for them. Compete in a fully unified way as you all share the grace of God for your team.

Bible Reading Plan:
John 20:10-18
Revelation 18
Job 39
Haggai 1-2

December 21

363

PERSEVERANCE

James 1:2-4

What is the most difficult part of the game for you to endure? Is it the long bus trips? Maybe it's the double sessions of practice in preseason? What is the final outcome of persevering through these trying times? What benefit could possibly come from such painful, hard work?

In his letter to his friends at chapter 1 and verses 2 through 4, the Apostle James tells us about such trials, "My brethren, count it all joy when you fall into various trials, knowing that the testing of your faith produces patience. But let patience have its perfect work, that you may be perfect and complete, lacking nothing."

The great promise of this passage is that the various trials produce patience or endurance in our lives. Just like conditioning produces endurance in our bodies, trials and tough times produce patience in our souls and endurance in our character.

When we can push through the tough times, like losing streaks, injuries and bench-sitting, we will find that we are more complete and better able to deal with life's bigger issues. We're catching onto this idea well when we see the trial coming and can welcome it as a friend, rather than cursing it as an enemy.

Bible Reading Plan:
John 20:19-23
Revelation 19
Job 40
Zechariah 1-5

December 22

REFRESHMENT

Philemon 7

Who refreshes your heart after a long practice? Can you see his or her face in your mind? Who breathes new life into your heart after a tough loss? What is his or her name? Such people are invaluable to your life. The Apostle Paul had such a person in his life and today's scripture tells us about him.

In Paul's letter to his friend Philemon at verse 7 we read these words, "Your love has given me great joy and encouragement, because you, brother, have refreshed the hearts of the saints." Like a wise coach, Paul was encouraged by how Philemon helped his teammates.

He received great joy and encouragement because of how his friend refreshed the hearts of others. Refreshing someone's heart is as simple as making an expression of love, comfort or encouragement.

We refresh our teammates' hearts when we offer congratulations for their performance in competition or practice. We refresh the hearts of coaches when we show good character. We refresh the hearts of those who are struggling when we walk beside them, encourage them and give them hope for the future.

As you compete today, refresh the hearts of your teammates and coaches. Give them your absolute best effort. In the process, everyone gets better and you spread joy and encouragement all those around.

Bible Reading Plan:
John 20:24-31
Revelation 20
Job 41:1-11
Zechariah 6-9

December 23

INVESTMENTS

Luke 12:34

In whom have you deeply invested your life? That surely includes family, friends, your sport team and possibly others. How have your feelings for those people changed as your investment in them has grown? Today's scripture will state clearly that affection follows investment.

Luke chapter 12 and verse 34 says, "For where your treasure is, there your heart will be also." Simple enough, your heart tends to follow what and whom you treasure.

There's no doubt that things like long seasons and losing streaks take a toll on a team's relationships. The promise in this verse is true even in such circumstances. Daily investments in your teammates, in the coaching staff and in those who support you will pay dividends in your hearts.

You will find that as you do the right things, your fondness for those in whom you invest will grow. That's true of even those you could find to be most annoying or distasteful. Invest more and the annoyance will diminish. Love more deeply and the distasteful attribute will fade in its importance.

Today, make your investments on the field of competition. Give your absolute best in support of a great team victory. As you give all that you have and all that you are to your team you'll find your heart full of a great treasure - teammates and friends.

Bible Reading Plan:
John 21:1-14
Revelation 21
Job 41:12-34
Zechariah 10-14

December 24

WORDS

Matthew 15:18

Have you ever heard your coach or a teammate say something outrageous and wondered, "Where did that come from?" Sometimes the most mild-mannered of us will utter some words that would make a sailor blush. Today's scripture reveals the source of such outbursts.

In Matthew chapter 15 and verse 18 it says, "But the things that come out of the mouth come from the heart and these make a man unclean." Jesus had been talking with some legalistic people who thought that their environment would pollute them, but He turns it back on them and points straight to their hearts as the real source of life-pollution.

When we hear others or even ourselves use speech to belittle or to hurt others, it's an indicator of our heart's condition. When we speak profanely or condemn, we're revealing our own hearts.

When you hear sarcasm it's revealing disappointment and resentment. When profanity is flying it's an indicator of anger and disgust. When harsh criticism is spoken, bitterness and envy are often in the speaker's heart.

As you prepare for today's competition, prepare your heart for clear and helpful communication. If some ugly things come flying out of your mouth, take it as a reminder that your heart needs some work. So does mine.

Bible Reading Plan:
Job 42
Malachi 1-4

December 25

VALUES

Luke 16:15

Have you ever found your value system to be at odds with that of your teammates or your coaches? Have you ever seen a player give lip-service to changing just to gain favor with the coach? Here's a poorly kept secret – the coach is not impressed. Today's scripture shows us why.

Luke wrote the following in chapter 16 and verse 15, "You are the ones who justify yourselves in the eyes of men, but God knows your hearts. What is highly valued among men is detestable in God's sight." Jesus strongly tells these people that God's not impressed by their posturing attitudes. He knows their hearts.

Good coaches can also see through the disguises of players who try to justify themselves. Some players seem to be constantly framing their failures with excuses and shifting blame to others. Coaches are not impressed with such attitudes. They can see their players' hearts.

As you prepare for competition, make a quick assessment of your value system. Check it against the one you know your coaching staff holds. If there's a conflict, strongly consider making a change. You're not fooling your coaches and you're certainly not fooling God. They and He can see your heart and they each want the best for you. Let today's contest be a demonstration of how well a team can compete when their hearts are in harmony.

Bible Reading Plan:
John 14:22-31
Revelation 2:18-29

December 26

CONSISTENCY

Matthew 15:8

When have you encountered people who seem to talk one way, but live another? Publicly they say one thing, but in private they do the exact opposite. Jesus knew people just like that and in today's scripture we hear what He thinks about them.

In Matthew chapter 15 and verse 8 we read, "These people honor me with their lips, but their hearts are far from me." Jesus is not fooled by these people's hollow words. He knows their hearts are distant and cold toward Him no matter what they say.

We've all had teammates who talk about team unity, but privately they criticize and condemn. You and I both know players who talk about hustle, but drag through practices. We have seen competitors who talk about teamwork, but play selfishly. The disconnect between their hearts and their mouths is seen by how they behave.

How we conduct ourselves is the best indicator of the condition of our hearts. Our words may belie the true nature of our attitudes.

As you prepare to compete today, draw near to God through prayer. A heart that is fully His will be in perfect alignment, speech and action working together in integrity. Make that your highest goal today.

Bible Reading Plan:
Job 28
Joel 1

December 27

A PURE HEART

Matthew 5:8

As you compete, how well do you know the mind of your coaching staff? How clearly can you tell what they're thinking as the competition progresses? Are your hearts in tune as you pursue victories? Today's scripture shows us how to relate intimately with our leaders.

In Matthew chapter 5 and verse 8 we read, "Blessed are the pure in heart, for they will see God." To see God is not so much like viewing a photograph or a video of His face, rather it's to have an intimate knowledge of what He's doing, what he values and what He's thinking.

It says also that it's the pure in heart that see Him in that way. Think about yourself and your teammates. When your heart is pure, your motives and intentions are selfless and generous, you seem to have clear lines of communication and there's a strong sense of team unity among you. This dynamic works in how we relate to God and how we relate to each other.

In today's competition, keep your heart pure and watch how your team is unified in heart. With a pure heart you may even get a glimpse of God's smile of approval.

Bible Reading Plan:
John 16:12-24
Revelation 6

December 28

HALL OF FAME

Hebrews 12:1

Do you have aspirations of someday being in your sport's Hall of Fame? What would it take to achieve such an award? Today's scripture gives us some hints.

The Bible speaks of a Hall of Fame, but it is a Hall of Fame of Faith. Hebrews chapter 11 lists these great people and then chapter 12 challenges us to live as they did. It says, "Therefore, since we are surrounded by such a great cloud of witnesses, let us also lay aside every weight and the sin which so easily entangles us and run with endurance the race that is set before us. Fixing our eyes on Jesus, the author and finisher of our faith."

When I read that I can see a basketball arena or a football stadium filled with Hall of Famers watching us play the game. They're cheering us on and want only the best for us. They have paid the price to achieve excellence in their lives and they want us to do the same. Join me in the powerful confidence that comes from trusting God for Hall of Fame qualities in our play, our attitudes and in our faith.

As you compete today and look out at the spectators, look at them in a new way. See the people that surround your arena of competition as people who came to see you play and more than that, they're on your side. See the place as being filled with the great players from the past and your teammates from the past couple of years. They're here to see you as you compete like a Hall of Famer.

Bible Reading Plan:
Job 31:24-40
Amos 7-9

December 29

GREETINGS

III John 13-14

As the year nears its close, I want to thank you for taking time to read these devotional thoughts. It is a great privilege and an honor for me to have such favor with you. I deeply appreciate it.

The Apostle John expresses well my feelings in his third letter at verses 13 and 14, "I had many things to write, but I do not wish to write to you with pen and ink; but I hope to see you shortly, and we shall speak face to face. Peace to you. Our friends greet you. Greet the friends by name."

We all have friends who have been displaced over the years. Whether childhood friends, teammates from our years in school or coworkers from adulthood, we've been separated by time and the circumstances of life. It's important to maintain these relationships, even if just by mail.

There is, however, no substitute for seeing each other face to face and enjoying the sweet communion of dear friends.

As valuable as writing to you is to me, speaking with you face to face is even better. I hope to do so very soon and to greet you, my friends, by name. Thanks again for all you, and all the people of sport, mean to me.

Bible Reading Plan:
John 18:19-27
Revelation 13

December 30

PERSEVERANCE

II Thessalonians 3:5

Here at the end of the year, I'd like to express my thanks for taking time to read these devotions. I also want to communicate the things I hope and pray for you.

As Paul was closing his second letter to his friends in Thessalonica, he wrote in chapter 3 and verse 5, "May the Lord direct your hearts into God's love and Christ's perseverance." He prays for God's direction toward two ends.

He prays that the Lord will direct them toward God's love that is daily assurance of His protection, presence and provision.

He also prays that the Lord will lead them toward Christ's perseverance, the ability to finish life well.

That would be my prayer for you as well. I pray that you'll have a day to day sense of the Lord's presence in your life. That comes through relationship with Christ Jesus. I also pray that you'll press through the difficult times of your life with the assurance that our Lord will never leave nor forsake you.

Bible Reading Plan:
John 21:15-25
Revelation 22

December 31

Heart of a Champion
Devotions for the People of Sport
Discussion Guide

For these discussions, each member of the group will need:
A copy of "Heart of a Champion – Devotions for the People of Sport" for personal, daily devotional reading.

A Bible for the daily readings suggested at the bottom of each page and for reference during the discussion of selected devotions and their scriptures. **The facilitator for the group will be the only person needing a copy of this discussion guide.**

There are a number of ways to approach using "Heart of a Champion" for discussions with people of sport. You may choose any one or any combination of the options listed below.

Have each person in your group read the daily devotions privately through the week and when you meet together, discuss the one for the day on which you meet.

Have each person in your group read the daily devotions privately through the week and when you meet together, discuss one (or more) of the devotions from the last week, as chosen by the leader or the group.
Have each person in your group read the daily devotions and the daily Bible readings at the bottom of each page privately through the week. When you meet together, discuss one (or more) of the devotions and/or the Bible readings which had particular significance that week.

Suggestions for discussion meetings:

In meeting with people of sport for quality time of prayer, study, discussion and fellowship, the setting is best determined by the opportunity you're afforded. This may mean a meeting with a team at the practice facility prior to practice or immediately thereafter. It may mean an early morning meeting at a restaurant including breakfast. It may mean a weekly study prior to team meetings. The opportunity with those whose lives you wish to impact determines the **where**, the **when**, the **how long** for your setting. There is plenty of flexibility within the forms listed as models.
    It is wise and helpful to begin and end the discussion meetings with prayer in some form. The discussion leader and his group should determine the form that prayer should take in their meetings.
It is normally best to arrange chairs in a circle or to meet around a table. This way the leader can see everyone in the group face to face. This is also the best arrangement for discussion between members of the group. Chairs arranged in rows or classroom style allows for the leader to see everyone, but inhibits discussion between various other members of the group.
    It's often wise to set a finite number of weeks or months for the group to meet together. This makes for a natural time to adjust details, to change subject matter, to add new people and for some people to grace-

fully leave the group. The group can then adjust and begin again with new focus, direction and energy.

Recommended process for leading the discussions:

Read and discuss the discussion questions, one at a time.
Leave time for them to think and express their ideas, tell their stories, share their feelings.

Don't worry about finishing the list of questions; your objective is to have them interact with each other and the Scripture.

Don't worry about times of silence, they might be thinking! If the question seems clumsy or confusing, rephrase it or shape it in a way that better fits your group. If it's helpful, you may offer your ideas or experiences as an example.

Encourage everyone to take part in the discussion and welcome all responses, especially the stories and experiences of the group.
Judge wisely the responses to questions that relate to truth and error with respect to the Scripture. Be ready to correct or affirm such responses.
Look for ways to take the questions to deeper levels of their hearts. The goal is to get to the fourth level and deal with matters of the heart.

Personal experience. These questions invite the group to share experiences they've had related to the themes in the text. These also invite everyone to participate and lead to later applications of scriptural principles.

Observation of text. These are mostly questions that are easily answered simply by observing the material in the text. These questions welcome everyone's participation and invite all into the discussion.

Interpretation and application. The principles seen in the scripture will lead the group to grasp the moral implications and personal applications of the text. They are now wrestling with God's will for them as Christian people of sport.

Matters of the heart. Some questions will probe deeply enough to challenge the members about their identity in Christ. They'll be confronted with their tendency toward performance rather than unconditional acceptance in Christ Jesus. The motives and attitudes of the heart are uncovered by these probing questions.

It is the role of the leader to ask the questions, to facilitate discussion and to ask follow up questions at the appropriate levels. Doing these things will result in your group being deeply impacted by the Spirit of God in all areas of life.

Heart of a Champion – Discussion Questions

January 1 – Pray, read the devotion, ask the questions and pray.
What is the value of the training you do every day in practice?
How efficiently could you perform on game day if you didn't train well?
What are the rewards of such training?

January 2 – Pray, read the devotion, ask the questions and pray.
What part of your sport comes so easily to you that you seem to effortlessly soar in it?
When does competition seem to flow naturally and relaxed?
What parts of your spiritual life flow easily?

January 3 – Pray, read the devotion, ask the questions and pray.
If athletic talent could be measured in dollars and cents, who would be the richest player that you know?
How generous is that player in relation to his/her teammates?
Who would be the poorest player that you know?
How generous is that person toward others?
Who is your team's most giving person?

January 4 – Pray, read the devotion, ask the questions and pray.
How do you relate to your teammates when they're at their best?
How about on their worst days?
Do you ignore them, avoid them or even run and hide?
What does your heart tell you to do?
How about family or others?

January 5 – Pray, read the devotion, ask the questions and pray.
How many of us would say that we have an ideal father?
Who among us has a dad 100% without fault or inconsistency?
How does/did your father view your life in sport?

January 6 – Pray, read the devotion, ask the questions and pray.
Can you recall a time in your sport career when things were so good that you didn't want them to end? Tell us about it.
What did it cost to get to that moment?
How quickly was it over?

January 7 – Pray, read the devotion, ask the questions and pray.
Why is this kind of fear good?
Why would the fool despise wisdom?
What are the results of each?

January 8 – Pray, read the devotion, ask the questions and pray.
When do you need encouragement most?
How would a sense of God's presence affect how you practice?
Perform in competition?
Relate to your teammates, coaches, and officials?

January 9 – Pray, read the devotion, ask the questions and pray.
Have you ever know a competitor who seems to have an unbending will

to win? Tell us a story about him or her.
What best helps you to focus on your goals?
How could God help you as a competitor?

January 10 – Pray, read the devotion, ask the questions and pray.
Who are the people in your lives who encourage your heart and
strengthen you to do well? List their names. See their faces. Recall their
words.
What if God was on your list of such people?
How does the Lord encourage you?

January 11 – Pray, read the devotion, ask the questions and pray.
Who are the most trustworthy among your teammates?
On a 1-10 scale, how deeply do you trust your coaches to do what's best
for the whole team?
On a 1-10 scale, how much do your teammates and coaches trust you?
On a 1-10 scale, how much do you trust God with your life?

January 12 – Pray, read the devotion, ask the questions and pray.
Have you ever felt betrayed by a coach or a teammate?
When did it happen? What was the situation?
How did you handle it?
How do you avoid betrayal and embrace loyalty?

January 13 – Pray, read the devotion, ask the questions and pray.
What is there about your life in sport that is so difficult or painful that
you wish it would just go away? (Injury? Losses? Broken relationships?)
How does one press through this pain to do the right thing?
What has been a difficult part of your pursuit of God's will?

January 14 – Pray, read the devotion, ask the questions and pray.
What is the most reckless, dangerous and risky thing you've ever done?
What's risky about the kind of love mentioned in the scripture?
Have you experienced it? When?
When have you taken risks to love a teammate?
Who are your risky-to-love teammates?

January 15 – Pray, read the devotion, ask the questions and pray.
Who are the smartest coaches you know?
Who are the strongest players you know?
How would their wisdom and strength compare to God's?
How could you tap into God's wisdom and strength?

January 16 – Pray, read the devotion, ask the questions and pray.
Which of these is a better descriptor of your frame of mind in competi-
tion: joy and peace or anxiety and rage?
When do you experience joy and peace?
When do you experience anxiety and rage?
How can we find more joy and peace in competition?

January 17 – Pray, read the devotion, ask the questions and pray.
Have you ever felt abandoned by your team during competition? Tell us
about it.

How could Jesus feel abandoned?
How did Jesus handle his feeling of being abandoned?
How is this a model for us?

January 18 – Pray, read the devotion, ask the questions and pray.
To whom have you given your heart? An intimate friend? Family? The
Lord Jesus?
Why guard one's heart?
What flows from one's heart that could be so valuable?

January 19 – Pray, read the devotion, ask the questions and pray.
Take a moment to recall a team from your past, which had great team
unity. What were the key attitudes from which that unity sprang?
What made that team so special? List the unifying characteristics and
practices.
What can you do to foster similar attitudes among your teammates?

January 20– Pray, read the devotion, ask the questions and pray.
Does your team seem divided at times? Over what issues?
Is strife at work to tear your teammates apart and to cause disharmony?
How do we bring about the healing of relationships and restoration of
teamwork?
How does love cover transgressions?

January 21 – Pray, read the devotion, ask the questions and pray.
What is it that we as Christian athletes can do to bring about a more
intimate relationship with the Lord?
Is there some program to work through, some book to read, a tape to lis-
ten to?
What makes for a closer walk with Christ?
Why does simply doing God's will lead to intimacy with Him?
What do people substitute for doing His will to gain depth of relation-
ship with Christ?

January 22 – Pray, read the devotion, ask the questions and pray.
When does your heart need direction?
Do you ever fell like you've gone adrift or that you're wandering through
life with no clear path?
What kinds of situations can cast you adrift?
How would Christ's perseverance enhance your life?

January 23 – Pray, read the devotion, ask the questions and pray.
What do you pray about your life in sport? Situations? People? Results?
Do you regularly talk with God about each situation or just when things
seem out of control?
Which kind of prayer do you think God hears well?
How can we pray on game day? For what and whom?

January 24– Pray, read the devotion, ask the questions and pray.
Can you recall an instance when a great player was disqualified from
competition due to poor off-field decisions?
What do you suppose was driving their hearts to make such foolish decisions?

What are some evil desires of youth?
Why are they so powerful?
How can you flee from them?
How does one pursue righteousness, faith, love and peace?

January 25 – Pray, read the devotion, ask the questions and pray.
For what are you most often corrected?
How do you respond to the correction"
How would one who ignores instruction lead others astray?

January 26 – Pray, read the devotion, ask the questions and pray.
Do you ever feel isolated, cut off, all alone? When? (In season or off season; pre-game, post game; injured or suspended…)
How do you handle those feelings?
How did Jesus handle them?

January 27 – Pray, read the devotion, ask the questions and pray.
How should we as Christians approach this issue?
When does this happen most?
Why do people do it?
How do others react to it?
How do you deal with it?

January 28 – Pray, read the devotion, ask the questions and pray.
What are your goals in competition?
How do you prepare to achieve them?
How could this mindset honor Christ?

January 29 – Pray, read the devotion, ask the questions and pray.
When does your sport demand courage of you?
Is it when you face superior competition?
Does playing through injuries require courage?
Is courage a factor in overcoming fatigue?
What role does courage playing overcoming adversity?
What are some situations?
How does obeying God relate to courage?

January 30 – Pray, read the devotion, ask the questions and pray.
When do you sense satisfaction from your coaches?
How do you respond to their gladness and encouragement?
When do you sense God's satisfaction with you?

January 31 – Pray, read the devotion, ask the questions and pray.
From where does peace come for your life?
When and where do you feel most at peace?
Do you ever feel peaceful in competition? When?
Could it be there is a source of tranquility that is internal rather than based on circumstances?
What brings you and internal sense of peace?

February 1 – Pray, read the devotion, ask the questions and pray.
What would it be like to compete for something that will not tarnish on your bookshelf?

What would be a prize worth striving for that never fades, but requires great effort and concentration of will to achieve?
Tell us about some of the trophies, medals, and other awards you have won.
What are some of the more enduring rewards of life that you've received?

February 2 – Pray, read the devotion, ask the questions and pray.
To whom do you look for guidance?
Who helps you make good decisions?
What would be the consequences of your not seeking the wisdom of others?
When do you seek their counsel?
For what kinds of decisions?

February 3 – Pray, read the devotion, ask the questions and pray.
Have you had times of competition that assaulted your belief in your teammates, your game plan or even in your own abilities? Tell us about one such instance.
What do we have to believe in when our strengths are called into question?
How does your belief in Christ overcome doubts and fears?

February 4 – Pray, read the devotion, ask the questions and pray.
How do you react when you're losing by a wide margin and your opponent rubs salt in your wounds with some trash-talk?
How does it feel to lose and to hear the snickers of the winners on their way to the locker room?
What should your attitude be in the face of such disrespect?
Who is someone you know who handles this well?

February 5 – Pray, read the devotion, ask the questions and pray.
What advantages are yours when you know your opponents are intimidated by you and your teammates?
Do you ever sense their fear?
Can you see them hesitate or compete tentatively?
Have you watched as the intimidated team was overcome by a momentum shift? Tell us about that.

February 6 – Pray, read the devotion, ask the questions and pray.
How do you prepare for competition?
How do you bring your mind into focus?
What do you think about and how do you keep your goals in sight as the season moves along?
For what do you hope in Christ?

February 7 – Pray, read the devotion, ask the questions and pray.
Have you ever had teammates who would mot take correction form their coaches?
What happened with them?
How readily did you take advice?
How about now?

February 8 – Pray, read the devotion, ask the questions and pray.
What would be the most important factors in your decision to attend a university? List these factors.
How would you have responded to Jesus' recruiting style?
Can you hear his call now?
How will you respond when God calls you to serve Him?

February 9 – Pray, read the devotion, ask the questions and pray.
What distinctions are easily made between your teammates? List these differences.
What can be done to override these distinctions and to unify your team?
How does a pure heart overcome the natural distinctions?

February 10 – Pray, read the devotion, ask the questions and pray.
Would you characterize yourself as a hard worker in practice or as a lazy player? Rate yourself on a 1-10 scale, 1 = lazy and 10 = untiring worker.
How would your coach score you?
How would your teammates score you?

February 11 – Pray, read the devotion, ask the questions and pray.
As a percent, how much or your sport skills are a gift vs. something you have developed? (90/10, 50/50, 30/70)
From where do these gifts come?
How is it that you're given certain abilities and others do not possess them?
How much of your talent is a gift and how much is a cultivated skill?
How should we use our gifts and abilities in relation to our teammates and coaches?

February 12 – Pray, read the devotion, ask the questions and pray.
Have you ever had a teammate of whom you'd say, "I'm glad he's on our team? Tell us about him or her.
Why would Joshua respond this way?
What could we learn from Joshua's attitude?

February 13 – Pray, read the devotion, ask the questions and pray.
What are some factors that can produce anxiety in you prior to a competition?
How does anxiety hinder an athlete's performance?
How does a kind word help?

February 14 – Pray, read the devotion, ask the questions and pray.
What are the limiting factors for you in relation to achievement? List the factors.
What is the greatest thing you think you are capable of accomplishing?
What is the highest goal you are pursuing?
Do you believe you're able to achieve everything God has called you to do?
What feeds your belief in God's call?

February 15 – Pray, read the devotion, ask the questions and pray.
How do leaders emerge from among your teammates?
Is there a personality type or a position on the team that automatically

makes one a leader?
What is the process of leadership development on your team?
Are there common traits to these leaders?
Who could be a Jephthah kind of leader among you now?

February 16 – Pray, read the devotion, ask the questions and pray.
What is the key to attaining a position of power and influence?
How do leaders and other people of prestige and authority attain their places?
How does it usually happen in your sport?
How would you describe God's way of leading?

February 17 – Pray, read the devotion, ask the questions and pray.
On a 1-10 scale, 1 = minimum effort and 10 = diligent, where would you score yourself?
Would you characterize yourself as a diligent, hard worker in practice or do you lean toward doing just enough to get by?
What might be the eventual outcomes of each of those attitudes toward training?

February 18 – Pray, read the devotion, ask the questions and pray.
What have you left behind to pursue your athletic career? List the things you've left behind.
What do you suppose that Jesus' disciples left when he asked them to follow him? List the things they left to follow Christ.
What have you left behind to follow Christ? Has it been worth it?

February 19 – Pray, read the devotion, ask the questions and pray.
How much are you a student of your sport?
How do you study your sport?
Do you know its history and traditions?
Who are the key figures in your own program's history? List their names.
Who has left you an inheritance of faith in Christ?

February 20 – Pray, read the devotion, ask the questions and pray.
What are the attitudes that rule your hearts?
List some prevalent attitudes you possess.
List some prevalent attitudes your teammates possess.
What would it look like for one's heart to be ruled by peace?
What would it look like for a team?

February 21 – Pray, read the devotion, ask the questions and pray.
How many newspaper clippings have your parents collected about your athletic career? Tell us about how you've collected memories.
Did you ever wonder at the attention you received for playing your game?
How has public attention affected you?
How did you handle it?

February 22 – Pray, read the devotion, ask the questions and pray.
Have you ever approached a competition filled with worry and apprehension because you didn't know if you would be successful?
How does worry affect your performance?

Have you ever faced an opponent who seemed unbeatable and wondered who could possibly be concerned for your feelings?
With whom can you share your anxiety?

February 23– Pray, read the devotion, ask the questions and pray.
How clearly does your coaching staff outline your game plan? Rate on a scale of 1-10, 1 = muddy and 10 = crystal clear.
How well do you study and implement each one?
Rate on a scale of 1-10, 1 = poorly and 10 = flawlessly.
How important is the communication to the implementation?
How can we improve on both ends?

February 24 – Pray, read the devotion, ask the questions and pray.
Do you have any teammates who you'd call arrogant, boastful or proud?
Tell us when you see these traits?
When might that be seen in you?
How should we view ourselves with respect to others on our team?
How does one communicate that he/she is ready to receive advice and wisdom?

February 25 – Pray, read the devotion, ask the questions and pray.
What do you do to quiet your mind and to keep some perspective about your life?
Where do you go to relax, reflect and to meditate?
How do you stay true to who you are when everybody is praising you?

February 26 – Pray, read the devotion, ask the questions and pray.
On what basis do your opponents or teammates boast? List the subjects of boasting.
Does anyone you know boast in the power of his God?
What is there about God one would boast?

February 27 – Pray, read the devotion, ask the questions and pray.
Are there ever opportunities to score or to make a great play that escape your notice? When does that happen?
Are there other times when it seems like someone is shining a giant flashlight on the situation and the whole game slows down for you?
Describe one of these moments?
How clearly can you see hope, inheritance, and power in your life?

February 28 – Pray, read the devotion, ask the questions and pray.
Has your success in athletics and the resulting popularity ever led to a loss of privacy for you? What happened?
How did you handle it?
How would you deal with it now?

March 1 – Pray, read the devotion, ask the questions and pray.
How subject are you to mood swings with wins and losses?
What brings you joy consistently?
For what and whom do you pray most often?
When is it easy to be thankful? When is it most difficult?
How can we maintain a joyful life?

March 2 – Pray, read the devotion, ask the questions and pray.
Have you ever been a part of a team that seemed destined to win? Tell us about that team.
How confident were you as you approached each competition? How did that confidence help your team?
How confident are you about today's challenges?

March 3 – Pray, read the devotion, ask the questions and pray.
Do you ever think about the irony that accompanies some of the video-tape exchange between your opponents?
Why would teams do this?
How did Jesus handle their conspiracy?
How can you do similarly?

March 4 – Pray, read the devotion, ask the questions and pray.
What is there in sport that can match the joy of winning? List other joy-ful things in sport.
What are the desires of your heart and the requests of your lips?
How does God respond to your requests?

March 5 – Pray, read the devotion, ask the questions and pray.
Who is the strongest, most powerful player you've ever competed with or against? Tell us about him or her.
What seemed to be the source of that strength and power?
What are some sources of power and strength to athletes?
If you could access an even greater, limitless source of strength and power for your life, would you want some?
How do we gain access to God's power?

March 6 – Pray, read the devotion, ask the questions and pray.
What goals have you set that are still unachieved? List those goals.
For what have you hoped and been disappointed? List the disappoint-ments.
How did these times affect you?
List some of your desires that have been fulfilled.

March 7 – Pray, read the devotion, ask the questions and pray.
As a young athlete, who were you striving to please?
What really pleases the Lord and what makes us pleasing to Him?
How would a sense of already being pleasing to God affect how you compete?

March 8 – Pray, read the devotion, ask the questions and pray.
Have you ever had a sense that God was calling you to do something?
Did the task seem too great or your resources seem too small?
Did the call of God overwhelm you and cause you to doubt whether you had really heard Him at all?
To what do you sense the Lord calling you now?

March 9 – Pray, read the devotion, ask the questions and pray.
In what parts of your sport do you find real delight? List those delightful situations.
Which situations or settings give you a wide grin?

How does one delight himself in the Lord?

March 10 – Pray, read the devotion, ask the questions and pray.
Here's a heart check–do you do what pleases your coaches all the time
or only when they are watching?
Do you do the right thing just to win their favor or because it's right?
How about some of your teammates?
How would this attitude change you?

March 11 – Pray, read the devotion, ask the questions and pray.
How did you come to be a part of this team?
Did you just show up and volunteer or were you chosen? Who chose or
recruited you? Tell us about the process.
How did you respond when chosen?
How strongly do you feel the responsibility that comes with the privi-
lege?

March 12 – Pray, read the devotion, ask the questions and pray.
Who's the best recruiter you've ever seen? Tell us about him/her.
What was it that made him or her special?
How good would Jesus be at recruiting?
What could have gripped these men deeply enough for them to leave
their livelihood and to follow instantly?
When and how did you respond to Jesus' call to follow Him?

March 13 – Pray, read the devotion, ask the questions and pray.
How successful is a star player without his teammates and coaches?
How well could that player compete if he took on the opposing team by
himself?
When have you seen someone do this? What happened?
How does one stay attached to his team?
How does one abide in Christ?

March 14 – Pray, read the devotion, ask the questions and pray.
Why do some athletes seem so fragile?
What is your most troublesome source of pain?
How is God glorified in your personal weakness?

March 15 – Pray, read the devotion, ask the questions and pray.
How would you rate the skills possessed by your teammates and your-
self? List some of these skills?
Are you so skilled that people will be reading about you in 1500 years?
Why or why not?
What would make someone that remarkable?

March 16 – Pray, read the devotion, ask the questions and pray.
Do your family and friends sometimes misunderstand you because of
your high commitment to sport?
What is it that puzzles them?
Do they occasionally think you've lost your mind?
Tell us about an instance when they thought you'd lost it.

March 17 – Pray, read the devotion, ask the questions and pray.
To whom and to what are you most committed? List some names and
the nature of the commitment. (Friend, spouse, teammate, coach, etc...)
What do you expect to come from those committed relationships?
Do you ever become disappointed by those to whom you're committed?
When does that happen?

March 18 – Pray, read the devotion, ask the questions and pray.
Think of someone you know from sport that inspires you because of
how he or she has endured opposition, but stayed true to his principles–
do you know anyone like that? Tell us about that person.
When have you been in a similar situation?
How can such an example help us to not lose heart?

March 19 – Pray, read the devotion, ask the questions and pray.
What would it be like to be going down the road, fully confident of
being on the right highway, but you're actually heading straight for a
washed out bridge that crosses a 1,000 foot cliff?
When have you been similarly put in peril by a decision in your life?
What did you learn from that time?

March 20 – Pray, read the devotion, ask the questions and pray.
When you think of power under control, what images do you see?
Which people? What words come to mind? Tell us about them.
Why would God choose to bless the meek and not just the powerful?
What would be the inheritance of sport people whose power is under
control?

March 21 – Pray, read the devotion, ask the questions and pray.
Whom do you represent when you compete? List all that apply.
Whom do you represent off the field of competition?
Whose signature do people see in your life?

March 22 – Pray, read the devotion, ask the questions and pray.
How secure do you feel in your game?
Is your position on the team rock-solid and secure or a little tenuous?
Rate on a scale of 1-10 how secure it is.
From where does your security for life in sport and life in general come?

March 23 – Pray, read the devotion, ask the questions and pray.
How do you measure an athlete's performance?
How is it measured in your sport?
What is your stand of measure for a player's effort?
How do you gauge a competitor's commitment, loyalty or teamwork?
How does your standard for your effort differ from your expectations for
others?

March 24 – Pray, read the devotion, ask the questions and pray.
How do you describe your teammates and opponents who compete
greatly?
What words or similes do you use?
Whose competitive spirit will you remember for life?

March 25 – Pray, read the devotion, ask the questions and pray.
Have you ever chewed some gum until the very last drop of flavor was gone? What did you do with it them?
What is salty about a person's character?
Why would one lose his saltiness? How?

March 26 – Pray, read the devotion, ask the questions and pray.
Do you have any short-tempered teammates? Do you know anyone who gets angry at the drop of a hat?
How even tempered are you? Are you easily angered?
What sorts of things set you off?
What does God think about these things?

March 27 – Pray, read the devotion, ask the questions and pray.
What are some counterfeit sources you see in sport?
How does one tap into true sources of strength?
What have been your best sources of strength for life?

March 28 – Pray, read the devotion, ask the questions and pray.
Have you ever had a coach or a teammate who could instantly bring peace and order to a chaotic situation? Tell us about that person.
What did he or she do?
How can you be that sort of person for your team or your family?

March 29 – Pray, read the devotion, ask the questions and pray.
Who among your teammates leads in such a way that others will naturally follow along? Tell us about that leader.
What difference does that make in your team's performance?
How can you develop into that sort of leader for your team?

March 30 – Pray, read the devotion, ask the questions and pray.
Have you ever wondered in your mind, "What's the use, we're not doing very well, why put up with the suffering of losing?"
What kinds of situations produce that feeling in you?
How do you press through suffering?

March 31 – Pray, read the devotion, ask the questions and pray.
What attitudes are most respected and appreciated by your coaches and team leaders? Let's list some respected attitudes.
What do you suppose would be the attitude most respected by God?
Why would God be so pleased with brokenness and contrition?

April 1 – Pray, read the devotion, ask the questions and pray.
How does a gentle answer do this?
Whom do you know who does this well?
How well do you do it?

April 2 – Pray, read the devotion, ask the questions and pray.
In whom have you made a great investment? Let's each list a person or a group.
What happens between you and those in whom you make such investments?

When do you see each investment pay off?

April 3 – Pray, read the devotion, ask the questions and pray.
Do you have any teammates or friends who seemed trapped by something? If so, by what were they trapped?
How was this person set free?
What could you possibly do to remove the obstacle from their paths?

April 4 – Pray, read the devotion, ask the questions and pray.
Might one of your teammates have a glaring weakness?
 Is that person aware of the weakness?
Do you make that weakness the defining characteristic of that person?
How do we overcome our tendencies to judge and to label?

April 5 – Pray, read the devotion, ask the questions and pray.
What situations in your sport tend to produce fear in you or your teammates?
How do you deal with fear when it appears?
Who can we trust when we're assaulted by fear and anxiety?

April 6 – Pray, read the devotion, ask the questions and pray.
How much respect do you get when you go back to your hometown to visit family and friends? Do they understand who you've become?
How do you handle the respect (or lack of it) when you go home?
Why should it be this way?

April 7 – Pray, read the devotion, ask the questions and pray.
Do you ever wonder about what God's purpose for you might be?
Have you ever contemplated why God would have you born in this generation and not a hundred years earlier, or later?
How will our great-grandchildren see our lives long after we've died?
For what purposes could God have created you?
How well do you feel you're serving them?

April 8 – Pray, read the devotion, ask the questions and pray.
Do you ever fell like the Lord must be on vacation?
Does it seem that your plight has gone unnoticed? Does it seem to you that everybody but you gets breaks?
When do you fell this way?
How do you overcome the feelings and affirm your trust in God?

April 9 – Pray, read the devotion, ask the questions and pray.
Which would provide a better foundation for your home, solid rock or a sandy beach?
What kind of foundation does your team have?
How would you describe your team's foundation?
What could make it more solid?

April 10 – Pray, read the devotion, ask the questions and pray.
Whom have you known long enough to have acquired an unshakable confidence in them? Tell us about him or her.
What do you suppose was in John Stockton's mind when he passed the ball toward Karl Malone in the middle of a pick and roll?

Do you have that kind of confidence in your teammates?

April 11 – Pray, read the devotion, ask the questions and pray.
How conscious are you of the possibility that today could be your last
opportunity to compete?
Who is there in your life that lives with a Mary-like sense of readiness?
What could help you be ready to take action like Mary?

April 12 – Pray, read the devotion, ask the questions and pray.
When do you feel the pressures of your life of competition most greatly?
Who among your teammates handles such pressure well?
How do you handle similar pressures?

April 13 – Pray, read the devotion, ask the questions and pray.
Where and with whom do you seek refuge when the pressures of com-
petition are getting to you?
Where do you suppose is the best?
How can we take refuge in God? What would you do?

April 14 – Pray, read the devotion, ask the questions and pray.
Have you ever had a sense that God was helping you as you competed?
Tell us about that instance.
Do you remember having healed from an injury more quickly than nor-
mal?
What was the injury and the recovery process?
Have you obtained help from God?
Have you told anyone about it?

April 15– Pray, read the devotion, ask the questions and pray.
What is the standard for measuring commitment, loyalty and teamwork?
How about for a family?
How about for friendship?
How does one lay down his life for a teammate? Friend? Family?

April 16– Pray, read the devotion, ask the questions and pray.
Who are your heroes in this game? Let's list them.
Wouldn't it be great to be like that player? Wouldn't you like to emulate
your mentor?
Who has been a sport mentor to you?
What qualities of your hero or mentor would you like to possess?

April 17 – Pray, read the devotion, ask the questions and pray.
What's the greatest mismatch in competition that you've ever experi-
enced? Describe that for us.
On which side of the mismatch were you? Were you the underdog or the
heavy favorite?
What was the outcome?
How does one prepare for such competitions?

April 18 – Pray, read the devotion, ask the questions and pray.
If one farmer sows 100 pounds of seed and another farmer sows 10,000
pounds which one will have the greater harvest?
How have you seen this principle work in your life?

How can we use this to our advantage?

April 19 – Pray, read the devotion, ask the questions and pray.
In your life as a competitor, have you ever experienced great courage and
an unnaturally calm spirit in the midst of tremendous struggle and fear?
When did that happen?
Who is a person like this in your life?
How does he or she do that for you?
For whom are you that kind of person?

April 20 – Pray, read the devotion, ask the questions and pray.
How do you approach the sport in which you compete? Is it just a game
to you or is there more to it than that? Rate on a scale of 1-10, 1 = just a
game and 10 = it's my life.
How do you practice? Do you apply all you have and all that you are to
improving your game or do you just try to get through practice and do
what it takes to keep the coach off your back?
How can your values be seen in your daily habits?

April 21 – Pray, read the devotion, ask the questions and pray.
When, in the course of a season, do you begin to lose a little steam?
When are you starting to run low on energy?
How do you press through these conditions to compete well?
What can you do to regain your strength and vitality?

April 22– Pray, read the devotion, ask the questions and pray.
Do you ever get tired, a little leg weary? Does it ever seem like you're
dragging an anchor back and forth through practice?
How do you come to Christ for this rest?
When do you experience such rest?

April 23 – Pray, read the devotion, ask the questions and pray.
What are your plans for this season? Do you have goals for your team or
for yourself? List some of these goals.
What are the keys to seeing your goals achieved?
How does one commit his/her work to the Lord?

April 24 – Pray, read the devotion, ask the questions and pray.
Have you heard about Kareem Abdul Jabbar's college basketball career?
Have you ever seem him play?
How have you adapted to changes in order to compete well?
How have you experienced God's strength in your weakness?

April 25 – Pray, read the devotion, ask the questions and pray.
Have you ever heard a disrespectful comment or seen a gesture by a
competitor inflame the competitive edge in his opponent and lead to his
or her team's defeat? Tell us about the incident.
Why would God be pleased by our expressions of respect?
How can you show proper respect to others in your sport experience
this week?

April 26 – Pray, read the devotion, ask the questions and pray.
Have you competed to the point of total exhaustion?

How does one continue to compete, even when at the point of physical breakdown and total collapse?
How does God strengthen you in such moments?

April 27 – Pray, read the devotion, ask the questions and pray.
What are some of the traditions in your sport?
Do any of those things ever violate your conscience or cause you to wonder if you should be involved in them? Which ones? Why?
How does one choose God's way over man's?

April 28 – Pray, read the devotion, ask the questions and pray.
Rewards for performing well in sport are numerous. What are some rewards you've attained?
How valuable are those rewards to you now?
What are some of the less tangible, but more valuable rewards in sport?

April 29 – Pray, read the devotion, ask the questions and pray.
Have you ever wondered why your path seems to zig zag sometimes?
Why am I here? How did I end up in this place when I was going over there?
At what points in your life have you had similar thoughts?
How has God directed your steps?

April 30 – Pray, read the devotion, ask the questions and pray.
How many people around the world would love to compete in your sport?
When do you feel the privilege that is yours?
How many would love to see what you see and hear what you hear?
What can you hear that can't be heard from the top row?
What can you see that non-participants cannot?
How can you express gratitude for such blessings?

May 1 – Pray, read the devotion, ask the questions and pray.
Have you ever stood in a stream and felt the power of the current pulling everything downstream?
Have you ever tried to outrun the wind on a March afternoon?
When do you feel a similar flow in your sport?
Does your spiritual life have a similar flow of power?
When do you feel it?

May 2 – Pray, read the devotion, ask the questions and pray.
Have you ever taken some heat for your convictions? Tell us about that situation.
Have you been criticized for doing the right thing?
How do you handle the criticism?
Why would the kingdom of heaven be theirs?

May 3 – Pray, read the devotion, ask the questions and pray.
Have you ever considered how very fortunate you are to participate in sport?
Where is your favorite place in sport?
How often do you get to go there?
Where do you experience God's presence most vividly?

May 4 – Pray, read the devotion, ask the questions and pray.
Have you ever felt that you were personally tainted by the cheap shot taken by a teammate or by the unethical tactics or gamesmanship of your coach? Tell us about that incident.
How did you handle that moment?
How often have you though of doing the same?
Why did you not do it?

May 5 – Pray, read the devotion, ask the questions and pray.
Who has been your most powerful opponent?
How does love overcome fear?
How is anxiety counteracted by self-control?

May 6 – Pray, read the devotion, ask the questions and pray.
How well do you control your emotions during competition? Do you blow up on occasion or do you stay under control? Rate yourself on a 1-10 scale.
How is self-control better than power?
Over what do you daily need self-control?

May 7 – Pray, read the devotion, ask the questions and pray.
What is your most prized possession?
What did it cost you?
How valuable is it to you?
How did you acquire it?
Which relationships are most valuable in your life?

May 8 – Pray, read the devotion, ask the questions and pray.
Which of these questions have you asked yourself? Will we have that dream season, undefeated and champions? Will we be winless and disheartened?
How did you answer yourself in pre-season?
How will did last season's results match your dreams?
How can we prepare to finish our lives well?

May 9 – Pray, read the devotion, ask the questions and pray.
How critical is good teamwork to your individual success?
How much of your success can you directly tie to your teammates and their support?
When do you most need your teammates?
In what ways can you further assist your teammates?

May 10 – Pray, read the devotion, ask the questions and pray.
Who is the greatest player you've ever known?
Did he or she do everything well or was there one small flaw in his or her game?
What was that flaw?
How do you think people perceived Jesus when He was on the earth?
What is one flaw in your life that Christ's power could restore?

May 11 – Pray, read the devotion, ask the questions and pray.
At this point in your sport career, in how many games have you compet-

ed? Could you count them?
Looking into the future, how many more do you think you have left?
How do we prepare ourselves to make the best of our remaining days?

May 12 – Pray, read the devotion, ask the questions and pray.
Have you ever been in a competition and observed how momentum
swings from one team to the other?
What causes momentum shifts in your sport?
When have you seen a 7 to 1 momentum shift in sports?
How does momentum shift in life beyond sport?
How do you dial with momentum shifts?

May 13 – Pray, read the devotion, ask the questions and pray.
Have you ever been afraid for your life? When and where was that?
How did the fear affect you?
How did you overcome the fear?
How does God's presence dispel fear?

May 14 – Pray, read the devotion, ask the questions and pray.
Have you had to battle gossip on your team? When?
How do we deal with this and what results from this kind of behavior?
What are we to do instead of repeating the matter?

May 15 – Pray, read the devotion, ask the questions and pray.
What would it take for you to compromise your integrity?
Which would be the most tempting? (Wins, money, fame, power, sex,
records...)
How much money would it take for you to shave points for gambling
interests?
What would be the consequences of such actions?
How does one guard his or her heart?

May 16 – Pray, read the devotion, ask the questions and pray.
Tell us about your adolescent dreams of championships.
What were your most grandiose childhood dreams?
How big to you dream now?
What do you suppose are God's dreams for you?

May 17– Pray, read the devotion, ask the questions and pray.
What's the longest losing streak you can remember suffering through?
Tell us about those days.
How long does your best winning streak seem in comparison? Describe
the feeling you had during this streak.
Why does it seem that losing streaks drag on, but winning streaks just
whiz by?
How should we pray when we're in such streaks?

May 18 – Pray, read the devotion, ask the questions and pray.
What is the most appropriate posture for a team leader? Is it standing
confidently?
Trick Question!
Why would Jesus do this?
How can we do similarly with our teammates?

May 19 – Pray, read the devotion, ask the questions and pray.
What do you have trouble believing when you consider your team's prospects for the season?
Can you believe you'll be conference champions?
Can you believe you'll have a winning season?
Do you believe you'll defeat your strongest rival?
Do you really believe you'll win today's contest?
Which of those seems beyond your grasp?
How can we overcome our unbelief?

May 20 – Pray, read the devotion, ask the questions and pray.
How do you respond to your coach's correction?
How do you react when a teammate tells you your technique needs improvement?
When do you sense the Lord's correction for your life?
How do you respond when the Holy Spirit prompts changes in your life?

May 21 – Pray, read the devotion, ask the questions and pray.
What would you do if you were given a blank check and allowed to write in the amount?
Would you write in a big amount or a more modest number?
What have been your most outrageous prayer requests?
What happened when you prayed?

May 22 – Pray, read the devotion, ask the questions and pray.
Where do you find strength for competition when you've become weary?
Who is your source of power when your legs, arms, back and even your mind is tired?
How does one's life in Christ strengthen his or her body, soul, and mind?

May 23 – Pray, read the devotion, ask the questions and pray.
Have you ever felt like your coaches or teammates expected more from you than you were capable of giving? When do you feel this way?
How do you handle expectations that seem unreasonable?
What do you think God expects of us?

May 24 – Pray, read the devotion, ask the questions and pray.
What are the characteristics of your life that show your true nature?
Let's make a list for each individual.
Do your actions accurately reflect the condition of your heart?
How can we demonstrate love, joy, and peace today?

May 25 – Pray, read the devotion, ask the questions and pray.
How would you describe the way you relate to your teammates, coaches, and friends?
When do you most need patience?
How do we show kindness in sport?
What does goodness look like in your relationships?

May 26 – Pray, read the devotion, ask the questions and pray.
When people talk about you, do the words faithful, gentle and self-con-

trolled come up?
To whom do you demonstrate faithfulness?
How gentle are you with people? Rate yourself on a 1-10 scale.
When do you most need self-control?

May 27 – Pray, read the devotion, ask the questions and pray.
Can you recall a time when your coaching staff told you something
about an upcoming opponent that triggered some questions? (They're
how big? Are they really that good? They're how fast? Why are we playing them? Can we compete with them?) Who was that opponent?
Did you dare ask the question or did you bite your tongue, afraid to ask
it?
Why would Jesus tell the disciples this?

May 28 – Pray, read the devotion, ask the questions and pray.
Do you have any teammates who seem to compete for themselves and
tend to shun their responsibilities to the team? When do you sense this
attitude?
Is there anything wrong with separating my personal competition from
the rest of the team? What is so wrong with that?
Should you pursue your personal goals if they conflict with the team's
goals? Why?

May 29 – Pray, read the devotion, ask the questions and pray.
Tell us about a time when your sport dreams were realized.
How did you celebrate your achievement?
How will you respond in the next similar moment?

May 30 – Pray, read the devotion, ask the questions and pray.
Which of your preseason goals seem to be presently impossible? Which
see totally beyond your grasp?
How do you stay focused when success seems so remote?
How do you define success?

May 31 – Pray, read the devotion, ask the questions and pray.
When has someone said something to you that saved you lots of pain,
heartache and suffering?
How did you take the warning?
How risky is it to warn a friend of approaching peril?

June 1 – Pray, read the devotion, ask the questions and pray.
Have you ever wanted a refuge, a place to hide from problems or adver-
sity? What were those problems?
Where does the Christian athlete go when trouble comes? How do we
handle great pressure or turmoil?
How does this work for you in practical terms?

June 2 – Pray, read the devotion, ask the questions and pray.
Do you ever get tired of practice? What part of practice is most tire-
some?
Does it seem that all your hours of training and practice seem to go for
nothing?
Why do we keep practicing anyway?

June 3 – Pray, read the devotion, ask the questions and pray.
Why do we have to practice all the time?
Why do we continually run these same drills on fundamentals? Haven't
we attained enough experience to do away with all this repetition?
What are your best skills?
How were those skills acquired?

June 4 – Pray, read the devotion, ask the questions and pray.
What part of practice and conditioning seems to be just plain old hard
work?
Has such a workout ever pushed you to the point of total exhaustion and
even tears? Tell us about one such workout.
What is a sport equivalent to harvest?

June 5 – Pray, read the devotion, ask the questions and pray.
What are some of the foundational principles of your sport?
From whom did you learn them?
How many of those principles apply to life beyond your sport?

June 6 – Pray, read the devotion, ask the questions and pray.
When did you become aware of your giftedness for sport?
How has your gift brought you before great people?
What other gifts do you possess which could give you favor with great
people?

June 7 – Pray, read the devotion, ask the questions and pray.
Which seems to be the tougher assignment for you, working a double-
team or a simple man-to-man defense?
How do certain of your teammates complement each other?
What is most helpful in building teamwork for you?

June 8 – Pray, read the devotion, ask the questions and pray.
Which of your opponents started the season intending to be first, to be
champions?
How many will finish that way?
How does this shape your attitude across a long season?

June 9 – Pray, read the devotion, ask the questions and pray.
What is your favorite thing about competition?
How should a Christian compete?
List some characteristics you would like to embody as a Christian com-
petitor.

June 10 – Pray, read the devotion, ask the questions and pray.
What is the value of the training you do every day in practice?
How efficiently could you perform on game day if you didn't train well?
To what percentage could you achieve without practice?
What are the rewards of such training?
How does your sport reward you?

June 11 – Pray, read the devotion, ask the questions and pray.
Have you ever competed in track? What events?

Do you remember running in a race and seeing someone caught running out of his lane? Was that person disqualified?
What could disqualify a person in life?

June 12 – Pray, read the devotion, ask the questions and pray.
Which is the better part of a baseball game, the first pitch or the bottom of the final inning?
Do you prefer to see, a football game's opening kickoff or the "Hail Mary" pass in the last seconds?
Does the opening tip of a basketball game or the desperation shot at the buzzer hold more excitement for you?
Why is the end better than the beginning?

June 13 – Pray, read the devotion, ask the questions and pray.
How deeply do you love your friends, teammates and coaches? Name one and rate your love for him or her on a scale of ocean (deep) to mud puddle (shallow).
How deeply are you touched by their personal moments of grief and pain?
When were you deeply affected by their pain?
Why is it worth the risk to share their pain and grief?

June 14 – Pray, read the devotion, ask the questions and pray.
In our society, who seems to be the greater, the player who scores 25 points and grabs 15 rebounds a game or the one who carries water to his or her teammates during the time outs?
Why would society see it that way?
Why would God value the servant more highly?

June 15 – Pray, read the devotion, ask the questions and pray.
How many hours do you spend in preparation for one game?
How about your opponents?
Does extra practice always make for more wins?
What other factors go in to making a team victorious?

June 16 – Pray, read the devotion, ask the questions and pray.
How can we as athletes fully please God with our efforts?
How can we best serve God's will in relation to our teammates and coaches?
Who do you know among your family or teammates who has a real burden to bear?
How can you help that person bear his load?

June 17 – Pray, read the devotion, ask the questions and pray.
How quickly are you provoked to anger during competition?
What pushes your angry button?
Would your teammates say that you are slow to anger or that you have a short fuse?
How do you control your anger?

June 18 – Pray, read the devotion, ask the questions and pray.
What are the most difficult tests for you as an athlete?
Do you find the athletic testing hard? How about academic tests?

How well do you measure up when your character is tested?
What situations regularly test your character?

June 19 – Pray, read the devotion, ask the questions and pray.
When does selfish ambition appear in your sport?
How is vain conceit harmful to a team?
How does one put others ahead of himself in a competitive world?

June 20 – Pray, read the devotion, ask the questions and pray.
How would you describe the sense of team unity experienced by this
team? Rate it on a scale of 1-10, 1 = fragmented and 10 = unified.
What are the benefits that accompany a team with great unity versus a
team that is full or strife, contention and selfish attitudes?
What can we do today that builds unity?

June 21 – Pray, read the devotion, ask the questions and pray.
Why do you compete in sport? What is your underlying motivation for
competition?
Which of these best describes your view of those against whom you
compete: worthy opponent, necessary evil, enemy, friend, or fellow competitor?
How well do you pull your weight for your team?

June 22 – Pray, read the devotion, ask the questions and pray.
Do you enjoy paying taxes? Do you pay them anyway?
To whom do you pay taxes? Make a list.
What claim does God have on your life? What do you owe Him? How
could you pay Him?

June 23 – Pray, read the devotion, ask the questions and pray.
What are the keys to success as an athlete?
What brings about the best life for us as Christians?
How does one apply his or her heart to discipline and ears to words of
knowledge?

June 24 – Pray, read the devotion, ask the questions and pray.
Can you remember a time when you defeated an opponent that was
highly favored over you? Tell us about that.
Who won?
Why is it that the better team doesn't always win?

June 25 – Pray, read the devotion, ask the questions and pray.
From whom did you learn your leadership style? Do you tend to emulate
a coach or team leader from past teams? Tell us about him or her.
Who might we find to be examples of poor leadership?
What was missing in their leadership?
How could greatness come from service?

June 26 – Pray, read the devotion, ask the questions and pray.
What is the difference between freedom and license? How are liberty
and anarchy different?
When does one cross the line from living freely to taking advantage of
others?

When is that line crossed in your sport?
How could loving service guard our freedom?

June 27 – Pray, read the devotion, ask the questions and pray.
Have you ever wanted to say something to a friend, but chickened out at the last minute because you thought it might seem silly or embarrassing?
What was it you wanted to say?
Did you later regret not saying it?
How can we be prepared for our next opportunity?

June 28 – Pray, read the devotion, ask the questions and pray.
How do you prioritize to know what's most important?
To whom do you look for values, direction and purpose?
Why would Jesus say this is the first and greatest commandment?

June 29 – Pray, read the devotion, ask the questions and pray.
How much thoughtful preparation goes into single competition for you?
Take a moment to calculate a number.
How much do you believe God thinks about you? How often are you at the front of His mind? Who could calculate such a number?
Why would God care to give such careful thought about each of us?

June 30 – Pray, read the devotion, ask the questions and pray.
Have you ever felt like you were out of God's reach? When did you last feel that way?
Have you ever prayed on game day and wondered if God was hearing you?
What led to those feelings?
When do you sense the Lord's strength?

July 1 – Pray, read the devotion, ask the questions and pray.
What is it that best motivates you to compete at your highest level?
What best stimulates some of your teammates?
How can you stir up our teammates to be their best?

July 2 – Pray, read the devotion, ask the questions and pray.
Have you ever seem a teammate or friend who seems to be bound by something?
What was it that had them restrained?
Are they still in chains or have they been freed?
How do we help the situation? What can be done to free them?

July 3 – Pray, read the devotion, ask the questions and pray.
When you come into game day, are you confident or fearful? Do you run to the field with great expectation or run away with great anxiety?
How much is your attitude affected by the nature of your opponent?
How do we put away our apprehension and take on boldness?

July 4 – Pray, read the devotion, ask the questions and pray.
How well do you get along with the people on your team? Give yourself a letter grade – A, B, C, D, or F.
How well with the coaching staff? Give yourself a letter grade – A, B, C, D, or F.

How well with your family? Give yourself a letter grade–A, B, C, D, or F. Think of the people for whom you had the worst grade; how can you give them real love today?

July 5 – Pray, read the devotion, ask the questions and pray.
How do you focus your mind on game day?
What is your pre-game routine?
How do you keep thinking about doing well and not about failure and loss?
How do you keep worry and anxiety from crowding into your mind?
How would meditation on Christ bring peace to your mind?

July 6 – Pray, read the devotion, ask the questions and pray.
Which of these would most people see as being greater, the driver of the team bus or the star player riding in the back?
Which would appear to be more important, the star athlete or the trainer who hands her a bottle of water?
Who would seem greater, the quest of honor at the team banquet or the person washing the dishes?
We know what most would say, but what do you think?
What would Jesus say?
Why would His values be different?

July 7 – Pray, read the devotion, ask the questions and pray.
Have there been moments in your sport career when you found yourself burdened by feelings or quilt or condemnation? For what did you feel that way?
How did you deal with those feelings?
How do you deal with a guilty conscience?

July 8 – Pray, read the devotion, ask the questions and pray.
Who was the most intimidating opponent you ever faced in competition? Tell us about him or her.
How did you perceive yourself in comparison with his or her abilities and stature?
Did your opponent see you in that same light?
How can we overcome a "grasshopper complex"?

July 9 – Pray, read the devotion, ask the questions and pray.
As we all know, the fundamentals of your sport are the beginning of success. How foolish would it look to compete at your level without knowledge of techniques and training?
What are some of those fundamentals?
What are some fundamentals of faith?

July 10 – Pray, read the devotion, ask the questions and pray.
Have you ever competed in a domed stadium or seen a game in one?
When and where was it?
Do you fully understand what holds the roof up? How does that thing stay up there with snow on it? From what does the roof hang?
How do the law and prophets hand on the greatest commandments?
How deeply have you committed yourself to loving God, then to appropriating His inexhaustible love toward others?

July 11 – Pray, read the devotion, ask the questions and pray.
How would you describe your attitude coming into today's game?
How well are you getting along with your teammates and coaching staff?
How well do the words of verse 4 describe you today?
How can we employ these attitudes today?

July 12 – Pray, read the devotion, ask the questions and pray.
What helps you to ward off fear when it comes?
How do you find confidence to combat such an enemy?
Who comes to your aid when you're gripped by fear?

July 13 – Pray, read the devotion, ask the questions and pray.
Who is someone from your sport, that if he was to walk in the room
right now, we'd all fell compelled to give up our seats, to offer something
to drink and to serve in any way possible? Who would be deserving of
such respect and admiration?
Who sacrifices like this on your team?
Ho can you lead like the Son of Man today?

July 14 – Pray, read the devotion, ask the questions and pray.
Who is there in your life that you love deeply, from the heart? Give us a
name.
How was that love formed?
How does a purified heart lead to a deeper love for our teammates,
friends and family?

July 15 – Pray, read the devotion, ask the questions and pray.
Who is the greatest source for wisdom in your life? Whose name comes
to mind?
For what parts of your life do you most need wisdom today?
How do you access God's wisdom and understanding?

July 16 – Pray, read the devotion, ask the questions and pray.
Have you ever seen the last place team, jump up and beat the previously
undefeated, first place squad?
How could that happen? When and where did that happen?
How much was overconfidence to blame?
How does one keep himself humble?

July 17 – Pray, read the devotion, ask the questions and pray.
When was the last time you were running in practice and your legs felt
like spaghetti?
Where could one find new strength and vigor for the day's competition?
How does this strength get from your heart to your legs?

July 18 – Pray, read the devotion, ask the questions and pray.
Do you know anyone who holds grudges or seems to have a recording
of every wrong ever done to him or her?
How is it and how are the affected by it?
How do we protect our hearts from these attitudes?

July 19 – Pray, read the devotion, ask the questions and pray.
Can you recall the feelings of arriving home after winning a championship or a victory over your fiercest rival? Tell us about that.
How did you keep your mind focused on your sport and not get distracted by all the noise?
How do you maintain your focus for life?

July 20– Pray, read the devotion, ask the questions and pray.
In whom do you place your trust? In sport? In relationships? In matters of faith?
How much do you trust that person? Give us a percent.
Could you trust him or her with your very life?

July 21 – Pray, read the devotion, ask the questions and pray.
Who is the smartest person you know? Whose face do you see?
Who knows more about your sport than anyone else does?
How smart are you?
How heavily do you rest on your limited understanding?
How do we tap into God's wisdom for life?

July 22 – Pray, read the devotion, ask the questions and pray.
What kind of things do you do for people you love?
How do you express your love for you family, friends, teammates and others?
How do we express a love for God?

July 23 – Pray, read the devotion, ask the questions and pray.
What are some essential qualities for an athlete to bring into competition? Make a list.
When does your sport require courage?
How do we recognize courage in a competitor?

July 24 – Pray, read the devotion, ask the questions and pray.
What makes up the daily workouts that you use to build your body?
What is the most effective in building up your mind?
How do you build your heart?

July 25 – Pray, read the devotion, ask the questions and pray.
What would it be like to receive a great inheritance?
What would the most valuable inheritance be for someone of wisdom?
How would one inherit honor?

July 26 – Pray, read the devotion, ask the questions and pray.
How much of your personal success do you owe to your team?
How many hours per week are reasonable for you to practice? Who determines the proper amount of preparation that is necessary for each competition?
To whom are you responsible for the most important parts of your life?

July 27 – Pray, read the devotion, ask the questions and pray.
What is it that best motivates you for competition?
What stimulates you to love people more?

What provokes good deeds in your life?

July 28 – Pray, read the devotion, ask the questions and pray.
Have you ever heard people speak of "once in a lifetime opportunities?"
Have you ever had one of those? Tell us about that opportunity.
Did you recognize it at the time?
How can we be as responsive as Mary?

July 29 – Pray, read the devotion, ask the questions and pray.
Is there someone in your life you can count on to always be the same?
Whose name did you think of?
Who do you now that you would describe as steady, faithful, and consistent?
For whom are you that person?

July 30 – Pray, read the devotion, ask the questions and pray.
Do you ever wonder if God has a real plan for your life?
When do you think about such things?
Is there ever a thought that maybe God has something in mind for you that would make you most fully satisfied and wholly fulfilled?
What do you think that might be?

July 31 – Pray, read the devotion, ask the questions and pray.
Have you ever suffered an injury and wondered where the Lord was?
When was that and how did it happen?
Why did He allow me to get hurt? Could it be in God's plan for me to be injured?
If harm is not His plan, why do we suffer?
August 1 – Pray, read the devotion, ask the questions and pray.
Have you ever lost hope in doing well? When did that happen?
Have you had a season where you dreaded competition because you expected to lose?
How do you turn that around?
How do we redeem our attitudes and expect the best?

August 2 – Pray, read the devotion, ask the questions and pray.
If you were to pick out one principle for competing in your sport as the most important, which would it be?
If there were one commandment for life that is primary, what would it be?
Which part of your life, heart soul, mind or strength, would you say is nearest 100% in commitment to Christ?
Which part is furthest away from 100% commitment?

August 3 – Pray, read the devotion, ask the questions and pray.
What sorts of things do you need on a daily basis to compete well? Let's make a list.
What could be the things that feed your soul that are also needed daily?
How and with what do you feed your soul?

August 4 –
Can you imagine how tightly you'd grip a rope if it were the only thing holding you from falling off a 500-foot cliff?

To what do you hold that tightly in sport?
What life principles do you hold on to that tightly?

August 5 – Pray, read the devotion, ask the questions and pray.
How do you respond when you see a teammate who demonstrates
strong commitment and devotion to his or her sport or to his or her
team?
Do you wonder why?
Have you ever asked him or her why he or she's so committed? What
did he or she say?
How do you communicate your commitment to Christ?

August 6 – Pray, read the devotion, ask the questions and pray.
What do you hate more than anything on earth?
When have you seen haughty eyes?
Why would God hate them?

August 7 – Pray, read the devotion, ask the questions and pray.
Have you ever had a teammate who lied to your coach or the team? Tell
us about it.
How did you react?
What did it do to your team?

August 8 – Pray, read the devotion, ask the questions and pray.
Have you ever been the victim of a cheap shot in your sport? Tell us the
story.
How did you respond to the incident?
How can love overcome the temptation to take a cheap shot?

August 9 – Pray, read the devotion, ask the questions and pray.
Do you remember hearing about some of the outrageous recruiting vio-
lations of recent years? What happened in that situation?
How about the academic cheating at some institutions?
Who dreams up that stuff?
Why do they do such things?

August 10 – Pray, read the devotion, ask the questions and pray.
Have you heard the story of Len Bias?
Can you relate a similar story?
Why would God hate this?

August 11 – Pray, read the devotion, ask the questions and pray.
How well do you handle press conferences or newspaper and television
interviews?
How do you handle it when a coach resigns or is fired?
What do you tell your friends when a teammate is suspended, benched,
injured or dismissed?
Do you tell the truth or do you concoct a story to cover the situation?

August 12 – Pray, read the devotion, ask the questions and pray.
Have you ever been on a team where someone is constantly stirring up
trouble between teammates or with the coaching staff? Tell us about that.
Why did he or she do this?

How did it affect your team?

August 13 – Pray, read the devotion, ask the questions and pray.
What sorts of things get you down during the season?
How do you handle those things?
How do you maintain your attitude?

August 14 – Pray, read the devotion, ask the questions and pray.
We talked elsewhere about the most important principle of your sport
and about the number one commandment for life. What might be principle and commandment number two?
How do we live out love your teammate as yourself, love your coach as
yourself, and love your officials as yourself?
How do we really apply love your opponent as yourself?

August 15 – Pray, read the devotion, ask the questions and pray.
When do you feel conflicted, like your heart is divided?
What are some often conflicting values in your sport?
How do you maintain a good conscience?

August 16 – Pray, read the devotion, ask the questions and pray.
With whom have you competed that had extraordinary vision for your
sport? Who seemed to be able to see things on the field of competition
that no one else could see?
What would it be like to see things as God sees them?
How can we begin to do so?

August 17 – Pray, read the devotion, ask the questions and pray.
When was the last time you did some honest evaluation of your abilities?
When have you sized up your competition to see how well you've done?
How could honest self-evaluation shape your attitude?

August 18 – Pray, read the devotion, ask the questions and pray.
Have you ever been a part of a great team? Tell us about that team.
Have you noticed how people around the team tend to boast and brag
about how good they are? Who boasted about your team?
In whom do you boast? In whom do you take pride?

August 19 – Pray, read the devotion, ask the questions and pray.
What were your preseason expectations?
Upon what were they based?
Upon what do your expectations of God rest?

August 20 – Pray, read the devotion, ask the questions and pray.
Which relationships do you pursue most vigorously?
How strongly do you pursue wisdom?
Where do you look for him/her?

August 21 – Pray, read the devotion, ask the questions and pray.
What sort of sacrifices have you made for your athletic career? What
have you given up to pursue a life of athletics? Let's make a list.
Has it been worth it? Why?
What do you sacrifice in daily worship of Christ Jesus?

August 22 – Pray, read the devotion, ask the questions and pray.
What sort of things do you value most highly?
What are some treasures worthy of protection?
Where do you keep items that are valuable to you?
What are the values that guide how you choose friends?

August 23 – Pray, read the devotion, ask the questions and pray.
Have you ever seen an athlete compete like he was stalking his oppo-
nent? Tell us about that person.
When you compete do you do it with passion and ferocity? Is it possible
that these kinds of ideas are in the bible?
What does God give you that feeds your soul?

August 24 – Pray, read the devotion, ask the questions and pray.
What is the most durable thing you can think of?
What is there in your life that will outlive you?
Why is love greater than faith and hope?
How have faith, hope and love proven durable in your life?

August 25 – Pray, read the devotion, ask the questions and pray.
Where do you look for wisdom about how to do things? Let's list some
people and places where we find wisdom.
What is the source of ultimate truth?
How do we find real life?
What are some situations when you experience the best of life?

August 26 – Pray, read the devotion, ask the questions and pray.
What could you look for that upon its being found pays the dividend of
life itself?
What could be so valuable that when it's attained bring s the best of life?
Why are wisdom and life so strongly connected?
How have you received favor from God?

August 27 – Pray, read the devotion, ask the questions and pray.
Who are the best leaders among your teammates?
How would you describe their leadership?
Would you say that they communicate freely or rather grudgingly?
Why is open communication important to leadership?

August 28 – Pray, read the devotion, ask the questions and pray.
What would happen if the greatest player you've ever heard of came to
your practice and wanted to play with your team?
How would you react?
How much respect would be given?
Whom do you similarly respect today?
How do you communicate such respect?

August 29 – Pray, read the devotion, ask the questions and pray.
For what do you hope with a great confidence that it will be realized?
List some of your goals for sport, life, and family….
Of what are you certain without ever having seen it?
How do you exercise your faith in Christ?

August 30 – Pray, read the devotion, ask the questions and pray.
When does failure sting the most sharply? Immediately or after a year or two?
What kind of failure results in personal loss?
Have you ever had a teammate who seemed addicted to failure? Tell us about him/her.
How would loving wisdom protect us from harm?

August 31 – Pray, read the devotion, ask the questions and pray.
What one thing could be added to your game that would make you the competitor that you've always dreamed of being?
What do you really need to be the most complete person you could be?
What have you received from God that makes you more complete?

September 1 – Pray, read the devotion, ask the questions and pray.
When you were a child, did you play with Play-doh modeling clay?
What did you make from it?
How much are you like Play-doh?
Are you soft and moldable or rigid and resistant to change?
What pressures in your life squeeze you into strange shapes?
How do you resist the pressure to conform?

September 2 – Pray, read the devotion, ask the questions and pray.
What happens in the process of metamorphosis for an insect?
How are people transformed?
Which parts of your life have been transformed?

September 3 – Pray, read the devotion, ask the questions and pray.
Do you wonder from time to time how you'll match up with your competition over the season? How do you think about this?
How good a player are you in relation to others on your team or on your opposing teams?
What are your standards for these judgments?

September 4 – Pray, read the devotion, ask the questions and pray.
Does your team seem divided at times? Is strife at work to tear you teammates apart and to cause disharmony?
If so, when do you sense the division?
How do we bring about the healing of relationships and the restoration of teamwork?

September 5 – Pray, read the devotion, ask the questions and pray.
When do you sense the privilege that is yours through sport?
What are some of the responsibilities that come with that privilege?
What are some narrow gate choices you have to make?

September 6 – Pray, read the devotion, ask the questions and pray.
What is your standard for greatness, for intelligence, for wisdom?
How are these things measured in the world?
How does God measure wisdom?

September 7 – Pray, read the devotion, ask the questions and pray.
Who among us likes to get his or hear ear chewed off by the coach?
Who enjoys correction?
Why is correction necessary?
When has wise correction shown you the way to life?

September 8 – Pray, read the devotion, ask the questions and pray.
Who is there in your life that loves sincerely?
How is sincere love expressed?
Whom do you love that way?
To what good things in life do you cling?

September 9 – Pray, read the devotion, ask the questions and pray.
How do we see God's favor in our lives?
What does it look like to have God's favor in sport?
How would God establish the work of our hands?
What do you do with your hands that God should care to establish?

September 10 – Pray, read the devotion, ask the questions and pray.
In whom do you most strongly trust?
If you were Mary, how much would you trust Jesus?
Why would she trust Him?
Who trusts you like this?
With what parts of your life do you need to trust Jesus more?

September 11 – Pray, read the devotion, ask the questions and pray.
How much trash talking do you hear on the field of competition?
How much of it do you do?
How should we think about such speech?
What is helpful to you in controlling your tongue?

September 12 – Pray, read the devotion, ask the questions and pray.
How may Hall of Fame members or All Americans end their athletic careers without the ultimate championship for which they had hoped and competed? How many can you name from your sport?
Are their careers less complete because of this?
When do you sense that your spiritual life is complete?

September 13 – Pray, read the devotion, ask the questions and pray.
What are the foundational principles upon which your sport is built?
Do they appear to be wise or foolish? How so?
How enduring will the lessons you learn from sport be?
Does your spiritual life feel rock solid or a little sandy?

September 14 – Pray, read the devotion, ask the questions and pray.
What is there in your sport that gives you a sense of belonging? What makes you feel like you belong to the team or the organization?
What gives you a similar sense of belonging to Christ?
How does that affect your daily living?

September 15 – Pray, read the devotion, ask the questions and pray.
What do you do for sport? Let's list everything we do for sport.

What would be on a fool's list?
How can we pursue wisdom like sport?

September 16 – Pray, read the devotion, ask the questions and pray.
What sort of person would be worthy of honor if he or she walked into this room right now?
How much do you honor your teammates?
How devoted are you to your team?
How can we express honor and devotion?

September 17 – Pray, read the devotion, ask the questions and pray.
With whom are you more likely to spend some time in conversation after a hard fought game, the first-time spectator or the friends and family who have invested years of life and love into your career?
Whose names come to mind?
Whom would you avoid?
What are some character traits that you distrust?

September 18 – Pray, read the devotion, ask the questions and pray.
Who has been the strongest influence on your athletic career?
Has there been more than one person who has made a significant impact in making you the player you've become? Who were some of those others?
Who would list you as such an influence?

September 19 – Pray, read the devotion, ask the questions and pray.
Have you ever seen an athlete compete who seemed to be completely in his or her own league? Who was that?
What was it that distinguished him/her from the rest?
Why would people fear those who are called by the name of the Lord?

September 20 – Pray, read the devotion, ask the questions and pray.
What are your worries as you approach a big competition?
How does anxiety weigh someone down?
How could a kind word cheer him up?
What are some kind expressions that cheer you up?

September 21 – Pray, read the devotion, ask the questions and pray.
Who are the coaches and players in your team's history that are still impacting your lives today?
What made them unique and impactful?
What will those who follow recall about you?

September 22 – Pray, read the devotion, ask the questions and pray.
Of what are you sometimes afraid? Are there some things that bring you fear and rob you of courage?
What are the situations that make your faith seem small?
How can we put off fear and take on courage?

September 23 – Pray, read the devotion, ask the questions and pray.
How would you describe the attitudes on your team as the youngest players relate to the eldest and to the coaching staff? Are they respectful and honorable or arrogant and rebellious?

What value does humility have among you?
How is humility expressed?
Why would God give grace to the humble?

September 24 – Pray, read the devotion, ask the questions and pray.
What would it be like to be a record holder in your sport, right at the
top of your game, only to watch someone else come along and immediately break all your records with apparent ease?
How would you feel if you were John the Baptist?
Which of your gifts and abilities are purely gifts of God?

September 25 – Pray, read the devotion, ask the questions and pray.
How do you maintain your focus on goals in sport?
How do we appropriate our faith in Christ toward our life as athletes?
What is behind you that you'd like to forget?
How would you express your ultimate goal in life?

September 26 – Pray, read the devotion, ask the questions and pray.
Do you enjoy a good relationship with your coaches?
How would you rate it on a 1-10 scale?
Do you have favor with them or do they seem to be angry with you a
lot?
How does this scripture reveal the source of many coach/player conflicts?
What are some shameful things that incite your coach's anger?

September 27 – Pray, read the devotion, ask the questions and pray.
Tell us about a place where you've competed which had an atmosphere
in which it seems almost impossible for visiting teams to win.
What are some attitudes that overcome atmospheres?
Which of these have been most helpful to you?

September 28 – Pray, read the devotion, ask the questions and pray.
Are there things to be learned by playing sports that cannot be learned
through books, seminars and lectures? What are some of them?
Why would God choose to hide wisdom from the learned and to reveal
it to the simple?
How do you use these truths in life outside of sport?

September 29 – Pray, read the devotion, ask the questions and pray.
When have you most recently suffered as a result of competition? Was
that suffering physical, emotional or mental in nature? Tell us about what
happened.
Did it seem like you were alone in your suffering?
How does one share in the suffering of a teammate or friend?

September 30 – Pray, read the devotion, ask the questions and pray.
What does true humility look like?
Whose name comes to your mind?
Why would John say what he said?
How can we express that same attitude?

October 1 – Pray, read the devotion, ask the questions and pray.
What are the keys to overcoming anxiety and worry?
What can we do that will lead to an active trust in God?
How can we approach the Lord and overcome our fears?
How does prayer affect your attitude?

October 2 – Pray, read the devotion, ask the questions and pray.
When have you seen someone win an award and thought the person
was just lucky or got a break of some sort?
Was that true or did he or she earn it?
Why does humility precede honor?

October 3 – Pray, read the devotion, ask the questions and pray.
How many bills have you had come due this week? List some of them.
Why would love be a perpetual debt to pay?
How can we pay on our debt this week?

October 4 – Pray, read the devotion, ask the questions and pray.
What are the most important items in your daily diet?
How many of us know what feeds our souls well?
What keeps your soul from starvation and running strongly?
With what do you feed your soul?

October 5 – Pray, read the devotion, ask the questions and pray.
What are the keys to success as an athlete? List some of these keys.
What brings about the best life for us as Christians?
Why is it our hearts we should apply to discipline?
Why is it our ears that we apply to words of knowledge?

October 6 – Pray, read the devotion, ask the questions and pray.
What is most pleasing to your soul?
What was pleasing to Jesus' soul?
How can we partake of the food Jesus talks about?

October 7 – Pray, read the devotion, ask the questions and pray.
Which of your athletic gifts is most important to you as a competitor?
Who is the giver of that gift?
What would be a proper response to your benefactor?
How can we serve each other with our gifts?

October 8 – Pray, read the devotion, ask the questions and pray.
What are the keys to seeing your goals achieved?
How would one go about the pursuit of athletic achievement?
How does one commit his or her work to the Lord?

October 9 – Pray, read the devotion, ask the questions and pray.
When has keeping the peace and building teamwork required great
effort?
What are some things that fight against a team's peace and work to
destroy their teamwork?
How can we promote peace this week?
How can we build each other up this week?

October 10 – Pray, read the devotion, ask the questions and pray.
What is the hallmark of a truly great coach?
What characterizes the best of team leaders?
Why would Jesus ask Peter the same question three times?
How can we "feed Jesus' sheep" on our team, in our families, and in our community?

October 11 – Pray, read the devotion, ask the questions and pray.
Who has more confidence about recovery from injury, the one who's never been hurt or the player who has come through the pain and has found renewed strength?
How is the player changed through the injury, recovery and rehab process?
How does Christ's suffering help you overcome sin?

October 12 – Pray, read the devotion, ask the questions and pray.
Have you ever wondered why your path through life has zigzagged sometimes? Tell us about some of those course adjustments.
When does it seem that your path to a championship has been sidetracked?
If this verse is true, why should we even have a plan?

October 13 – Pray, read the devotion, ask the questions and pray.
Which of these statements seem true?
    A) Difficult times develop character, or
    B) Hard times reveal the character that's already in a person or in a team.
What had Paul suffered?
Why could he see the suffering as so insignificant?

October 14– Pray, read the devotion, ask the questions and pray.
Who is your model for the ideal teammate?
What does he or she do that makes him or her such a great teammate?
How can we lay down our lives for our teammates this week?

October 15 – Pray, read the devotion, ask the questions and pray.
When do you sense the real healing in a once injured knee, in the training room or while chasing a loose ball?
When does the confidence return, while looking at an x-ray or after making the difficult cut toward the basket?
How does Jesus check your heart in a similar way?

October 16 – Pray, read the devotion, ask the questions and pray.
How well do you control your emotions during competition? Grade your self-A, B, C, D, or F.
Do you get easily distracted or do you stay under control?
Why is self-control so important to our life in Christ?

October 17 – Pray, read the devotion, ask the questions and pray.
Tell us about a time when suffering and pain come along to meet you.
How do you usually respond to suffering?
How does suffering make us better?

How will knowing this affect your attitude the next time you're visited by pain and suffering?

October 18 – Pray, read the devotion, ask the questions and pray.
Who is your dearest friend?
For whom do you care deeply, family, friends, teammates, and coaches?
What is the source of those affections? (church, team, family, school, job)
How durable are those relationships? Pick one and rank on a 1-10 scale of durability.
How does being loved so deeply affect your daily life?

October 19 – Pray, read the devotion, ask the questions and pray.
Whom do you respect more, the player who talks a good game or the one who shows his game on the field of competition?
Whose face came to your mind as the all-talk no-game competitor? Tell us about him or her.
How can we love our teammates in deed and truth this week?

October 20 – Pray, read the devotion, ask the questions and pray.
From whom have you taken instruction in the game?
Who else provides wise guidance for your life? List the coaches, teammates, and opponents.
Who would have done this for Jesus?
How can we follow Jesus' example from this verse?

October 21 – Pray, read the devotion, ask the questions and pray.
What are the situations in your life that have required perseverance?
How has that shaped your character?
How do you see the process in this verse at work in your life?

October 22 – Pray, read the devotion, ask the questions and pray.
What could happen during a practice or a competition that would cause you to lose heart?
From where would you draw the power to press through such circumstances?
How does God's mercy fuel your heart?

October 23 – Pray, read the devotion, ask the questions and pray.
How do you get your mind to calm down when worries and fear come your way?
How do we trust God when everything we can see points to failure and despair?
When has God's peace guarded your heart and mind from despair?

October 24 – Pray, read the devotion, ask the questions and pray.
What's the most miraculous thing you've ever seen on the field of competition?
Why did God enable Jesus to do signs and wonders?
What marvelous things could happen on your team because of your relationship?

October 25 – Pray, read the devotion, ask the questions and pray.
Tell us about the trophies in the school's trophy case, which have been won over past decades of competition.
How is it that they so soon fade, tarnish and gather dust? Have they somehow lost their luster since the days of championships won?
What kind of trophy would never grow old?

October 26 – Pray, read the devotion, ask the questions and pray.
How would forgetting things from your past improve your focus for competition?
What does it look like to train toward what is ahead?
What could be the prize for which Christ called you heavenward?

October 27 – Pray, read the devotion, ask the questions and pray.
In what parts of your sport do you have to really strain to perform well?
How easy or difficult is it for you to stay focused on that which is ahead?
In what parts of your life in Christ must you strain toward what is ahead?

October 28 – Pray, read the devotion, ask the questions and pray.
The goal before you is the same with every contest: to win and to honor God in the process. How accurately does that statement reflect your approach to sport?
Through what kinds of adversity must you regularly press?
How can you help your teammates to press on?

October 29 – Pray, read the devotion, ask the questions and pray.
What do you find to be a trial while competing in your sport?
What parts of your character are tried in that process?
How deeply are you affected by those trials?
What is there to greatly rejoice in during those trials?

October 30 – Pray, read the devotion, ask the questions and pray.
Have you ever heard your coaches talk about the rhythm or the game or not hitting your peak too soon in a season? What did they say about it?
How important is timing in the life of an athletic team?
How important is it to life in general?
Why would Jesus resist the efforts to make Him king?
How can we work hard to manage our emotions and focus our concentration in order to best contribute to a winning effort for our team today?

October 31 – Pray, read the devotion, ask the questions and pray.
When do you feel like your body is wasting away and your strength is drying up?
How can we have our hearts renewed and find the strength to press through such feelings?
How can we continue to find new strength through renewed hearts and press through the hard times?

November 1 –
How do we find power and renewed life for our bodies and emotions after the long months of a season?
What can give us renewed vigor and an injection of energy?

When do you experience renewed strength due to your life in Christ?

November 2 –
What are some situations in your sport when finishing well is most important?
Which parts of your life seem to be in need of more work?
Which parts feel like they're near completion?

November 3 –
What kinds of things do you do in the process of preparing for competition?
We all know the value of physical preparation, but how important is it to prepare your mind?
Why is it important to rest in Christ's grace?

November 4 – Pray, read the devotion, ask the questions and pray.
What happens when one competes in an out of control way?
What are the penalties in your sport when one gets out of control?
What value might self-control have beyond competition?
How does one develop self-control?

November 5 – Pray, read the devotion, ask the questions and pray.
Upon what are your confident expectations for this season and today's competition built?
In whom or what do you fully place your hope for something?
Are those people or things fully trustworthy?
Why is Jesus fully trustworthy?

November 6 – Pray, read the devotion, ask the questions and pray.
Who is the one person in your life that can calm the most fearful situation?
How does he or she restore peace?
When do you most often experience Jesus' presence?

November 7 – Pray, read the devotion, ask the questions and pray.
What is the largest crowd before which you've competed? Was it nearer one hundred, one thousand or ten thousand? When and where was that?
How did that crowd affect you? Were you inspired or intimidated by it?
3. Who would be in your Hall of Fame crowd?
4. How would a crowd like that affect your performance?

November 8 – Pray, read the devotion, ask the questions and pray.
What is the single greatest hindrance to you as you compete?
How can these things be overcome?
How does one lay aside lifestyle patterns that weigh us down?

November 9 – Pray, read the devotion, ask the questions and pray.
What kinds of things could entangle someone during competition?
What sorts of sins entangle people's lives?
How does one get free form such sins?

November 10 – Pray, read the devotion, ask the questions and pray.
How would you characterize your season of competition, more like a

sprint or a marathon?
Which one requires more perseverance, the ten-second race or the two-hour race?
How do you train for perseverance in life?

November 11 – Pray, read the devotion, ask the questions and pray.
Have you ever met someone who seems to glow with enthusiasm and zest for life?
Have you ever talked with that person and asked from where that glow comes? What did he or she say?
Through what kinds of trials have you persevered? What might be the reward for your perseverance?
What might the crown of life look like?

November 12 – Pray, read the devotion, ask the questions and pray.
Do you have some precious metals at home in your jewelry box? How valuable are your rings, watches or necklaces?
What could be worth more than silver, gold, or platinum?
Why are wisdom and understanding more valuable than gold or silver?
How does one acquire wisdom?

November 13 – Pray, read the devotion, ask the questions and pray.
How does one maintain a good attitude in the midst of difficult times?
How does one's character affect these situations?
How have you seen this process work in your life?

November 14 – Pray, read the devotion, ask the questions and pray.
Upon what or whom do you focus your attention just prior to the start of a competition?
What does it mean that Jesus despised the shame of the cross?
How can we follow His example from this verse?

November 15 – Pray, read the devotion, ask the questions and pray.
Who are the people with authority in your world of sport?
What is your attitude toward such authorities, is it one of submission or defiance? Is it more like obedience or rebellion?
Why should that matter to us?
How can we build proper attitudes toward authority?

November 16 – Pray, read the devotion, ask the questions and pray.
Have you ever been in a competition and had the awareness that this might be a once-in-a-lifetime experience? Can you look back and see such occasions? Tell us about one such occasion.
Why would Jesus say what He did?
How does one prepare to be always ready?

November 17 – Pray, read the devotion, ask the questions and pray.
Who do you suppose has the greatest knowledge and the most skill of anyone in your sport?
How would your grasp of the sport compare with his or hers?
Who do you suppose has the greatest understanding about all of life?
How strong is your grasp on life's big questions relative to His?
How can we tap into God's limitless store of wisdom and knowledge?

November 18 – Pray, read the devotion, ask the questions and pray.
Do you remember your first impression of your coach? What did you think of him or her?
How about the first time you met your teammates? How would you describe that first impression?
Now that you know them better, are they what they appeared to be at first glance?
What is the difference between an appearance and righteous judgment?

November 19 – Pray, read the devotion, ask the questions and pray.
What's the toughest part of your training as an athlete?
Why do your coaches have you continue to do something that is so difficult?
How is the correction we receive from God similar to that we get from our coaches? How is it different?

November 20– Pray, read the devotion, ask the questions and pray.
How do you handle people who criticize your team or your coaching staff?
What, if anything, do you say to them?
Who are your strongest critics and how should we respond to them?
What are some ways we could wisely deal with criticism?

November 21 – Pray, read the devotion, ask the questions and pray.
How has strength and flexibility training improved your game?
In what ways is your team better with it than you would be without it?
Beyond the physical dimension, how can we strengthen and restore our teammates who are at less than 100%?

November 22 – Pray, read the devotion, ask the questions and pray.
When was the last time you challenged your teammates to do something spectacular?
How would you speak to a teammate who seems to be trapped in something that has boxed him in?
What sorts of factors could have a teammate trapped?
What words would you use to call your teammate or friend to freedom?

November 23 – Pray, read the devotion, ask the questions and pray.
How strongly do you value your team's leadership?
Is their behavior, on and off the field of competition, something that you would imitate?
What characteristics would you want to make your own?

November 24 – Pray, read the devotion, ask the questions and pray.
Which would seem to be more productive: strength and self-sufficiency or sacrifice and interdependence?
Why do most people choose the former and not the latter?
Why is it better to sacrifice and to reproduce?

November 25 – Pray, read the devotion, ask the questions and pray.
Who has more authority on your team, the wet-behind-the-ears freshman walk-on or the Head Coach? Why is that true?

How about between the new graduate assistant and the fifth year captain of the team?
Explain your answer to this tougher question.
What does it cost one to bear this authority?

November 26 – Pray, read the devotion, ask the questions and pray.
As you learned the basics of your game, how important was it to have an example to watch?
Who were your best examples?
How valuable is it to you to have videotape to watch of well-executed plays?
What is the value of having experienced players on your team to demonstrate the proper techniques and skills for excellent play?
How can we most practically serve our teammates this week?

November 27 – Pray, read the devotion, ask the questions and pray.
What's the most enduring part of this game?
What about your sport fades in significance rather quickly?
How can you make investments of eternal significance with your life?

November 28 – Pray, read the devotion, ask the questions and pray.
Which is better: to know your team's playbook inside and out, or the flawless execution of one of those plays? Why is that better?
Which parts of God's plan for your life do you find most difficult to execute?
Why is faithfully doing better than simply knowing the right thing to do?

November 29 – Pray, read the devotion, ask the questions and pray.
What do players regularly do that is a genuine gesture of respect?
How can we show proper respect for our teammates, coaches, opponents and even the officials? (Discuss them in order.)
Why should we even care about that?

November 30 – Pray, read the devotion, ask the questions and pray.
Who is the best player you've ever seen at finishing a play? Tell us about him/her.
Who is best at finishing the season with strength and charging into the playoffs? Tell us about that team or person.
What had Jesus finished?
Why is that important?

December 1 – Pray, read the devotion, ask the questions and pray.
What are the keys to playing the game naturally, freely and in a relaxed way?
How do we prepare for game day in such a way as to allow us to play with great freedom?
What does Jesus say is the preparation for a life of freedom?
How do you do that?

December 2 – Pray, read the devotion, ask the questions and pray.
Who is judged more strictly by the press for your team's standing in the conference, the head coach or the freshman walk-on?
Who gets fired if the team doesn't meet the expectations of the adminis-

tration, the coaching staff or the starting line-up?
Those answers are obvious, but why are they true?
Why would teachers of God's truth receive a stricter judgment than other believers?

December 3 – Pray, read the devotion, ask the questions and pray.
Do you have to sneak into the practice facility to practice? Why or why not?
What kind of people would have to sneak in and would always worry about being found and kicked out?
Do you come in through the door, or do you have to crawl in through a window?
What allows you such easy entrance?
What is the difference between a person being one of Christ's sheep and being a "spiritual wannabe"?

December 4 – Pray, read the devotion, ask the questions and pray.
Who among your teammates is the best student of the game?
Whose knowledge of strategy and fundamentals can help shape the outcome of a contest?
How is that wisdom evident to the rest of the team?
Tell us about some people who display Christ's wisdom in their lives.
How can you be similarly wise?

December 5 – Pray, read the devotion, ask the questions and pray.
What does it cost to be a good coach or teammate?
How much more does it cost to be a head coach or a team captain?
How can team leaders give up their lives for their team?

December 6 – Pray, read the devotion, ask the questions and pray.
How do you react when teammates or fans criticize your coaches' decisions?
What attitudes might be revealed by those various reactions?
Why is it important to guard one's attitude?

December 7 – Pray, read the devotion, ask the questions and pray.
Who is the greatest example of total commitment in your sport?
Who has really committed him/herself 100% to your team and to excellence in competition?
How would you rate your level of commitment on a 1-10 scale?
How did Elisha demonstrate commitment?
Who could you do similarly?

December 8 – Pray, read the devotion, ask the questions and pray.
In which part of your sport do you have the greatest sense of strength or power?
How central is that feeling to your enjoyment of the sport?
In what does it seem the Lord delights?
Why would that be true?

December 9 – Pray, read the devotion, ask the questions and pray.
How do you judge your teammates' performance on game day, by their appearance during pre-game or by their play during the competition?

In whom have you seen a vast difference between outward appearances and matters of the heart? What was the evidence of the difference? Why would God view people this way?

December 10 – Pray, read the devotion, ask the questions and pray.
When does it seem sometimes like the coach is getting on you more than some of the other players?
When does it seem like your parents expect more from you than you can give?
When do you feel like you're being overly disciplined or treated unfairly?
Why would our Lord and our coaches reprove and discipline us?

December 11 – Pray, read the devotion, ask the questions and pray.
What do you do for sport?
What is sporty about wickedness to a fool?
How is wisdom like sport to a person of understanding?
Which is more like sport to you?

December 12 – Pray, read the devotion, ask the questions and pray.
How have you chosen your friends? What was the process?
With whom do you hang out?
What kind of people do you spend the most time with?
Why is it the companion of the fool, rather than the fool, who suffers harm?

December 13 – Pray, read the devotion, ask the questions and pray.
Which comes first, honor and awards or hard work and a humble attitude? Why is this true?
How has this worked in your life?
Where are you in that process?

December 14– Pray, read the devotion, ask the questions and pray.
Which is more draining to your heart for competition, physical fatigue or a sense of hopelessness and despair?
Explain your answer for us.
How do you find renewed strength through hope?

December 15 – Pray, read the devotion, ask the questions and pray.
What kinds of situations are there among you teammates, which if mentioned, immediately stir up controversy and dissension?
Which issues in your family can most easily provoke a fight?
How do we handle such hot potatoes?
How can we avoid needless provocation?

December 16 – Pray, read the devotion, ask the questions and pray.
Whom do you trust when you're being overcome by anxiety?
Who is trustworthy when your life is in distress?
How difficult is it to trust anyone when you're full of doubt?
How can we build trust and the confidence which comes with it?

December 17 –
Can you recall a time when you felt like your whole store of energy was poured out in competition? Tell us about it.

Who pours new life into your heart when you've been totally poured out?
How does one receive this transfusion of love from God?

December 18 – Pray, read the devotion, ask the questions and pray.
What are some of the most treasured moments from your sport career?
Are there some souvenirs or mementos from those events? Where do you keep them?
When you anticipate the coming competitions, how eager are you for their arrival?
Where do you keep your dreams and aspirations?

December 19 – Pray, read the devotion, ask the questions and pray.
What are the situations in your sport that bring fear, doubt, pain or disappointment?
Is there anything that could guard your hearts from the onslaught of these thieves? What is it for you?
How do we gain access to the peace of God?

December 20 – Pray, read the devotion, ask the questions and pray.
To whom are you a treasure? Who recalls the events of your life as a precious commodity?
How strongly do you think they hold to those memories?
What was there about Jesus that Mary would treasure in her heart?
Whom do you treasure in this way?

December 21 – Pray, read the devotion, ask the questions and pray.
What are some of the more painful parts of life in sport that teammates share?
What are some more pleasant shared experiences?
What are some of the experiences, which have built your team's bonds of love?

December 22 – Pray, read the devotion, ask the questions and pray.
What is the most difficult part of the game for you to endure?
What is the final outcome of persevering through these trying times?
What benefit could possibly come from such painful, hard work?
How does patience in trying times make us more complete?
How can we cultivate joy in difficult days?

December 23 – Pray, read the devotion, ask the questions and pray.
Who refreshes your heart after a long practice?
Who breathes new life into your heart after a tough loss?
Who do you call for encouragement?
Whose hearts do you refresh? How?

December 24 – Pray, read the devotion, ask the questions and pray.
In whom have you deeply invested your life?
How have your feelings for those people changed as your investment in them has grown?
What are some ways we can make investments in our team?

December 25 – Pray, read the devotion, ask the questions and pray.
Have you ever heard your coach or a teammate say something outrageous and wondered, "Where did that come from?" Tell us that story.
What is in a person's heart that corrupts his/her speech?
How can we change our hearts and thus our tongues?

December 26 – Pray, read the devotion, ask the questions and pray.
Have you ever found your value system to be at odds with that of your teammates or your coaches? Over what did you differ?
Have you ever seen a player give lip-service to changing just to gain favor with the coach? Tell us about it.
Why would God's value system be different from most men's?
How can we align our hearts with God's values?

December 27 – Pray, read the devotion, ask the questions and pray.
When have you encountered people who seem to talk one way, but live another?
What is this behavior called?
How do we get our speech and action to better match?

December 28 – Pray, read the devotion, ask the questions and pray.
As you compete, how well do you know the mind of your coaching staff? How clearly can you tell what they're thinking as the competition progresses?
What about God can the pure in heart see?
How would having a pure heart affect your relationships with teammates?

December 29 – Pray, read the devotion, ask the questions and pray.
Do you have aspirations of someday being in your sport's Hall of Fame?
What would it take to achieve such an award?
How would a crowd of Hall of Famers affect your approach to competition?

December 30 – Pray, read the devotion, ask the questions and pray.
How do you express your greetings to friends and family? (Phone calls, cards, e-mails, letters, face to face...)
Who comes to mind as someone you should contact as you read this scripture?
When and how will you greet them?

December 31 – Pray, read the devotion, ask the questions and pray.
When do you feel the Lord directing you into God's love?
When do you most need Christ's perseverance?